Notorious C.O.P.

Notori

Derrick Parker with Matt Diehl

ST. MARTIN'S PRESS ✹ NEW YORK

Notorious C.O.P.

The Inside Story of the TUPAC, BIGGIE, and
JAM MASTER JAY Investigations from
the NYPD's First "HIP-HOP COP"

www.stmartins.com

Library of Congress Cataloging-in-Publication Data

Parker, Derrick.
    Notorious C.O.P. : the inside story of the Tupac, Biggie, and Jam Master Jay inves-
tigations from the NYPD's first "Hip-Hop Cop" / Derrick Parker ; with Matt Diehl.
        p. cm.
    ISBN-13: 978-0-312-35251-6
    ISBN-10: 0-312-35251-4
    1. New York (N.Y.) Police Dept. 2. Crime—New York (State)—New York—Case
studies. 3. Criminals—New York (State)—New York—Case studies. 4. Hip hop—
New York (State)—New York. 5. Detectives—New York (State)—New York. I. Title.

HV6795.N5 P37 2006
364.106'097471—dc22

                                                                                2005055180

First Edition: July 2006

10 9 8 7 6 5 4 3 2 1

To Joseph Pollini: you made me what I am today . . .

CONTENTS

NOTE TO THE READER

The names and identifying characteristics of some individuals described in this book have been changed.

ACKNOWLEDGMENTS

FROM DERRICK PARKER:
In January 2002 I decided to retire from the NYPD. Although the decision was made with mixed feelings, I felt that it was the right thing to do. I want to apologize to my many friends of all ranks for not saying good-bye or having a retirement party. It took me some time to write this book, but when you read it you will understand why.

I especially want to thank my parents for having me, my many brothers and sisters, friends; special thanks as well go to my business partner, Glen, and my other partners, A.J. and Harvey. I want to especially thank Adam Lublin (without you we could never get this done) and Matt—you're the best and working with you was fantastic. I also wish many thanks to Joe Pollini for believing in me, and to Retired Chief Louis Anemone many thanks. A very special thanks goes out to Retired Detective Lloyd Henry—you played a big role in my life. On the hip-hop side, I can't forget Eric B. and A. J. Calloway, as well as all the great artists that have inspired me with their music. As well, I can't forget Becki Heller and St. Martin's, and Kim Goldstein and the Susan Golomb Agency, for their tireless efforts. Much thanks as well to Steve Brownstein from Papa, Depaola and Brownstein and Craig Bruno of Bruno, Gerbino, and Soriano, LLP, for their sage legal guidance.

FROM MATT DIEHL:
First off, I especially wish to thank Derrick Parker for being an exemplary human being, a stand-up guy, a great, generous collaborator, and for having lived a life so fascinating to write about (a special shout-out to Derrick's family for their hospitality).

Adam Lublin, meanwhile, deserves praise as the visionary architect that brought this project together. Of course, huge thanks to Becki Heller and all at St. Martin's for their passionate belief in this project; Kim Goldstein and all at the Susan Golomb Agency; Rich

Green, Greg McKnight, and all at Creative Artists Agency; and Matthew Guma and Ink Well Management. Other crucial supporters deserving notice include Mike Brillstein and my legal team, Jamie Feldman and Jonathan Shikora.

My good friend and longtime journalist colleague Evelyn McDonnell deserves special praise for her part in bravely breaking the "hip-hop cop" story in the first place, and for being a brilliant writer, period. I would also like to thank all the amazing writers that have tackled this tough topic and inspired me over the years. They include, in no particular order: Danyel Smith, Elliott Wilson, Sacha Jenkins, John Leland, Chuck Phillips, Anthony Bozza, Keleefa Sanneh, Cheo Hodari Coker, Serena Kim, Jon Caramanica, Joseph Patel, Ronin Ro, Sia Michel, Randall Sullivan, Bonz Malone, Alan Light, Anthony DeCurtis, Greg Tate, Ethan Brown, Douglas Century, Kris Ex, Neil Strauss—the list could go on and on . . . A special mention must go to Joe Wood (R.I.P.) for inspiring me as a writer so early in my career. Also, many thanks to the artists that made hip-hop the fascinating, vital culture it is today, and to the magazines, newspapers, and editors that have supported me throughout my career.

Lastly, much thanks also to my family and friends, who have tirelessly supported and endured me through this project. You know who you are: to paraphrase the late, great Tupac, you are appreciated. . . .

Notorious C.O.P.

IT'S LIKE THAT, AND THAT'S THE WAY IT IS:
The Unsolved Mysteries of Hip-Hop Tragedy

The allure of breaking the law is always too much for me to ever ignore.
—Jay-Z, "Allure"

You're nobody 'til somebody kills you . . .
—Notorious B.I.G.

UF-61

Date of Occurrence: 10/30/02.

Classification: Homicide.

Approximate Time of Occurrence: 1930 hours. Referred to Detective Squad.

IT was around 1:00 A.M. when my cell phone rang. On the other end of the line was A. J. Calloway, then the host of the Black Entertainment Television network's hit show *106th and Park*—the *TRL* of the hip-hop generation. I could tell from his trembling voice A. J. had bad news.

Male/Black.

Age: 37

Date of Birth: 1/21/65

Wearing black jeans, black leather jacket, white shell-toe Adidas.

"Did you hear what happened?" A. J. said.

On T/P/O victim was found facedown, apparently suffered from a gunshot wound, D.O.A.

It had to be something more than just gossip: A. J. always keeps his cool, but tonight he sounded a little shook. Okay, *real* shook.

"No, what's up?" I replied.

Victim identified as Jason Mizell (Jam Master Jay).
103 P.D.S. notified.

"Jam Master Jay got shot," he said.

All I could say was, "Holy shit." We knew what was about to happen: we'd been down this road before. Tersely, we said our goodbyes. A. J. had other people to call. So did I.

Witnesses uncooperative.
No suspects, leads at this time.

They say everything comes in threes. It happened in Las Vegas. It happened in Los Angeles. And now it had happened here. In New York. My own backyard. Less than a mile, in fact, from where I grew up. It was a familiar story. A hip-hop superstar had been killed. In full view of witnesses. And the murder would never be solved—at least not by conventional law enforcement. I started feeling sick to my stomach.

I knew my phone was going to start ringing off the hook. The streets were gonna start talking, and talking loud. The clubs, corners, barbershops, boulevards, avenues, and back alleys where I used to hunt the truth were abuzz, and I couldn't turn my ears off from the murmurs of the street. The news that Jam Master Jay had been killed awoke the homicide detective that had been laying dormant inside me.

I couldn't say it out loud yet, but I knew it already in my heart: badge or no badge, I was going to solve the Jam Master Jay murder and continue my mission to stop the cycle of violence and distrust that had claimed the lives of our greatest hip-hop icons. *Boom!* The "hip-hop cop" was back.

Gutted, I started calling all my old street informants, trying to find out whatever I could. Reaching out to my contacts in Queens's homicide division, where I'd worked so many years ago, I finally got in touch with Bernie Porter, a detective from the 103rd Precinct in South Jamaica. Porter confirmed the story going around: Jam Master Jay had been killed in his Jamaica, Queens–based recording studio. But, he added, NYPD didn't have much to go on, and furthermore, witnesses weren't cooperating.

"Surprise, surprise," I thought to myself. I told Bernie if he needed my help to give me a call. He never did, but I could already feel myself getting pulled in. While Jam Master Jay's murder would've been any homicide detective's nightmare, for me—as the New York Police Department's original "hip-hop cop," as I became known first by my law-enforcement colleagues and eventually by the media—it was worse than a nightmare.

Hip-hop is in a state of crisis, yet nobody on either side is making the right moves to quash it. Due to its tragic legacy of violence, hip-hop supremacy could end at any time: just let one well-placed AK-47 spray at an awards show and it's all over—and considering what's gone down at those awards shows, that's a pretty fuckin' likely scenario. So when I got the call about Jam Master Jay's abrupt death that fateful night in 2002, it felt particularly bittersweet. His murder seemed so symbolic to me: if a tree is already dying, how can it survive when you remove the roots?

In fact, I was no longer a homicide detective when I first heard the tragic news that hip-hop legend Jam Master Jay, the innovative D.J. for rap's first worldwide superstars, Run-DMC, had been shot and killed in his recording studio on October 30, 2002. I had actually retired from the New York Police Department (NYPD) nine months prior, but I was having trouble suppressing my investigative instincts. After spending twenty years on the force, they kicked in like a reflex.

I started as a twenty-year-old beat cop walking seedy Times Square streets during Ed Koch's infamous mayoralty before moving on to the Bronx for undercover narcotics, ending up straight outta Brooklyn as a first-grade homicide detective with a gold shield under Rudy Giuliani's iron-fisted administration. Working homicide, I'd investigated well over three hundred murder cases; on the job, I

saw more dead people than that little kid in *The Sixth Sense*. I've
seen bodies chopped up in sections and then neatly disposed of in
little plastic bags. I found one victim's bones tossed on the Van
Wyck Expressway. In another case, I saw a man's face blown clear off
by a shotgun, his eyeballs blown out their sockets, leaving a hole in
his head like a window. Through that "window," I could see the
dude's brain membrane. Yup, just another day on the job. Talk to
any big-city detective and you'll probably hear similar stories—but
that's not why you're reading this. Ultimately, what I became most
known for inside the NYPD (and in the media) was my status as the
first hip-hop cop.

The NYPD would've liked to keep my existence as the hip-hop
cop secret. If it wasn't for a particular newspaper article, I probably
wouldn't even be writing these words today. That article was the shot
heard 'round the world, reprinted as far as Australia and bounced all
over the Internet.

On March 9, 2004, *The Miami Herald* published a story by Evelyn McDonnell and Nicole White headlined POLICE SECRETLY
WATCHING HIP-HOP ARTISTS. In it, McDonnell and White revealed
that Miami law enforcement were "secretly watching and keeping
dossiers on hip-hop celebrities," even "[photographing] rappers as
they arrived at Miami International Airport."

According to Evelyn McDonnell, she became aware of Miami law
enforcement's covert hip-hop surveillance through a not-so-covert
human screwup. After that, McDonnell, *The Miami Herald*'s chief
music reviewer, wrote an article profiling local Miami rapper Jacki-O.
She then received an e-mail from a Miami Beach–based police detective named Rosa Redruello asking her for information. "I collect
intelligence on all current rappers and record companies in the
South Beach area," Redruello explained in the note. McDonnell was
taken aback. "It was pretty shocking," she explains in hindsight.
"When I realized it was from a police officer, I knew this was a big
deal. I e-mailed the woman back and said 'Sorry, I can't divulge my
sources—but I'd love to hear more about what *you* do.' "

That's right—Miami law enforcement's clandestine hip-hop surveillance wasn't discovered via an intense investigative exposé; no, a

detective made it easy and sent a *fucking e-mail.* The first rule of law enforcement is the same as the code of the streets: keep your mouth shut—especially when talking to a journalist. Covert activity in any police department is kept undercover for two reasons. One, so those under surveillance don't realize they're being watched; two, exposure of such surveillance usually results in a public-relations disaster. As such, McDonnell and White's article exploded Miami's tensions like a volcano.

"Racial profiling" was already a hot-button topic for law enforcement across the nation; to many, the revelation that major urban police departments were targeting rappers and the hip-hop industry was further evidence of this practice. But racial profiling was an especially huge issue in Miami, according to McDonnell's collaborator Nicole White. "Black lawmakers were concerned by the profiling element," White explains today. "A lot of money was at stake, and that was the main concern."

The fallout from *The Miami Herald* piece was immediate. In particular, local tourism was threatened, and Miami was already walking on thin ice where race issues were concerned. After the city had refused to officially welcome South African activist/leader Nelson Mandela in 1990, Miami suffered a debilitating three-year tourism boycott by African-Americans. In later years, racial tensions exploded over incidents that occurred when hundreds of thousands of black revelers descended upon Miami for Memorial Day celebrations.

Since then, however, Miami had become a tourism mecca for hip-hop artists and their fans, with South Beach's glitzy, upscale clubs, hotels, and recording studios all catering to the blinged-out rap pack. Rappers were spending big money in Miami and showing off the city's high life in music videos, and as a result its luster as a glamorous A-list vacation spot had been restored. But now that was threatened. Following McDonnell and White's article, the American Civil Liberties Union (ACLU) and other civil-rights groups immediately threatened major lawsuits. And music industry insiders were pissed. "Russell Simmons was very upset," McDonnell says. "Damon Dash went on record: he was very upset that incidents from his past were still haunting him. Luther Campbell was very upset. Fat Joe found it all depressing because he thought in Miami he was getting away from that kind of surveillance. The hip-hop community in general was like 'We knew it was going on.'"

Quickly, I found myself in the eye of this hip-hop hurricane. Eventually it came out that members of Miami P.D. had attended training sessions in "hip-hop crime" from NYPD detectives. I directed those training sessions, but what caused even greater controversy was the admission that Miami had in its possession a dossier known as the Binder, which I also had created in my tenure in the NYPD's hip-hop squad. "We knew there was a guy in New York who had retired who was responsible for the Binder," McDonnell explains, "but the police wouldn't give us Derrick's name."

It didn't take them long to put two and two together, though, as all the evidence that was never meant to get into the public's hands led directly to me. As the NYPD's rap expert, I was commissioned in 2001 to create the Binder, a printable database detailing the associations and background of every rapper with a known criminal arrest. It would grow to be numbingly complete, numbering over a thousand pages. The Binder covered everyone from boldfaced hip-hop superstars like Puff Daddy, 50 Cent, and Jay-Z to obscure wannabes like E-Money Bags. It listed every case each rapper ever caught, every felon they ran with, every beef they had with rival rap crews—along with personal information like photos, Social Security numbers, record-company affiliations, and last-known addresses. Not surprisingly, the Binder caused a great outcry when it was leaked, and I ended up taking the hits.

The resulting episode reminded me of that scene in *Scarface* where Al Pacino's Tony Montana character states, "You need people like me so you can point your fucking fingers and say, 'That's the bad guy.' So what dat make you? Good? You're not 'good'—you just know how to hide." After the Binder surfaced, I was that "bad guy"—everyone else was hiding. Like the name of Tupac's best-selling album, all eyes were on me, ready to throw blame my way for one of the biggest law-enforcement controversies in decades. To the

American Civil Liberties Union (ACLU) I was suddenly public enemy number one.

Additionally, I found myself in the crosshairs of rappers as well: "I got the rap patrol on the gat patrol," Jay-Z rhymes on his hit "99 Problems."

My own people, though, truly left me out in the cold. The NYPD, my family for two decades of my life, which I departed as a detective with the highest rank of first-grade, couldn't take the heat and left me out to dry. "New York denied everything," McDonnell says. "It was like a game of whodunit?" Indeed, NYPD brass basically denied my existence, implying I was a lone wolf, a renegade working solo—even though I had taken my orders directly from the top: police commissioners Howard Safir and Bernard Kerik. Under Safir, who served under Rudy Giuliani's mayoral administration between 1996 and 2000, I was instructed to create a squad devoted to hip-hop crime. However, it was Giuliani's last commish, Bernard Kerik, who pushed me to create the Binder following the notorious 2001 shooting involving Lil' Kim outside the New York City hip-hop radio station Hot 97. Kerik would later become not just a bestselling author but also the first major scandal of President George W. Bush's second term in office: Kerik's nomination for director of Homeland Security ended in scandal involving allegations of mistresses and tax improprieties. Yet as the tough but innovative boss of the NYPD, any spike in hip-hop-related violence and the subsequent threat to the public seemed to personally galvanize him.

Kerik didn't exactly run to my defense when the shit hit the fan, however. When the NYPD began receiving criticism in the press for their involvement in hip-hop surveillance, they made me the scapegoat. I was even called an "Uncle Tom" by my fellow African-Americans, which hurt. To many in the media, the activist black community, and the hip-hop world, the existence of a law-enforcement unit created strictly to keep tabs on hip-hop was evidence that young black men were being unfairly targeted. The actions of my hip-hop squad were compared to the F.B.I.'s COINTELPRO program, created in large part to destroy radical black activists during the civil-rights era. Like everything in life, however, the truth is far more complicated.

In fact, as the NYPD's hip-hop cop, I led a paradoxical existence— I was a "po-po" that loved hip-hop music, yet wasn't afraid to put the cuffs on a rapper if he was breaking the law. Because of the way I dressed and the color of my skin, many of my fellow officers mistook me for a perp; later, they would suspect, because of my appearance and knowledge of the hip-hop industry, that I was too close to it, in too deep to be an objective upholder of the law.

I often felt that it was my critics whose subjective cultural assumptions clouded their perspective. To the ACLU types on my case, I'm *black,* okay? I grew up in the same 'hoods, like Bed-Stuy, Brooklyn, and Hollis, Queens, as many of the most famous rappers; I'm more likely to be racially profiled myself than to engage in any racial profiling. No, as the hip-hop cop, I was always clear about what my job was—to go after criminals and to protect the public.

That didn't mean persecuting rappers just because they tended to be young, black, rich, and angry (although during my experience with the Giuliani administration it verged on that—that's when my disillusionment with the NYPD really began). Often my job entailed protecting *rappers themselves* from the criminal element that attached itself to them like a barnacle. Sometimes my very presence at a concert or club would *prevent* a crime from happening. I was able to stop a lot of hip-hop-related crimes from happening that the public never even heard about, ones that never made it to the papers.

More often than not, I had to go to war against the cultural ignorance of my fellow officers, too many of whom assumed that all rappers were evil criminals, regardless of the facts. The NYPD often finds itself confused about how to deal with hip-hop crime—it's very interested in it, but doesn't know how to deal with it. Not every cop is knowledgeable of, or cares about, the codes of the streets rappers adhere to.

Still, if law enforcement wants to close cases, it needs to approach the hip-hop community with more sensitivity. Just as you wouldn't deal with a well-known Mafia don like a common criminal, the same goes for crime involving high-profile hip-hop figures. It seems like common sense, but alas, the NYPD doesn't always share my views. For example, in 2001, Jay-Z was arrested outside the midtown Manhattan nightclub Exit for illegal gun possession. Cops had allegedly found a loaded handgun on his bodyguard during a search of his vehicle; the weapon wasn't even in Jay-Z's personal possession. At the time, I begged the commanding officer to not make Jay do a "perp walk" past the rabid paparazzi lurking outside the precinct house, but it was no use. All perp walks are good for is humiliating suspects, and Jay-Z was no ordinary perp—why would the cops treat him different from, say, Liza Minnelli in the same situation? Humiliating Jay-Z served no purpose except to make him and other rappers cooperate *even less* with law enforcement than they already do. Ultimately, in fact, the charges against Jay-Z were dropped. Why should rappers help the police if cops are going to alienate them just to prove who's *really* boss? I couldn't blame the rappers' attitudes sometimes, because every day I saw what was causing them.

Despite headlines portraying me and the NYPD as obsessive rap haters, I've always been passionate about hip-hop. That seems surprising coming from a cop, I know. And as a seasoned detective, I knew that someone had to try to build bridges between law enforcement and hip-hop—or the murders of Jam Master Jay, Tupac, Biggie, and others would never be solved. And as rappers became high-stakes, headline-grabbing prey for ambitious detectives and district attorneys, I had to protect myself from peers who were all too eager to knock me down and nab my spot.

The war between law enforcement and hip-hop is an ongoing saga showing no sign of stopping; I, myself, got caught in that crossfire many times. Law enforcement and hip-hop have a lot in common. They're like two sides of the same coin, warring cousins inextricably linked to each other's destinies: each eyes the other with suspicion through cracks in the fortress walls each has sequestered itself into. Both cultures are wracked with corruption, driven by ambition, stunted by stubborn egos, closed to outsiders, and fiercely protective of their tribal codes. There's no way "po-po" and hip-hop could exist without each other, and yet there's no way they can seemingly get along. This would prove to be hip-hop crime's deadly Catch-22.

Indeed, by the time I formed the rap unit within the NYPD's intelligence arm, there was a dire need for a liaison between the hip-hop community and law enforcement. Hip-hop has had a volatile relationship with the police for too long. And, as an African-American man who's seen it from both sides, I can understand *why* better than anyone. Young black males have long complained that police treat them like criminals even when they're not, and hip-hop's omnipresence on urban streets soured the bad relations even further. Many in law enforcement saw the flashy, brazen, blinged-out hip-hop lifestyle as a taunt, but it was rap's lawless braggadocio in its lyrics that soured relations between hip-hop and cops once and for all.

The spark hit the gasoline back in '88, when the prototypical Los Angeles gangsta-rap group N.W.A. (an acronym for Niggaz With Attitude) released their scabrous protest anthem "F*** Tha Police." For N.W.A.—whose members included future superstars Dr. Dre and Ice Cube—"Fuck Tha Police" was a throwing down of a gat-wielding gauntlet: "When I'm finished, it's gonna be a bloodbath of cops dying in L.A.," Ice Cube threatened on his verse.

Law enforcement's response to "F*** Tha Police" was immediate. Cops started refusing to provide security at rap concerts, while rappers themselves complained about new, increased harassment. The F.B.I. even threatened N.W.A.'s right to free speech by sending them a letter threatening to go after the group if it didn't curtail its lyrical provocations.

The contentious battle didn't stop there, however. Archetypal gangsta rapper Ice-T escalated the situation when he released the song "Cop Killer" in 1992 with his heavy-metal group Body Count "I'm 'bout to kill me somethin'—A pig stopped me for nuthin'" goes one typical verse. Texas police called for a boycott of the song, and cops nationwide took "Cop Killer" as a call to arms against rappers. The tension didn't end there. Snoop Dogg's early '90s breakthrough hit "Deep Cover" called for a "187 on an undercover cop"—"187" being police code for murder. Meanwhile, an ongoing slew of threatening "cop killer" rhymes keeps the hostile mistrust between police and rappers alive, like those on Philadelphia rapper Cassidy's 2005 street hit "I'm A Hustla": "Cops wait, wait for a drought, then I make a flood/Try to take my cake, you gone take a slug."

Between angry rappers and angry cops, I worked the middle chasm. During the last four years of my law-enforcement career, I was responsible for creating and directing what alternately became known as the "hip-hop task force," "hip-hop squad," or the "rap intelligence unit" within the NYPD's Intelligence Division; it was never given an official name, as its function was intended to remain clandestine and mysterious, unknown to all but department insiders.

As the hip-hop cop, I found no shortage of controversy. I had a front-row seat to watch over this potent cultural phenomenon, yet I was afraid I might see it die. It was the greatest job, but also ruthlessly challenging. I was proud that my hip-hop squad was placed in "Intel," as it's the department's most elite division. Go any higher, and you'd be in the F.B.I.; in fact, in Intel we often collaborated with the Feds on big cases.

The reason a hip-hop task force was created was because, in fact, it was urgently necessary. By the end of my tenure, hip-hop-related crime, in fact, had become an epidemic involving murder, robbery, extortion, money laundering, bribery, witness intimidation, and drug trafficking—most notably crack cocaine. The hip-hop industry had grown into one of the NYPD's main concerns, as evidenced by my placement in Intel: there, my hip-hop squad worked alongside the units devoted to organized crime, gangs, security for politicians and judges, and, of course, most important of all, security detail for Gracie Mansion, the stately, historic home for New York mayors since 1942.

Some NYPD guys know the Mafia like the back of their hand; others are forgery experts, others do warrants. Me, I know hip-hop, homicide, and the music industry like George Steinbrenner knows the Yankees' batting lineup. Even before I was commissioned to start a rap-intelligence unit, I was always known around the NYPD as the go-to guy and all-around expert in rap-related crime. The big bosses let it be known loud and clear throughout the force: if a crime occurred involving a rapper or someone in the hip-hop industry, Derrick Parker was to be notified pronto.

It appeared I was preternaturally disposed to become the hip-hop cop. I've spent nearly all of my professional life working the streets of New York's hardest-knock neighborhoods that, in retrospect, would be seen as the legendary spawning ground for rap music and culture: Brooklyn, Queens, the "Boogie-Down" Bronx. I'd grown up with rap as the soundtrack to my life and had always loved the music—and like many, I've been sucked in by the drama that follows it like a shadow.

As a fan (and even sometime performer), I had always kept my foot in the music industry, which inadvertently helped me in my law-enforcement career. Starting in the early '80s, I'd immersed myself in the music world. I'd hit all the hot spots, attending legendary hip-hop clubs like the Latin Quarter to check out budding rappers like Heavy D and Big Daddy Kane before they became stars. I'd hang out in black-music industry spots like Bentley's and Chas & Wilson's, and at urban music conventions like Jack the Rapper, where I'd network with everyone from Russell Simmons and Puff Daddy to Suge Knight and Snoop Dogg.

My law-enforcement career coincided with two key developments: the rise of crack cocaine as urban America's deadliest plague and the growth of hip-hop music out of a ghetto fad into a permanent part of the mainstream pop-culture landscape. With my involvement in and passion for music, I had unwittingly created the ultimate deep cover. Even before I started a "Rap Intelligence Unit," I was a one-man "mod squad." My clashing personas proved awkward sometimes: when I made the rap scene, people would always ask me, "Are you a promoter?" Often, I so blended into the hip-hop world that my fellow cops would be fooled. I had the same response for both camps: "Nah—I'm 'po-po'!" That wasn't always the answer either wanted to hear.

As drug dealers started swarming around rappers at clubs and concerts in the birth of the crack era, I was always there, waiting in the wings; I was invisible, but I kept my eyes and ears wide open. My double life followed me everywhere. I started noticing heavyweight drug dealers and known felons attaching themselves to music celebrities—often the same criminals I was chasing for my day job. The coincidence haunted me. Before my eyes, my police work and music-business interests started to converge.

As a result, in my decades spent working my way up through the NYPD's ranks, I've seen hip-hop grow from ghetto subculture to the most dominant pop-cultural force operating today. Behind the lurid tabloid headlines and stereotypes, hip-hop has grown into possibly the second greatest African-American art form after jazz. I've put my life on the line for it many times, spending most of my career trying to protect its legacy. I've watched rap spawn superstars from Eminem and 50 Cent to Ice Cube and Wu-Tang Clan, with hip-hop becoming not just the most popular music genre worldwide—it's evolved into the lingua franca for the disenfranchised everywhere.

Rap has moved from serving as the voice of urban America to dominating the heart and soul of people of all ages and races, from heartland American suburbs to Asia, Africa, Europe, and beyond— and it's brought its problems with it. But if there's one thing I've learned having hip-hop under my microscope all these years, it's that, despite its vitality, the rap game has got itself stuck on death row, and the appeals are running out. To me, Jam Master Jay's murder was the ultimate indication of that prognosis.

In fact, the night Jam Master Jay was killed I was working security at a nightclub in downtown Manhattan's Soho district called NV. NV was a glamorous, exclusive hangout favored in particular by the hip-hop elite, which was once the site of a rap-related shooting. It later closed down. Ironically, it was one of the main places I used to do surveillance as the hip-hop cop. Now in post-retirement, I found myself on the other side of the game.

The minute word of it hit the streets, Jam Master Jay's killing was sure to be a massive case, with huge media exposure and controversy. Still, the way NYPD had been dealing with rap-related crime since I left the force made it clear to me that they would probably botch the investigation.

The problem was, Jam Master Jay wasn't even *in* the Binder. Jay had no criminal record to speak of, and he was no "gangsta" rapper, either—when Run-DMC began in the '80s, rap wasn't as criminally minded, and Run-DMC often focused on uplifting positivity and Afrocentric black pride over gun talk in their songs. Jam Master Jay was never perceived to have committed any violence in his life. A family man with a wife and two daughters, Jay—born Jason Mizell in 1965—died at thirty-seven years old, much older than most of the young hotheads typically causing trouble in rap circles.

Jam Master Jay was truly one of the most beloved figures in the rap community, both for his easygoing charisma and his musical innovations. Despite his star status, Jay was a benevolent mentor, frequently encouraging up-and-coming rappers' careers; he was instrumental in helping now-famous rap star 50 Cent get his first major-label record deal. But Jay was most legendary as one of the seminal figures in the development of "turntablism," where hip-hop D.J.s transformed record players into musical instruments, cutting and scratching musical phrases off vinyl to create a whole new sound. Jay was both innovator and virtuoso—what Picasso was to the paintbrush, Jam Master Jay was to the turntable.

Most perplexing of all, Jay had few, if any, known enemies. Indeed, Jam Master Jay wasn't involved in any of the highly publicized "beefs" between rival rappers that make headlines—and often end in violence. There was nothing in Jay's background like the dispute between thuggish West Coast rap kingpin Suge Knight and his Death Row Records crew and Sean "Puff Daddy" Combs's New York–based Bad Boy posse. Their beef had already claimed the lives of two rap icons. Tupac Shakur, who was signed to Death Row, had been murdered in a drive-by shooting in Las Vegas in 1996, while Bad Boy's premier artist Notorious B.I.G. had been slain one year later outside a party at the Petersen Auto Museum in Los Angeles.

That wasn't Jay. Yet, as I would later discover as I delved deeper into the case, Jam Master Jay had taken to carrying a firearm for the first time in his life in the weeks before his killing; as I investigated further, other lurid details that contradicted his public image started to come out of the woodwork. Yes, Jay's murder was one of the strangest cases I'd encountered in my career as an investigator. And when I saw the unmarked Chevy Impala tailing my truck as I drove away from Jam Master Jay's funeral, I knew it was only going to get stranger. . . .

Soon after I heard about Jay's shooting, I got a call from my friend Eric B., a rap icon in his own right as the D.J. half of legendary rap duo Eric B. & Rakim. Eric B. doesn't talk just to talk: when he's serious about something, he makes sure you know. This was one of those times: Eric needed my help. "Lydia and the other witnesses, they're very afraid," he told me. Lydia High was one of the key witnesses in the Jam Master Jay case, and a good friend of Eric's. She was also Jay's personal assistant and the receptionist for his recording studio. It was no surprise, then, that the authorities suspected that Lydia saw more than she let on—or maybe even that she was involved as a perpetrator.

More than anything, Eric was worried for the witnesses' safety, as the police were doing little to protect them. "They don't know why someone wanted to kill Jay, and, as witnesses, if that someone may now want to kill them," he intoned gravely in his deep voice. The hardcore investigator in me kicked in; furiously I started taking notes. According to Eric, the NYPD was being very intimidating in their interrogation, scaring the witnesses even more than they already were.

"Cops on the scene put Lydia in handcuffs the night of the murder, yelling at her and berating her just hours after her friend was killed in her presence," Eric explained with frustration. "Can you believe that?" I could. Soon enough I would experience just how hard charging my former peers were acting in the case.

Despite the tensions and danger remaining around the incident, Lydia still wanted to attend Jay's funeral. "But Lydia doesn't have any money for security," Eric tells me. "She can't afford it, and she's afraid to attend the service without serious protection." He asked

me if, as a favor to him, I'd be Lydia's security. I agreed gladly; besides, my hunger to seek the truth hadn't left me when I left the
force. I wanted to see what was going on from the inside for myself.

Before the funeral, I took precautions to protect Lydia. I contacted both Malcolm Smith, a state senator from Queens, and Rev.
Floyd Flake, a respected figure in the African-American community
and a senator himself, to arrange for Lydia to enter from the
church's back door. I didn't want Lydia to enter through the main
entrance—she was still too vulnerable as an eyewitness. I packed a
9mm pistol in my waistband, just in case.

The funeral was held on November 5, 2002, at the Allen A.M.E.
Cathedral in Queens. The ceremony proved very tasteful, passing
without incident. Jay's big-name pals were out in force—rap celebrities like Salt-N-Pepa rubbed shoulders with basketball players and
music-biz insiders like executive Andre Harrell and mogul/socialite
Russell Simmons, who was Run-DMC's manager and co-founded the
legendary Def Jam label. Simmons's brother Joseph—aka Reverend
Run, the "Run" of Run-DMC—eulogized his late bandmate with
great sincerity.

"Jason helped build hip-hop," Simmons intoned in the commanding voice so familiar from Run-DMC hits. "And his job is finished." Jay's friends in the crowd wore black bowler hats and white
shelltoe Adidas in honor of the D.J's trademark style. (Later in my
investigation, I would discover that one of Jay's killers had attended
the funeral, sporting a bowler and shelltoes himself. But I'm getting
ahead of myself.)

After the memorial service, Lydia decided she wanted to attend
Jay's burial, too. This wasn't part of the original agenda, but I
turned my black Nissan Xterra to join the procession moving toward the Valhalla Funeral Home anyway; I wanted her to fully grieve
her close friend Jay, so that day I was going anywhere she wanted to.
The thing was, I wasn't alone in that thought.

On the way to the burial, I saw an unscript police car creeping behind me. When Lydia and her girlfriend Missy (who had joined us for
the ceremony) noticed the car, too, they became increasingly agitated.

"Damn, we didn't do anything!" Lydia cried. "Why are the police following us?"

"They're probably just following the funeral procession," I responded, trying to put her at ease. "They're here because they don't want anything to happen."

It was a reasonable enough explanation. I almost believed it myself.

Lydia, Missy, and I made it through the entire burial ceremony, which was even more emotional and intense than the memorial—I found myself choking up as I threw a rose onto Jay's coffin before they lowered it into the ground. Lydia had trouble tearing herself away: we waited until everyone had said their last goodbyes, making our group one of the last to leave. As I drove away from the funeral home in the Xterra, Lydia was still wiping tears from her eyes. That's when I saw the unmarked Chevy tailing us again in the rearview mirror.

At Francis Lewis Boulevard and 104th Avenue in Hollis, Queens, the Impala finally made a move. When it put on its siren to pull us over, Lydia started freaking out.

"The man just got buried," she sobbed. "Why don't the cops just leave us alone?" My words couldn't console her, with good reason. As the cops got out of the car, I saw one of them was my friend Bernie Porter, accompanied by a white detective I didn't know. As I got out and walked over to Bernie to find out what was going on, Lydia cracked the window slightly and started yelling.

"Why don't you just leave us alone?" she screamed as the white detective quickly approached my car. Before I knew what was happening, the white detective began yanking on the door handle, trying hard to get it open as he ordered Lydia to unlock the door. "Let me *in*!" he bellowed. Tears began streaming anew down Lydia's face.

I was *shocked*—this guy was really coming on strong. Okay, I'm not that surprised; after all, the detectives were from *Queens*. They have what cops from other boroughs call the "Queens Marines" mentality. They take short cuts that don't lead anywhere—like this: they don't know how to treat the community, and then they wonder why they can't get witnesses to cooperate. Enraged, I rushed over to stop him.

"Hey, Detective, don't do that," I told him. The detective ignored me, continuing to violently wrench the locked door. He was pulling so hard, I was afraid he would tear it off.

"She's given me her permission to enter the vehicle," he shouted back.

"Nobody is giving you permission to enter *my* car," I responded. The detective kept ignoring me until Bernie Porter spoke directly to his partner.

"Cut it out—this is *Derrick Parker's* car," Porter instructed him wearily. My name didn't appear to hold much weight with this hot-head until Porter spelled out my real deal for his partner: "Derrick's a retired detective—he was in charge of Intel's rap squad."

This made Mr. Queens Marine back off, but it was too late. The damage to Lydia was done. "She'll never cooperate with the police after this," I thought to myself. Jam Master Jay's body was barely in the ground, and the cops might have already blown it, probably irreparably, with a key eyewitness in the case.

Seeing this kind of behavior from the cops, I was worried whether the Jam Master Jay case would ever be solved. When I called Bernie Porter before, he told me they were having trouble getting witnesses to talk. Now I saw why—with interrogation tactics like these, the witnesses were more scared of the police than they were of the killers. It was all too typical, too familiar. I knew at this moment that the Jam Master Jay case would never be closed by the NYPD. Just like the Tupac shooting in Las Vegas and the Notorious B.I.G. murder in Los Angeles, now New York had its own unsolved murder of a superstar rap icon. Congratulations, law enforcement, you've done it again.

Like its predecessors, Jam Master Jay's case will most certainly remain unsolved, despite all the headlines and outcry. It's a disturbing pattern that the highest-profile murder cases involving rap celebrities will never be solved. Nearly a decade after they happened, both Tupac Shakur's and Notorious B.I.G.'s killers remain at large and unprosecuted, and these were no ordinary victims.

Biggie and Tupac were luminaries not just to the black community, but to the world; next to the mighty Rakim, they are largely
considered the two greatest rappers in hip-hop history, with tens of
millions of records sold between them. The mythology and rever-
ence surrounding Tupac puts him somewhere between Elvis and
Nostradamus. In his music, Tupac always predicted his own death at
a young age; his killing turned him into a martyr, a Malcolm X–type
figure for younger generations. Ironically, his albums sell better now
that he's dead, and his lyrics read now like prophecies. While Tupac
is considered rap's greatest, most heartfelt storyteller, Notorious
B.I.G. had perhaps rap's greatest "flow." Big's barrage of too clever,
armor-piercing wordplay remains unparalleled, his cadences taking
on a unique, spontaneous musical flair that rivaled the best jazz players. And Jam Master Jay, well, he's one of those that put rap on the
map in the first place. With Run-DMC, the group that first took hip-
hop to international success, Jay helped pave the way for many future generations of Biggies and Tupacs.

These icons are famous and beloved worldwide, yet when it comes
to solving rap-related cases, well, something is rotten in New York
City. My mission took on new urgency when I saw how the NYPD
and the Queens D.A. were going about trying to solve the Jam Master Jay case: not only were they culturally unequipped to deal with
the hip-hop community, they were unwilling to give the case the resources it needed to close it. I was enraged; you can't just do business as usual when dealing with rap-related crime. After personally
putting in over one hundred hours of unpaid time, I eventually un-
covered what really happened in the Jam Master Jay's murder. While
the NYPD and other law-enforcement entities continue to bungle
the resulting investigations, other high-profile hip-hop crime incidents keep piling up.

Of late, the hip-hop crime story grabbing the most headlines is
the F.B.I.'s investigation of Murder Inc., record-label home to massive stars Ja Rule and Ashanti. Murder Inc.'s head Irv "Gotti"
Lorenzo, his partner/brother Chris "Gotti" Lorenzo, and other associates were arrested, charged, and released on one-million-dollar
bail, accused of using their label to launder drug money for Ken-

neth "Supreme" McGriff, one of the most dangerous, most feared
drug lords to come out of the Queens crack game. I'd been following McGriff's crime career for years on the force, along with many,
many other detectives and agents. McGriff has even been fingered
by 50 Cent as a suspect in the now-infamous 2001 shooting that left
nine bullets in the not-yet-famous rapper. "50, who shot ya?/You
think it was 'Preme, Freeze, or Ta-Ta?" 50 wonders aloud in the
song "Fuck You."

After many hairpin turns, the Gottis were ultimately acquitted of
all charges in a stunning defeat for the government. I have my own
personal insight into the Murder Inc. case: for three months during
2003, I worked as personal security for Chris Gotti, right at the moment the Feds' investigation in Murder Inc. was heating up. If I was
Murder Inc., I would have been worried—*real* worried: the Feds
have an over 90-percent success rate of convictions. That the F.B.I.
put Murder Inc. in their sights shows that hip-hop itself has a lot of
work to do before the police stop targeting it. It also reveals what can
happen when real criminals and big business commingle, a trend
that, despite such high-profile cases, shows no end in sight.

To me, the Jam Master Jay case represented something different.
With it, I found myself on more of a personal mission, as in many
ways I *identified* with him. Just like Jam Master Jay and the other
guys in Run-DMC, I was raised in Hollis, Queens, around the same
time they were. Through my youth, I always saw Jay around the
way. They were everywhere: Jay, Run, and DMC would drive constantly through the 'hood, back and forth, hanging out on Hollis
Avenue all the time. I saw them before they were stars, watched
them come up, and cheered when they finally made it. In fact, Run-
DMC formed in 1982, the same year I joined the force, and released
their classic first single "It's Like That/Sucker M.C.s" just one year
later.

Run-DMC were true icons in my world, pioneers, but more than
anything we *knew* them—that meant you had the ability to be closer
to them. Their success was our success; when Jay died, it was our
death, too. Understanding his murder became a lens through which
I could comprehend what was going on in society—why all this

deadly chaos was happening again in the rap game, and why it was getting worse, not better.

At nearly the same moment as Run-DMC were growing to international fame in the '80s, crack cocaine began dominating the inner-city drug trade. Suddenly, a subset of people who shared similar backgrounds were making a lot of money, more than they'd ever seen, either by selling crack rocks or rhyming into a microphone. Often the drug dealers and rappers were from the same neighborhoods—in the case of someone like Murder Inc.'s embattled label founder Irv "Gotti" Lorenzo and convicted felon drug dealer Kenneth "Supreme" McGriff, they'd been childhood friends. Suddenly cocaine-referencing songs like Grandmaster Flash's "White Lines" seemed like art imitating life.

The crossover happened quickly. Drug dealers, murderers, and robbers all saw the money rappers were making and wanted a piece themselves. Rap became the new crack game; it was just too damn tempting for the bad guys. Known drug dealers and felons started attaching themselves to hip-hop artists as security guards, managers, road managers, label backers, *whatever*. Drug money might fund, say, studio time for an aspiring rapper, always with an implied payback attached. Sometimes the drug dealers and gangbangers wanted to get on the mic themselves.

Today, it's almost required that you have a prison record before you make a record: hip-hop's biggest stars, from Jay-Z and 50 Cent to Snoop Dogg and The Game, all boast of their time dealing drugs, gangbanging, or both. Indeed, the thugs didn't leave their nefarious ways at the coat check when they joined the hip-hop party: more often than not, criminals didn't see the music business as their chance to go legit, but to expand operations. The results left hip-hop in an extended cycle of violence, murder, and corruption that has yet to end. That's what I was fighting.

As the NYPD's hip-hop cop, my primary duty was to protect the public. For example, if a shooting occurs at a rap concert or at an awards show, the danger multiplies—thousands of people are put at risk in a riot-type situation. I strived to prevent things like that from ever happening; if I was successful, I felt I'd done my job. But I also wanted to protect the rap artists themselves, either from rivals set-tling a score or someone just trying to jack them for their chain. By protecting rappers from their foes, often one can prevent a potential riot from happening in the first place. On a personal level, however, as a rap fan I more than anything wanted to protect the rap-music industry from destroying itself.

Now, not everyone in the rap community is a felon or gang-banger; even if a rapper has a past, it doesn't mean they're still out there committing crimes. "I was dirty before," gangsta-rap origina-tor Ice-T admits. "But my act is clean [now]. I'm square as a pool table, twice as green. I wouldn't steal a nickel off the mantelpiece, man. If you selling dope, you can't even buy me a hamburger." Nor does every rapper hate the police, either. "Hey, I like cops," claims Wu-Tang Clan star Method Man. "NYPD fuckin' rock!"

Some major figures in the hip-hop community feel that if rappers actually start policing themselves first, then the real police won't come on so strong. "It's kind of the rappers' fault," explains DMC, co-frontman of Run-DMC. "If you didn't present that [gangster] im-age, you wouldn't give 'em nothing to worry about. But you wanna get out there being all rah-rah and thugged-out and 'Yo, I'm Scar-face' . . . of course you're gonna get checked. You bring that upon yourself. Some of us are stupid enough to still ride around with unli-censed weapons. Either get a bodyguard or get your life together—you don't need to be out there still doing that stupid shit."* Too often, however, there's that one bad apple—and his twenty-strong, armed-to-the-teeth entourage—around to do exactly that "stupid shit."

At the same time, I understood a lot of the animosity rappers held toward the police—some of it very much justified. I always felt one of my duties as the hip-hop cop was to protect rappers from the NYPD itself. Police first need to establish trust and at the very least learn to communicate with the hip-hop community; if they don't, many police departments will continue to leave more and

---

* All quotes from this and the previous paragraph come from the article "50 Cent Arrested For Gun Possession," mtvnews.com.

more hip-hop-related crimes unsolved. Only when law enforcement starts solving murders like Tupac's, B.I.G's and Jay's will true bridges to hip-hop get built.

Throughout my career, I've worked under some of the most controversial, innovative police administrations in New York, and therefore the world. As an NYPD insider, I've experienced the insights, infights, and growing pains that come from changing eras of politics and law enforcement, all set to a hip-hop thump. As the department's top hip-hop cop, I found myself on hand for some of the most headline-grabbing cases involving some of the biggest names in rap. There was the Club New York shooting involving Puff Daddy, the rapper Shyne, and Jennifer Lopez; Puffy would find himself associated with so many criminal investigations, he got to know me by name. Then there was the funeral of superstar rapper Notorious B.I.G., the event that truly galvanized the NYPD as to the seriousness and scope of hip-hop crime. In addition, there were incidents involving Wu-Tang Clan, 50 Cent, Nas, DMX, Mobb Deep, Lil' Kim, and others. Not all of these artists were the perpetrators in the crimes—many were victims—but hip-hop was always the connective tissue; many details never made it to the papers. Indeed, there were whole *crimes* that the media never even heard about, let alone the public. As the original hip-hop cop, no one has been where I've been.

In the NYPD I was often alone, an outsider inside the system; my methods sometimes clashed with the powers that be and threatened police tradition. But when faced with hip-hop's gray areas, I knew routine police work wouldn't get the job done. But as rap gained notoriety in the public eye, holding on to my spot as the top hip-hop cop became harder. Ambitious detectives saw the hip-hop crime beat as a quick means to advance their career, and my peers started trying to sabotage me to get ahead. Subsequently, after two decades of public service, I left the force with a bitter taste in my mouth. My work wasn't done, however. It never is.

If I've learned anything in my experience as the top hip-hop cop, it's that the gray areas run grayer than anybody ever expected. Indeed, all sides in this game—from rap and law enforcement to big business—have their work cut out for them: there are hard lessons each has to learn when it comes to flying straight and cooperating with each other. I've been face to face with killers, drug dealers, and hip-hop's greatest lyricists—sometimes all at once. I've turned the hardest, most cop-hating felons into bean-spilling informants. That just went along with the job: after what I've been through as the hip-hop cop, I've seen it all.

Most of all, when it comes to hip-hop, the rule book *is* different. After all, nothing is quite like the music business—least of all the crime associated with it. There's always been crime in the music business, regardless of race, nationality, ethnicity, or religion. Jewish organized-crime figures like Roulette Records head Morris Levy regularly flouted the rule of law while chasing cash in the early days of rhythm and blues and rock and roll. Later, in the "Rat Pack" era of Frank Sinatra and Dean Martin, the Italian Mafia famously entrenched themselves in the music industry, dominating it for decades.

Today, the rap industry is going through the same phase: similar to how organized crime behaved during prohibition, bad guys now are moving in because there's a lot of money there, legal and otherwise. It's like any other criminal enterprise, just with a lot more flashy allure and heated racial politics added, all set to a beat you can dance to. In my case, I've only ever looked at criminal activity, not skin color: as a black man myself, I have no interest in persecuting other blacks for no reason. Unfortunately, hip-hop-related crime remains largely in the African-American community, although it's spreading to other racial groups and even other countries around the world. Like a virus, it recognizes no borders: as rap spreads its influence beyond the United States, countries ranging from England to South Korea are finding hip-hop crime growing in their midst.

Hip-hop crime remains on a nonstop roll, and while the NYPD and other police departments around the country are interested in it, they still didn't know how to deal with it. In terms of hip-hop, law enforcement has a lot on its plate. A rash of incidents spanning from the dusk of 2004 to the dawn of 2005 through today shows that rap-related crime remains a more unabated threat than ever. A man was stabbed at the 2004 VIBE Awards following an assault on Dr. Dre; authorities charged Dre's protégé, G-Unit soldier Young Buck, for the stabbing. Buck has since proclaimed his innocence. R&B star R. Kelly claimed that he was the victim of an assault involving a member of Jay-Z's entourage. Lil' Kim was sent to prison for perjury. Death Row Records mogul and recidivist criminal Suge Knight continued to find himself in conflict with the law, including an incident in Miami that left him shot in the leg. Meanwhile, 50 Cent started so many beefs during this period, he might as well be a butcher—including one spat with his own protégé, Los Angeles–based rapper The Game; a clash between Game's and 50's entourages resulted in a man being shot at a popular hip-hop radio station. Of late, crime has infected all corners of the rap community: both established rap stars (DMX, Ja Rule, Snoop Dogg, Beanie Sigel, C-Murder) and those new jacks on the come-up (Young Jeezy, Game, Cassidy) have found themselves linked recently to any number of serious violations of the law.

And that's just what made the papers. Hip-hop crime has now become a full-blown epidemic. Everywhere rappers go, the threat of violence hangs in the air, and persecution follows: while that's always been true on some level, the stakes are higher now. Federal authorities now feel emboldened to shut hip-hop down, especially as, thanks to hip-hop's economic power, big business has never felt more comfortable getting in bed with known criminals. As long as large corporations like Reebok continue to do major deals with the likes of, say, 50 Cent and Jay-Z, the Feds will be watching and waiting for any misstep. It's not a game.

So yes, while this is my story, it's really the history of something much, much bigger: how hip-hop grew into the global power it is today, set against crucial issues affecting real people. As such, this is only the beginning: unless extreme measures are taken, things are only going to get worse with hip-hop crime.

More than anything, both hip-hop and law enforcement need to take a real good, hard look at themselves. They say hip-hop is all about being "keeping it real"—well, money, let's get down to some *real* talk then. To the truth.

Do you think you can handle it? Do you think you can handle the truth? If so, read on.

It goes a little something like this . . .

2.

THESE ARE THE BREAKS:
The Birth of Hip-Hop—and the Hip-Hop Cop

BEFORE I was the hip-hop cop, I was merely "hip-hop." The culture had started as inner-city party music in late 1970s New York, and it was immediately the beat of the street—and the soundtrack to my life: since its inception, rap went with the territory of being a young black male. The first hip-hop record I ever heard was the same one everybody else did—"Rapper's Delight" by the Sugarhill Gang, arguably the first ever rap single, released all the way back in 1979. But me and other original hip-hop heads back in the day had been hearing hip-hop in its original form long before it ever made it to wax. Little did we know all these good-time party grooves would change musical history.

At first, the D.J.s were the stars of this new scene—old-school heroes like Grandmaster Flash, Lovebug Starski, and Kool Herc—and I saw them all, anywhere from impromptu outdoor parties in ghetto parks to legendary hip-hop clubs like the Fever in the Bronx and uptown's Harlem World. Back in the day, rappers merely served the D.J. as hype men: their "raps" were not songs so much as uplifting chatter to get the crowd excited at parties. My favorite back then was Eddie Cheeba, who was always getting the party started on the mic—I loved that guy, and Kurtis Blow, too, who was a big name in the clubs. The hip-hop D.J., on the other hand, was in the process of inventing a kind of renegade sonic alchemy on the turntables that would jumpstart a hip-hop revolution.

During the '70s disco era, club disc jockeys figured out how to layer and blend disco's thumping beats together seamlessly, sometimes creating one long, hypnotic, seemingly endless groove out of two songs. Around the same time, in West Indian enclaves in outer New York City boroughs like the Bronx and Brooklyn, reggae D.J.s would play "dub" versions of songs, isolating and repeating fragments of, say, a bassline or snare hit to moody, atmospheric effect. Old-school hip-hop D.J. innovators like Herc, Flash, and Grand Wizzard Theodore would blend these approaches and add their own, taking these moves even further to create new music out of old sounds.

Using two copies of the same vinyl record on two turntables, early hip-hop D.J.s would locate the funkiest instrumental portion of a song (known as the "break" in D.J. slang) and replay it over and over again by cutting and mixing between the tables, creating an irresistibly percussive, dynamic groove. Soon, D.J.s were "scratching" minute fragments and phrases of the beat to create their own new dance-floor rhythms (Theodore, for example, is generally known as the inventor of the scratch technique). The sources for this new sound were surprisingly catholic: while many "breaks" came from great jazz or soul classics from the likes of, say, James Brown, others came from more obscure or surprising sources. In Run-DMC's early days, for example, the group's M.C.s would drop rhymes over Jam Master Jay cutting up the funky drum break in Aerosmith's 1975 hard-rock hit. "Walk This Way"; in 1986, Run-DMC would cover "Walk This Way" to create rap's first international smash hit.

Run-DMC proved crucial in turning rap from inner-city subculture into a worldwide success story, largely because they represented a key trend: emphasizing the rapper as the hip-hop group's main attraction. Early rap groups like Grandmaster Flash and the Furious Five named themselves after their D.J.: Run-DMC, on the other hand, took their name from its two rapping frontmen, who had started fashioning their syncopated chatter into songs with infectious choruses that sounded great blasting out of radios. Now, instead of the mute D.J. hiding behind turntables, rap music had recognizable faces and personalities that could be marketed for real. Once rap songs started cracking the Top 40, its march to world pop-cultural dominance had begun.

By the mid-'80s, hip-hop's transformation from a D.J.-driven phenomenon to pushing the rappers forward as headliners was complete. Major record labels started signing rappers to deals; soon enough, hip-hop groups like Run-DMC and the Beastie Boys would be selling out stadiums. In addition to bringing rap commercial success, Run-DMC's greatest contribution was bringing the street vibe to the forefront of the genre. Rap music was always street music, but before Run-DMC, rappers tended to look more like disco holdovers: groups like the Furious Five resembled the Village People in their feather headdresses, spikes, and leather getups more than what would become known as "b-boy style." Run-DMC, meanwhile, were real b-boys; they dressed like cats on the street really dressed. In picture after picture from the era, they rock Kangols, black Lee jeans, fly eyeglasses like Cazales, and shelltoe Adidas with either the fattest laces possible—or no laces at all.

Even though the members of Run-DMC were no gangsters, they looked, in fact, like the media stereotype of a street thug, and the in-your-face, aggressive blare of their music seemed to second that. Not surprisingly, the moment Run-DMC began making the scene in the early '80s was also when the *real* street thugs started making inroads into hip-hop, as I would discover. And it would be the street life's growing intersection with rap that would result in the murder of Jam Master Jay.

Me personally, I loved Run-DMC most of all. They looked like the guys I knew from around the way, from where I grew up. They looked like the dudes playing basketball in the parks I played in, the fly guys hanging around the streets, avenues, and boulevards I ran up and down every day. That's because, like me, Run-DMC came from the outer-borough area of New York City known as Hollis, Queens. Hollis is one of the premier hip-hop hotbeds thanks to Run-DMC: LL Cool J hails from there as well, and today's hip-hop boldfaced stars like Irv Gotti and Ja Rule got their start in and around Hollis, too, watching Run-DMC perform impromptu shows at local parks like 192 Park. "I was at 192 Park when Run-DMC invented 'Here We Go' [one of Run-DMC's greatest songs]," Ja Rule told Rafer Guzman in a 2004 *New York Newsday* article. In the same piece, Guzman wrote, "If Run-DMC are the Beatles of hip-hop, then Hollis is their Liverpool"—and he's right.

Basically, if you were from Hollis, you considered Run-DMC family, and to me, family's always been something worth fighting for. In 1961, I was born Derrick James Parker to a big family with a classic New York melting-pot ethnic background—mostly African-American mixed with a little Jewish, a little Italian, and who knows what else. My family was so big, my dad had to make bunk beds out of wood because he couldn't afford to buy beds for so many kids. I was actually born in another hip-hop hot spot, Bedford-Stuyvesvant, Brooklyn—and I continued to visit the area every Sunday to see my grandparents (as well, I would later work in Bed-Stuy as a homicide detective). But I always say I became a man in Queens. My family moved to Hollis when I was four, and growing up there was perfect: I always say "I'm from the 'hood, but I'm not really from the 'hood." *That's* Hollis.

Growing up, Hollis, Queens, was the perfect mix of urban and suburban. It's a largely African-American community, and certainly many of the issues facing inner-city America can be found there. At the same time, there's a kind of middle-class upward mobility that's empowering. Families live in Hollis, and people there take pride in caring for their homes. It's the kind of place where all that "be all you can be" talk actually doesn't fall on deaf ears: when I was growing up, Hollis was the kind of environment where you could both stay in touch with the community *and* make it happen for yourself.

Hollis to me was America's melting pot. My mother called me the all-American kid, and I suppose I was. I wasn't looking to throw my life away and be stereotypical, no way. Basketball was my thing—I idolized Dr. J, and rocked an Afro and Converse Chuck Taylors just like him—but music was my real passion. Then again, me becoming a cop was probably inevitable.

After I spent three years at St. John's University in nearby Jamaica, Queens, my parents, tapped out by the financial challenge of taking care of such a large family, could no longer afford to pay for my college education. Joining the NYPD seemed like my best option. Of my ten brothers and sisters, almost all of them are involved in law enforcement, which is no surprise. My father was first a marine sergeant and later a member of the sanitation police, and he always encouraged civil service. He was also committed to the idea of doing good, of doing your part for the good of the world. "I'm going to go out there and make a difference," I said to myself when I signed up for the Police Academy in 1982. I've tried to live up to that; in my twenty years as a cop, I've never had to fire my gun, and I wanted to rise as high on the force as I could.

Working my way through the NYPD, though, I always kept a foot in the music industry, promoting various parties and even performing occasionally as a singer; in 1988, I recorded a solo R&B single called "Single Man," which attracted the interest of talent scouts from major labels like RCA. Music was in my blood—literally. My grandfather on my mother's side was Willie Bryant, a legendary entertainer back in the day, the master of ceremonies at Harlem's Apollo Theater back in its old-time prime. Willie's wife, my grandmother Lillian, also came from showbiz—she was a dancer on Broadway. Grandpa Willie even acted on the TV show *The Untouchables*; his character's identifying quirk was that he could pass for white. "Passing" was another legacy my grandfather gave me—due to my light skin, in undercover operations I could pass for black, Latino, Italian, whatever. This chameleonic ability helped me fit in as the hip-hop cop, too. I was always there in the background at concerts and clubs, and no one knew whether I was a fan, a promoter, or what.

I found I had to be a chameleon on the job, too—it helps to be able to blend in at the NYPD, believe me. Police work was changing because crime was changing; it had to evolve, even if that meant some kicking and screaming. I would see the NYPD through many eras. I started in the anarchic Ed Koch days, and later served under David Dinkins's administration. I worked under Giuliani's brash first police commissioner, Bill Bratton, who's now in charge of the

Los Angeles Police Department (LAPD). Back then, however, Bratton's main goal was to modernize and streamline the department into a stealth crime-fighting machine: he even got the NYPD into the computer era with the COMPSTAT (Computerized Analysis of Crime Strategies) program, which revolutionized crime fighting. Under Bratton, even minor quality-of-life crimes like jaywalking and subway-turnstile jumping were brutally enforced like never before. Bratton was too successful: in the process, he alienated both the old guard and Rudy Giuliani, who felt Bratton was getting too much credit—and too many headlines—for reduced crime rates. Bratton was replaced by Howard Safir, under whom the hip-hop squad began. After Safir, of course, came Bernard Kerik, a hard-hitting yet inventive commish who had his own way of running things, too—and his own passion to crush hip-hop crime.

When I started in the early '80s as a rookie beat cop in the Midtown North precinct, I saw wild, wild times. Walking the blocks around Forty-second Street and Hell's Kitchen, I dealt with more pimps, prostitutes, panhandlers, and three-card monte players than I could handle. It was fun—the time of my life. At the same time, I was experiencing hip-hop's glory days in their uncut magnificence. It was an exciting time—everything in society was changing and transforming. *Especially* the NYPD. And I was on the frontlines for all of it.

At the time, law enforcement was in the midst of change and identity crisis. Even by the '80s, the Women's Liberation movement of the '60s and '70s hadn't exactly made much impact on everyday police culture. Back then, male cops didn't like to have women partners, and not just because your knees got bruised when they pulled up the bench seats in the Chryslers when it was their turn to drive. Police brutality was more casual back then, too—I remember seeing a sergeant punch out an obnoxious drunk kid during a Who concert at Shea Stadium like it wasn't anything. But these attitudes and traditions wouldn't last for long.

The complexion of the force was starting to change, too, resembling more of the demographic reality of New York's ethnic populations. The NYPD had always been dominated by Irish clans, but you were now seeing entire African-American families like mine, where nearly every member of the family wore some kind of badge. Most of all, when I joined the NYPD, I didn't want to be a "quota sergeant" and get promoted just because of my race. I hated that people stigmatized blacks as dumb—that we could pass Police Academy tests with lower grades than our white peers. I wanted to prove those ideas wrong in my performance. Exuding ambition in everything I did, when I got into the force, I studied how its hierarchies moved, who got promoted, and why. I was going to make sure I wouldn't be a beat cop forever.

As well, I discovered that police work is like a litmus test for racial issues. During that early era of my career, law enforcement mirrored what was happening in the world: society was changing, *period*. After Midtown North, I moved on to the 101st Precinct in the beach slums of Far Rockaway, Queens. There I really learned about the streets. If someone wanted to move out of the vicious 'hood of Bed-Stuy, well, Far Rockaway was the next step; unfortunately, more than a few of those people were criminally minded, and brought their badness to the beach. It was a no-man's-land out there—the suits over at One Police Plaza didn't care much about the poor Jews, blacks, and what cops called the "shanty Irish" populating Far Rockaway. The neighborhood was changing quickly, and the racial mix was starting to explode. The area was severely impacted by the "busing" era of desegregation, where black kids were bused to schools in white neighborhoods. We were constantly getting called in for race riots where white kids would turn the buses over and throw rocks at their new classmates of different skin color.

When I started at the NYPD, hip-hop was just creeping into consciousness on a national scale; hip-hop's growth into the juggernaut it is today mirrored my twenty years spent as a New York cop. Hip-hop's rise brought racial issues into America's pop-culture mainstream— and soon the world's. And as hip-hop went on its collision course with crime, racial issues within the NYPD, LAPD, and other police departments around the country bubbled back to the surface. It's not just always about racism per se—although that can certainly play a part. For many officers, the rap game simply remains a different world, a different language, and a hostile one at that.

This cultural divide still affects police work severely. If a cop interacts with a young black male (and even those of other races) dressed in hip-hop fashion, in many cases that officer brings whatever cultural prejudices he or she has toward hip-hop in addition to their own ideas about race. Prejudice, ignorance—whatever you want to call it—it affects police work detrimentally. I can say that, from my experience, cases like both Tupac shootings, the Puff Daddy incident at Club New York, the Biggie Smalls murder, and many others were compromised by such attitudes. Later in my career, when fellow officers started gunning for my spot and trying to take me down, race proved a definite factor as well.

From my perspective, then and now, too many in law enforcement remain culturally unequipped to deal with criminal developments in the hip-hop world. That lack of cultural knowledge and experience may not be their fault, but their unwillingness to learn in the face of a growing epidemic is. And it's not just non-blacks in law enforcement who represent this tendency. Too often, law enforcement higher-ups of whatever race put African-American officers on hip-hop crime cases simply because they're black. The thinking behind that tendency is that, since hip-hop was created by African-Americans—that much they get, anyway—then a black cop will automatically have a special decoder ring for sifting through the culture.

After the Biggie Smalls murder in Los Angeles, the LAPD sent out two black detectives to work with me in New York. I was puzzled—they didn't know anything about hip-hop. "My kids listen to that stuff—not me," they would tell me. At the same time, the few law-enforcement professionals that have dedicated themselves to really getting at the roots of hip-hop crime aren't always black, either. LAPD detective Russell Poole is as straight arrow and Caucasian as they come, but he forced himself to consider all the angles in his investigation into Biggie's murder, to the point where he had to go against his own department and was ostracized.

It's *complicated*, man. The thinking seems to be that race will provide a cover of some kind in such delicate situations. If I had white partners in the hip-hop squad, say, then when everything came down, the racial-profiling angle might have more credence in the eyes of some. It's *bullshit*. I'm not saying I cared about the race of my partner at all—what I cared about was his ability to get cases solved. And if you're going to solve cases, you've got to know your beat backwards and forwards. For the most part, the cops I knew didn't know hip-hop culture and didn't care to know. It's kinda like some cops' attitudes toward gang crime—you know, as long as those savages are killing each other, who cares? I've heard that too many times, in too many variations, from someone wearing a badge.

Politics. Racism. Ignorance. Ambition. In addition to the crimes I had to solve, the investigations I had to navigate, these were the challenges facing a hip-hop cop in the NYPD—my crosses to bear, all from within my own department. From my peers in blue. And as hip-hop became more and more prevalent throughout society, the stakes kept getting higher and higher on both sides, as I would come to discover. The bodies kept dropping, and as usual I was caught in the middle.

WHITE LINES:
Undercover in the Boogie-Down at the Dawn of Crack

This is only the beginning
Until this point the crack has been winning.
—*Kool Moe Dee, "Monster Crack," 1986*

Crack!! It got my niggaz addicted
Crack!! But got my niggaz convicted.
—*Cassidy, "Crack," 2005*

THE A-Team, the Supreme Team: these names hold special currency in pop culture. When fans of '80s television hear "A-Team," they think of the kitschy show about a mercenary vigilante posse starring famously mohawked celebrity Mr. T as the gang's muscle. When old-school hip-hop heads hear "Supreme Team," however, they think of The World Famous Supreme Team, a seminal group of hip-hop D.J.s known for their scratching sessions on WHBI, one of the New York area's earliest hip-hop radio stations, and some of rap's classic early singles like 1984's "Hey D.J." and their hit collaboration with Malcolm McLaren, "Buffalo Gals."

For those of us entrusted with the seemingly impossible job of keeping the killing-field streets of New York's outer boroughs crime-free during the late '80s, however, the A-Team and the Supreme Team were like the organized-crime Super Bowl, urban death squads devoted to murder and money. That their monikers carried the flashy arrogance of '80s hip-hop wasn't a coincidence. In my investigations into the A-Team and the Supreme Team, I would discover nascent links between the growing hip-hop world and new-style organized crime. These links would prove resilient: decades later into the millennium, it would be the Supreme Team's associa-

tion with the hip-hop label Murder Inc. that would place its principals Irv and Chris Gotti into the crosshairs of a F.B.I. investigation.

What gave ruthless gangs like the A-Team and the Supreme Team
maximum power and resources came down to one thing, and one
thing only: crack cocaine—the deadliest, most profitable drug trend
to hit the ghetto since heroin. In fact, crack is probably worse than
heroin; it's far more addictive, easier to imbibe, and cheaper to
make. Without the birth of crack in the inner city during the early-
to-mid '80s, the A-Team and Supreme Team would never have existed.

Smoking or "freebasing" cocaine was always the quickest, most
intense, and seductive high, but dealers struggled to find a suitable
method, as most freebasing methods proved typically too flammable
for common usage: the comedian Richard Pryor, for example, infa-
mously received severe burns while attempting to smoke cocaine in
1980. But by the mid-'80s, when dealers figured out they could create smokeable cocaine "rocks" by mixing the narcotic with baking
soda, a new holocaust was born. Crack got its name from the distinctive crackling sound a cocaine "rock" makes when ignited, yet
soon after it debuted it would leave a fracture through the urban
poor like an earthquake.

Today's rappers brandish their crack-dealing credentials as a
badge of street authenticity: 50 Cent's songs relentlessly eulogize
his days as a Queens crack hustler. Biggie even wrote the definitive
audio guide to selling rock, "The Ten Crack Commandments"
("Rule *numero uno*—never let no one know how much dough you
hold"). Crack in fact has been a subject of rap songs since the old-
school. As early as 1983, songs like Grandmaster Flash and Melle
Mel's anti-cocaine anthem "White Lines" were noting the sale of
"rocks"; by 1986, however, rappers had moved to endorsement—
"I'm never dusting out 'cause I torch that crack," rapped the
Beastie Boys on their hit of that year, "Hold It Now, Hit It."

Yet for those who lived in the 'hood, all crack brought was misery
and death. Makeshift ghetto drug labs sprung up in project apartments. Crack dens overflowed to capacity with zombied-out base-
heads. Prostitution skyrocketed to feed the addiction. Crack babies

flooded urban hospitals. And drug gangs used murder to regulate the streets, their bloody duels for street-corner supremacy felling many an innocent bystander with gunplay. It was war on 1980s city streets, and as an up-and-coming undercover narcotics operative with the right complexion, I had a front-row seat for all the action. I would even see crack infiltrate the NYPD. It was that heavy.

I didn't intend to be there, though—my entrée into the crack game was a coincidence of grand proportions. I was just looking for a promotion. After two years as a beat cop, I wanted out—I didn't want to be patrol and wear a uniform forever. I learned a lot as a beat cop. My senior partner, Steve Weiss, taught me Yiddish for one. From others I learned about how cops could get free steak dinners "on the arm" at restaurants, and how old-timers would turn your locker upside down if you didn't respect their fraternal codes of conduct. And after months of busting three-card monte dealers and panhandlers, I finally got my first "real collar," arresting a business-man wielding a .357 Magnum in front of a midtown office building. My peers gave me a party: "Congratulations, you're now a full-fledged cop!"

In just two years, I'd gotten more experience than I'd ever bar-gained for. As a part of a Neighborhood Stabilization Unit—and one of very few blacks in it—I'd seen my share of action; as one of the youngest guys working the Citizen Complaint Review Board, I'd experienced great insight into the inner workings of the NYPD and how it interacts with the citizens its assigned to protect. Going from Hell's Kitchen to working the slums of Far Rockaway, I'd really learned the streets, and I was itching to put all that knowledge to good use. After all, I didn't want to be stuck in a squad car forever. Steve Weiss, who had twelve years on the job, pushed me. "Der, you're a young guy—you're not meant to be on the beat," he told me. "Maybe you'll be a boss, a super-detective. You won't know un-til you try." *I* knew I didn't want to do patrol forever: I wanted a de-tective shield. At the time, there was one fast track to becoming detective, especially for a minority: undercover narcotics.

At the time, NYPD didn't need investigators in the narcotics division—they had those positions filled. But the NYPD was crippled in the most crucial area: they had nobody to go out and buy drugs undercover, and they needed minorities to do it. I put in my application; soon enough, they called and said "Parker, you passed—you're going to go to the Bronx." In particular, "Organized Crime Control Bureau, Bronx Narcotics"—that's how the assignment read. I got sent to the team 7A module, in the 7th district. Each district had a pool of four, with two undercovers on each team. It was so out of control: we all worked out of a tiny third-floor room with just a desk. Only time you had a typewriter is when you could find one—my colleagues had to bring their own. Everyone was playing their part: the white guys had hippie long hair, the girls dressed in street fashions, Hispanic guys rocked flashy earrings.

The Bronx was the hottest narcotics division in the country—the capital of where drugs were most prevalent not just in New York, but in the United States. The South Bronx in particular was the lab where all inner-city drug trends incubated, but I wasn't prepared for how hot the next trend was gonna get. No one was.

I started at Bronx Narcotics in July of 1984, right as the crack epidemic was poised to blow big time. When I started in narcotics work, it was like joining the army one day to pay for your college education, only to have George W. Bush declare war against Saddam Hussein the next day and ship you off immediately to Iraq. I was in for the ride of my life—of *anyone's* life.

I had almost no personal exposure to narcotics, which was a blessing and a curse. It was a blessing because drugs held no allure for me. Sure, growing up in the 'hood during the '70s, I saw kids smoking joints and sniffing cocaine in school. I had friends that did drugs at parties. It was the 1970s—most kids did drugs. Not me—I wasn't into that; I was more into sports. And after some guy dosed my brother with angel dust, well, I didn't want to do drugs after I saw how it messed him up. I wasn't looking to throw my life away. I didn't want to fit anyone's stereotype of what it is to be a black man—I wanted to be my own man, and that attitude came into my police work early on. But my inexperience was a curse because I had no idea what I was getting into: one of crack cocaine's earliest and most active hotbeds in the country.

I knew undercover narcotics work was dangerous. I knew undercover cops had died in the line of duty. A lot of undercovers suffer from depression, a result of having to become something that they are not: to do the job, you had to become a drug addict, a drug dealer, like an actor. You're living a fast life that's not yours, handling real drugs, and you've got to be very convincing—or you could be killed. Sometimes, dancing so close to the flame, undercovers can cross the line into addiction and dealing themselves.

My mother was worried. I was barely into my twenties, and she didn't want me to do that dangerous stuff; all she could do was pray for the best, and as a Jehovah's Witness, she prayed a lot. Worry didn't just come from my family. A lot of guys I worked with on the force said to me, "You've got to be crazy *and* stupid to do undercover narcotics." I think I was little bit of both; I thought going undercover would be *exciting*. I fantasized about my new job like it was a TV show. After all, I was going to the *Bronx*, a place where you can buy drugs like orange juice. I had no idea how exciting this assignment would prove.

The Bronx Narcotics office was predominantly Irish—all the bosses, anyway: there was maybe one black or Hispanic boss at any given time, but they were a rarity. Even rarer were nonminority undercover operatives themselves. When I met a white undercover guy named Jeff Beck—no relation to the famous British rock guitarist of the same name—I was shocked: Beck looked like a shorter version of Tom Selleck, not a street thug! I was like, "Wow, they got a *white guy* to go undercover—where's *he* gonna work?" The Irish bosses were like our keepers—either you were gonna be good or bad. There was a merit system in place: if you were a good undercover, everybody wanted you. If you were bad, you were out. I was determined to succeed.

Scarier still, for such an intense job, there was surprisingly little training. Sure, they sent me to "undercover school," but that didn't teach me very much: I did some target practice at the shooting range, they showed me boring movies, I learned how to analyze drugs, *blah, blah, blah*. It wasn't much of a training course—just enough so the department could say you had training. Besides, the bosses figured that my being black gave me innate insight into the job: my real training consisted of them saying, "Hey, you're a minority—you know what you gotta do." The bosses were excited because of my chameleonic complexion. "Parker, you can be anything—black, Hispanic, Indian," they would tell me in amazement.

Race issues were always in the air at Bronx Narcotics, and we dealt with them mostly through dark humor. One of my fellow officers was an Irish guy with big red cheeks that I called "the Klansman." We'd make racial jokes—I'd say, "I wouldn't go into your neighborhood because there's too many Klansmen up there." I teased them, saying, "I know you're going to beat up some black people." And they would jokingly talk about busting black and Hispanic dudes right back at me. During buys where I was deep undercover, they'd handcuff me during the bust and throw me down a flight of stairs. I wanted to kill them. They said, "Derrick, we had to make it real good." Really, they could have crippled me, but I had to laugh it off. We had to make a joke of it just to get through the day.

Where you felt race issues most, however, was on the street. One day, our lieutenant tells me, "I need you to go out with Jeff to be a 'ghost.'" A "ghost" is an undercover or investigator who blends in and watches another undercover make the buy so that he leaves the set without being robbed or cut. You see, as our token Caucasian undercover, Jeff Beck was having problems doing buys. As a ghost, I went with Jeff to this chicken joint on Boston Road, where the dealing was so rampant the line ran out the door, and those people in line weren't there to buy the food. While we're inside, a sergeant waited in the car with the backup team.

As Jeff and I waited, a stocky black guy came out from behind the counter and addressed the crowd. "Who here is affiliated with NYPD?" he yelled. Jeff, who's six or seven guys ahead of me, started laughing. The black guy walked up to Jeff and started slapping the shit out of him, saying, "We're not selling to you, *cop*." I went for the gun in my waistband, but then I paused—I didn't know what to do. After a little more punishment, Jeff leaves, and I end making the buy. Ironically, Jeff's race made my cover more believable.

I couldn't believe how fast moving and *nuts* a scene it was. Bronx Narcotics was a trial by fire from minute one. I was the new kid, so I had to make all the buys. "Your face isn't recognizable," they explained. It was one hell of an initiation. We had quotas just like parking-ticket quotas. Each detective had to take two collars a day. "Who's getting on today?" the boss would yell at us first thing. "I see three investigators here—that means get me *at least* six collars." A bad day in Bronx Narcotics was a day with no collars: the captain would say, "You're *kidding*," then proceed to tear you a new asshole.

During the drug-crazed '80s in the "boogie-down" Bronx, however, collar-free days were few and far between. A typical day started with me and my more senior partners, Zulma Moreno and Wilfredo Ceberello, piling into my orange 1979 Volkswagen—back then, you used your own car and the department would pay for it. We'd begin with an attack plan, which often would originate from what's known in law enforcement as a "kite." A "kite" is a report or tip that a citizen calls into the front office desk via community drug hotlines. The sergeant would tell us, "Go down to 192nd Street and Jerome Avenue—we got a kite that says they're selling mescaline."

Sarge would always warn me, "Don't get out of sight of the investigators because you're not wearing wires. Don't go inside any house or apartment—and don't walk too far off the set." We called the area where the drug deal was going to happen the "set"—like a movie set. Me, rocking a beard and street clothes, I was the actor on the set, the bait. I'd walk up to a dealer on the corner and expound on some variation of, "Yo, what's up, man—got mesc? I was here last week—remember me?" Back then, a mescaline tab ran three, four bucks; I might haggle a little to make my rap seem authentic.

As soon as I'd completed the buy, I'd walk back to the car and "name," or positively identify, the dealer. I'd describe the dealer to the attending investigators, naming all identifying characteristics— black male, black shirt, doo-rag, white tennis shows, bandanna, whatever. I tried to make buys off people who were very distinguishable and easy to describe; if they were, say, wearing a fat gold chain with a skull, or had a scar on their face, or something else unusual about them, it made our job much easier. Then I would lie in wait while the team would coordinate around the whole area; the area around the dealer would become so tightly infested with cops that when the dealer tried to run, he wouldn't get far. Once the arrest was made, the sergeant would order the dealer to look up into the sky, into the sun, so he couldn't see who was identifying him. I'd drive by, make a positive identification, then *boom!* He'd be booked, and another dealer was off the street.

Back then everything was so rampant and out in the open, and 192nd and Jerome, as well as 141st and Alexander, were real hotspots for nitty-gritty South Bronx drug activity. On 141st and Alexander, dealers would hide in vestibules, then run up as I walked past. "Heroin, mad dog, I got it all," they would say. "Yo, what you need?" I'd see people on the corner strung out. I even saw a young mother pushing a baby, selling drugs out of the carriage. I was buying heroin so openly, it was a joke. It was a lot of fun, though. You were really *out there;* this was real life at its realest.

I wasn't afraid to go into the streets. I'd hang out and check out girls, buy soda at local bodegas like I lived in the neighborhood. I learned the streets pretty quick. Then again, it was easy for me to fit in, because I looked like I belonged.

At the time, I drove a black Pontiac Firebird and dressed "street"—fat laces on Adidas shelltoes, track suits, puffy snow parkas, gold earrings, my hair wild with a beard to match. It wasn't an act: hip-hop was everywhere, and was what I loved. Everybody listened to D.J.s like Marley Marl and Mr. Magic, who had a great show on WBLS radio called "Rapp Attack"; Magic was legendary for being the first D.J. to play hip-hop on New York radio.

Though it was still New York street music, hip-hop was getting bigger and bigger. LL Cool J, who my brother Ralph knew from the neighborhood, was just starting to bubble. I saw Run-DMC in Hollis at parties, just as they were hitting. We used to go to Jamaica Park, where Murder Inc.'s Irv Gotti would D.J. as a teenager, and, of course, we went to the clubs. I'd been hitting the clubs since I was teenager—I'd had no problem getting in because my moustache made me look older. Hip-hop events were different back then: they were all about the D.J.'s scratching skills and dance music all night long—songs like "Last Night a D.J. Saved My Life" by Indeep, "I Wonder If I Take You Home" by Lisa Lisa and Cult Jam, and Shannon's "Let The Music Play" were spun alongside socially conscious raps like Grandmaster Flash's "The Message" and "White Lines." There were hip-hop parties everywhere—in sweaty Bronx basements, in cramped Brooklyn apartments, and in Manhattan hotspots like the Latin Quarter, Bentley's, the Palladium, and the Roxy. Hip-hop wasn't so violent during this era: it was about gathering, about people, about music, about having fun. Yes, drugs were usually around—people used drugs so openly back then. People were using drugs in clubs socially, weed and cocaine mostly. They weren't lighting up crack in clubs. Not yet.

They would soon enough. Bubbling right alongside hip-hop was the burgeoning crack industry, and the two would quickly find themselves on a collision course. In '82, when I started at the NYPD, crack was just starting to percolate; nobody even knew what to call it. The changeover really happened around '83 or '84, as crack activity started multiplying exponentially. Almost overnight, seemingly, crack became an epidemic; no one, not even the NYPD, thought crack would be as big of a scourge, of a cancer, that it became.

Pretty early in my undercover narcotics tenure, I found that almost every time I caught a kite, the investigators said it was about something called "crack." I was like, "Holy shit—what is this thing?" Crack was different because there was so much more of a demand. And it was easy to make: dealers could cook it up at home without a lab, making their operations even more mobile. Crack was a phenomenon that would change the face of police work, of organized crime, and of hip-hop, all in one fell swoop.

As the crack game took center stage, my job became more and more dangerous. For one, after proving my proficiency in street buys, I graduated to going "inside." I was going after the heavies, doing big buys inside apartments, homes, warehouses—wherever major quanti-

ties of drugs were being bought and sold. There was major prepara-
tion necessary for this kind of undercover work. For one, I had to get
a confidential ID with an alias, so I went to One Police Plaza, where I
got a fictitious license with a fake name. Uniform cops didn't know
who I was—nine times out of ten, cops would stop me and pat me
down. I didn't want them to know who I was; you never knew if uniform cops were "dirty" or not.

Every Tuesday and Thursday, we'd do our "inside" jobs. Going
"inside" required patience, not to mention cojones of steel. These
assignments usually ran something like this: we would go into a
building, say 1851 South Street, Apartment 2A, where I'd be told to
ask for, say, Matilda; or maybe we'd go to an Hispanic nightclub
around Fordham Road and Kingsbridge, where I'd be setting up the
owner, who was selling coke from behind the bar. Then I would have
to make the first buy, what we called the "A" buy. The first time I
went in, I'd be like, "*Papo*, if you guys really got that weight, then
money's not a problem. Gimme a sample—I'll take a hundred
bucks' worth and if it's good, don't worry, I'll be back." We'd then
go back within ten days and make the "B" buy. After two successful
buys, we'd apply for a search warrant, which we'd have to execute
within ten days—search warrants were crucial.

We were allowed to have shotguns and .38 pistols. I'm a decent
shot, in the 90th percentile; they used to tell us in the Police Academy, "Don't shoot 100 percent perfect because they could bring that
into court—they can say you're a trained marksman and use it
against you." We always had .38s when we were working undercover:
I had a short snubnose Walther PPK 380, which held eight or nine
rounds. I'd strap mine up with duct tape and make it look like a piece
of shit a street thug would carry, not like a shiny, clean police-issue
weapon. My Pontiac Firebird, meanwhile, worked great as an undercover vehicle; no one ever suspected me as a cop with a flashy car like
that.

People always trusted me and let me into their house—but that
didn't mean there wasn't a risk once I was inside. One time my sergeant bet me I couldn't go into this one particular apartment and
buy coke. This one was a more dangerous game than usual: the deal-

ers that worked there would search you with a gun to your head. Because they were gonna search me, I couldn't wear a wire: we could record the setup on a bugged office "hello" phone, but once I was in, I was on my own. We'd always have an emergency plan, though: if I wasn't out in thirty minutes, the sergeant would order my backup to go in.

In this case, half an hour might've been too long—I was nearly dead within a minute of going "inside"; all the backup cops would've found when they barged in was my bloody corpse. But I got lucky. As soon as I stepped inside the door of the apartment, these two Dominican guys pushed me against a wall and slapped a .44 magnum against my temple. "Who sent you?" they spat at me through gritted teeth as they searched me for weapons. They don't find anything, even though I had a Walther PPK pistol in the small of my back—that's how stupid they were. After breathing a sigh of relief, I told them, "Hey, I was here with Tito last week."

"Tito Valentine?" they responded, looking at me sideways. The shooter pointed the gun in my direction again.

"I don't know his last name like that," I say.

"What, are you a cop or something," the shooter snapped back as he cocked the .44. "You think you smart?"

Thankfully, his partner calmed the situation: "This guy, he's okay, put the gun down!" I was shook, but I never allowed myself to break a sweat. In narcotics, there's always uncertainty—you don't know what your day is going to be like. Or if it's going to be your last.

NARC DAYS, DARKER NIGHTS

Kool Moe Dee had a rap hit out around this time called "Wild, Wild West," and the title perfectly described what we were going through in the Bronx when it came to drugs. It *was* like the Old West, shootouts and all. By '85 to '86, drug-related homicides were a daily occurrence: people were dropping like crazy all around us, and sometimes they *were* us. Undercovers were routinely getting killed on the job. Crack was big business by now, so there are more arrests, more buys. And more shootings.

This was the beginning of the real drug-war era, when the corners started to get hot. Territories started to figure in to the equation, from the Dominicans in Harlem to the brothers in the Bronx: guys would say, "Yo, you can't sell here, this is *my* corner." For dealers, controlling territory was everything. Dealers started marking up crack vials to denote their turf. They began appearing with a signature color: some vials came with a green top, others had white tops. If a dealer sold "green tops" in a "white top" area, he could get killed. On the corner, dealers became lawless: like Tupac rapped, they just didn't give a fuck. If a cop came up, these dealers wouldn't run—they'd just start shooting. As a result, our raids became more and more intense, and each one was a chance to catch a bullet. I'd make my three buys and go home at the end of the day, shaken. Death was always close by, and I felt it getting closer to me all the time. If anything, I'd welcomed death into the party, challenging him. As a narcotics cop during this era, I was doing buys that were more dangerous. It was like I was a crazy person. You had to be a little crazy just to survive.

My partners in undercover narcotics were just as nuts—we were a walking loony bin, but with badges and guns. On my team, Jose Arroyo was the *craziest* guy—I loved working with him. Jose was young, with one year less experience on the force than I had. We were quite a pair, me and this skinny little Puerto Rican kid sporting a ton of gold chains. Every day he'd be like "Yo, yo, *yo*—let's go to the South Bronx and kick some ass!" I was like "Yeah!" Jose, of course, spoke Spanish, which gave him an advantage with big drug dealers, who tended to be either Puerto Rican, Dominican, or Colombian. You had to be Hispanic if you were going to be a good officer. Thankfully I looked mixed—people didn't know *what* I was. They'd speak Spanish to me; everything was "Hey *papi*" this, "Hey *papi*" that.

It wasn't just us that had a screw loose—our team's supervisor, Jimmy Wood, was the craziest cowboy in the wild West of South Bronx undercover narcotics work. Jimmy was a real New York character: Caucasian, around five feet eight inches, long hair, moustache, and the best at what he did. Jimmy started as an undercover, and he knew the game inside and out. That man knew how to buy drugs. If you said you couldn't buy drugs on a corner, he'd laugh at you; if you couldn't keep up with his manic pace, he'd get rid of you. Jimmy Wood's big thing was buy operations—major buys. I'm talking motherfucking *Scarface*-type buys, know what I mean? Back then it was $5,200 for an eighth of a kilo, which we called "kis" (pronounced like "keys"): if we were doing a ten "ki" buy, well, you can do the math. And the drugs were getting stronger and more lethal, too—we were getting lab results back that said the cocaine we were recovering was up to *92 percent pure*. That meant that the local dealers were now connected to the real big boys in Colombia, in Peru, and wherever else the coke came from. They were getting their coke direct from the dudes who were manufacturing it, and as a result, the stakes grew even higher.

Major buys with real weight proved to be the highest in high-tension: your life depended on a wire—literally. When you started doing major buys, you had to be wired up with a broadcast-recording device we called a "kel." On a big buy, Jose would be point man, I'd be the wing man, the muscle, the guy with guns—and if I was packing heat, it had be an automatic. An automatic weapon signaled to street cats that I was *somebody*, that I had earned my notches.

On the office "hello" phone, we'd make first contact—"Hey man, I'm looking to buy some weight." "Weight" was slang for major cocaine inventory. We'd talk in drug-dealer code, like "I'm looking for the 'keys' to my house"; of course, "keys" meant "kis." If you could get the "keys" up to $50,000, it was a major buy—the guy on the other end of the line was a real player in the drug game, and someone worth taking down. So many nights I'd find myself sitting in an unmarked car with $50,000 in cash stuffed in a Samsonite briefcase, just lying in wait for the right moment. In narcotics, brand names are important—we always used Samsonite. Once you made a deal, you'd tell the dealer, "I got the money in the car. I'm going to put it in a briefcase and I'll be right back." The money was always in a locked Samsonite so they can't flush it or destroy it. At that point, I'd tell the backup team to get ready. As the police were ramming the door down, the dealers would attempt to scram down the fire escape: when they tried to open the Samsonite, it wouldn't open—just like in the commercial. As they're struggling with the lock, we'd recover everything and lock the guys up.

Jimmy Wood knew how to set up an attack plan, and how to get the most product from a dealer. Jimmy had funny rules that lightened the tension: he'd always say, "If you go through the door before the shotgun guy, you have to buy everybody a case of beer." Jimmy was fond of "door-knock warrants," which allowed law enforcement to get a battering ram, crash the door down, and go inside. Jimmy had a friend that worked with us, Sgt. Pete Dunne, who was another nutball narc vet. Pete was crazier than Jimmy. One day we were about to bust this guy selling drugs on a block up in the South Bronx. Just as we were about to do the raid, a garbage truck passed by. Pete asked the sanitation guy driving if he could borrow the truck for a minute. Pete then backed it up into the building where the dealer was and knocked the cinderblocks right out! Lemme tell you, that guy was definitely surprised. We weren't afraid to go in apartments with guns blazing, either. The problem was, with the adrenaline so high, you could never predict exactly what was going to happen. If you went in with the shotgun guy behind you, he could take down four or five cops with friendly fire. You didn't want to be in front of the shotgun, but most of the time you didn't have a choice.

It was crazy dangerous, doing major buys, but it gave you a real buzz, one I imagined was almost as addictive as crack itself. We were gambling with our lives, figuratively and literally. Jose and I would make bets with other teams over who could buy the most drugs; even our boss, Jimmy Wood, would place bets with other sergeants on how many kilos we could pull in. It was like a game—the most dangerous game.

Summer was our busiest season: people were everywhere on the streets, and it was more dangerous at night—so I naturally worked more nights than ever. There was no precedent about how many buys you could do; I could do ten buys a day. Ten buys meant ten reports, ten vouchers, ten "sign and seals" (the sergeant would sign and seal the evidence so it couldn't be tampered with); there was a lot of grueling paperwork involved. And then there were court appearances for the cases we were pulling in, which meant testifying in front of grand juries. At the time I was a single guy, more into being flashy, picking up girls, and having fun in my off hours. I'd hit the clubs and party all night; then in the morning I'd go to court or do a bust, get out and start all over again. I was *tired*. Undercover narcotics started as an eighteen-hour-a-day job, but soon turned into a 24/7 thing. I was getting more and more courageous—or foolish. I'm more of a daredevil. I was changing.

It was hard not to take the job home with you—every day I saw shit that shook me to the core, that tested my morality. When you're undercover, it's like you're a role player, like on *Alias*, and it's hard to ever step out of it. Once in the role, I'd start negotiating with the lingo. If a dealer tried to give me less. I'd be like, "*Papo, please*—I got my own scale." Sometimes it's harder to play the role than others. One day we scheduled a buy off a loose kite that indicated this guy Juan was selling drugs out of his apartment on Walton Avenue. So I go to Juan's apartment two or three times to buy drugs, and in the process I got to know him a little. I was setting him up for a felony and *mucho* jail time, but at the same time I start feeling sorry for him. Juan had family problems. He was beating his wife, slapping her around. I would have dinner with him sometimes, and I would ask him, "Why you gotta hit your wife?" My undercover name was Mike, so all the Hispanic suspects called me "Miguel."

"Yo, Miguel, why don't you mind your business?" he'd shoot right back to me.

"I can't see you treating your wife like this," I'd respond. He was getting hot under the collar, but I wasn't going to sit there and let him beat his wife in front of me. My sergeant was listening to all this on the wire, all the while getting really pissed and worried. But me, I had to do it the right way: if this buy was gonna go down, it had to be calm. I needed *breathing room*.

Afterward, I remember the sergeant chewing me out. "Don't forget what we do," he told me. "That guy's a drug dealer and you're a *cop*." I knew that, but the situation still haunted me. I was like, "This isn't right—Juan ain't a totally bad guy. He has no direction; he just wants to get out of the situation with his bills and his family." But after another meeting, sure enough I set him up for a kilo.

Boom! The pressure of the crack epidemic was getting to those of us working on the drug war's front lines. We were beginning to crack ourselves. We'd work five days a week, and sometimes more: a guy might come in Monday and go home for the first time the next Sunday, sleeping the week away on precinct-house bunk beds between buys. Check-cashing day in Bronx Narcotics became the most fun day: those two Thursdays of the month, we did nothing but let off steam. You could cash your checks at Pauline's, the bar downstairs from the precinct where we'd all hang out after hours. Pauline's was named after its tough-gal owner, Pauline O'Sullivan, a classic New York character of mixed Jewish and Irish descent. Sometimes the sergeant would send you down to the bar with ten checks, and Pauline would stash the money until we came by later. Pauline's deal was she'd cash the checks but keep the change, and that'd pay for the drinks.

The partying at Pauline's grew more intense, more desperate, as the crack war soldiered on. On the streets, it was us versus them, all day, every day, and the toll it took on us came out commensurately in how hard we partied. Gambling skyrocketed amongst my peers: the dice and poker games spiraled out of control—guys were losing so much cash, they'd have to borrow money so their wives wouldn't suspect anything was amiss. That wasn't the only thing guys were keeping from their wives: womanizing was rampant. After a long night partying at Pauline's, it wasn't unexpected to hear someone say, "I'm going to my *goumada*'s house." *Goumada* is an Italian mob term borrowed by cops to describe a girl you're keeping on the side. Maybe you give her a little bit of money, maybe she lives in the ghetto, has kids, whatever. During the week you had one wife, the *goumada*, and on weekends you had the "real wife," whom you'd lie to and tell you're working overtime.

Infidelity, gambling, alcohol abuse—you could find it all in Bronx

Narcotics; pretty soon, you could add cocaine itself to that list. As cocaine was so prevalent in our consciousness, I shouldn't have been surprised when I started hearing about undercovers testing positive for drugs and getting booted off the force. It was just too tempting. I was working with this girl—we'll call her Carlotta—who ended up putting me between a (crack) rock and a hard place. Me and Carlotta, we were real close, or so I thought. We'd ride around together as undercovers; we'd even carpool to and from work, as she was from the Linden Boulevard area in Queens near where I lived.

Carlotta was always tired, wide-eyed and glassy, chain-smoking cigarettes all day. I would ask her what was up and she'd say, "Oh, me and my boyfriend were partying all night." I thought she was talking about alcohol. Her hagged-out look gave a nice authenticity to our busts—little did I know how authentic.

One day I'm in the office when word comes down that someone has stolen two officers' paychecks and cashed them at Pauline's. Supposedly the only person in office when this all went down was Carlotta. Carlotta, however, denied it vehemently. Our sergeant started an investigation, and it turns into this whole big thing. Then they started questioning *me* about the checks.

When I came back to work on Monday, Carlotta and I were sent to go to buy some "smoke," aka marijuana, from some West Indians on White Plains Road and 225th Street. We rolled up there with another sergeant from our unit named Kevin Duffy. Weed was less of a priority than crack, but our lieutenant was breaking Duffy's balls about the numerous complaints from the neighborhood. These West Indians, they were selling *pounds and pounds* of pot up there. Whatever they were selling, the West Indian gangs were some of the most dangerous around: they were the first to bring automatic weaponry into the domestic drug game. I liked going to the West Indian neighborhoods: we'd get spicy beef patties and champagne colas from a local Jamaican restaurant, then go make our buy.

As we were driving over to the West Indians' drug spot, Carlotta turned to me and said, "I've got something to tell you. I have a drug problem." *Whoa!* I pulled the car over and put my head down. "I don't want to hear any more," I told her. But it got worse. "Look,

I've got to have *someone* to talk to—you're my only friend," Carlotta continued. "And I stole those checks, too." Now she's put me on the *spot*. I was already the middle of this criminal investigation about the checks, and people were looking at me with three eyes, like I knew what was going on and was saying nothing. And it was my partner all along.

Carlotta had put me into a bad place. Once I got home, I called the lieutenant in charge of our division, a straight-laced Irish-Catholic named John Creegan. Everybody hated him because he was so by the friggin' book.

"You don't know how I tossed and turned about this," I blurted out to Creegan, whom I'd woken up in bed. "I got a situation: Carlotta has a drug problem and she stole the checks." "It takes a lot of courage to tell me this," he said; he knew what this info was going to do to the squad. After I hung up with him, Carlotta immediately called me. "I don't want to put you in this mess," she said. "I'm going to resign, turn in my shield and gun, and pay back the money I took." When it came out it was Carlotta behind the theft, everyone looked at me. Their stares said what was on their minds: "How did you not know she was doing drugs?" It wasn't my business. A lot of memories you try to forget, but this one I couldn't shake. It was like crack was a reoccurring nightmare that just wouldn't go away. Crack's tragedy affected everyone.

Carlotta wasn't the only cop on drugs I came into contact with. In narcotics, a special case fell into my lap. I didn't want to do it—I still feel bad about it—but I had no choice. I was asked by Bronx Narcotic's commanding officer to assist a case involving crooked cops—including two sergeants—who were suspected of doing drugs. I'm like, "I don't want to be involved in this mess," but the Commanding Officer (C.O.) wasn't having it. "It's a black party, so I need a black undercover," he told me. "And this order is coming from headquarters. From the *chief*." I didn't have a choice.

In narcotics most of work is done with informants we call "C.I.s": that's an acronym for "confidential informants." They always say don't trust informants—they can tell on you if you do something. Informants are to be handled with care; you have to make sure your relationship is strictly professional and you're not "buddies." You can't forget that the informant is a criminal working off his time, who's made a deal in a court case. Sometimes, though, they get confused and think they're cops, as I discovered about the informant who ratted out the cop-cocaine parties. He fancied himself a chameleon and wanted to pull his own stunts: in his mind, he was one of us.

The C.I. took me to the spot where the cops were having their all-night cocaine fiestas. Where one of the sergeants lived was the po-po party palace: a nice apartment up in the Bronx, carpeted, patio, the whole bit. We walked in to a blast of loud R&B, the party in full swing. The C.I. and I were standing around having a drinking when the sergeant, a woman, greeted us.

"What's up?" the C.I. said to the sergeant. "Got some coke?" "Who's this guy?" the sergeant responded, pointing to me. "That's my man—he's cool," the C.I. explained. This guy was so good, he had the sergeant eating out of his hand: the C.I. got her to take us into a bedroom, where she opened up a shoebox full of coke. She and the C.I. started doing lines out the box. "How about your man does a line?" she asked, passing me a straw. She was just being gracious—she assumed if I was there I must want to do *something*.

I couldn't get out of it, so I took the straw and held it against the side of my nose and wrinkled my nostrils. Instead of snorting it, I let the powder fall out into my hand. The sergeant was so fucked up, she didn't even notice, and she just kept partying and laughing. When she stepped away for a moment, though, the C.I. turned to me excitedly. "See? I told you they were doing coke," he blurted out a little too loudly for my taste. "Shut up—don't talk like that here," I whispered at him through gritted teeth. I never trusted this C.I., and the whole scene made me feel dirty. He wanted to get close to me, but I wouldn't let him.

The next day, I told the detective in charge of the investigation what I saw, and he made all the suspects do a piss test called a "dole." When the results came back positive for cocaine, they were all fired. Still, I felt bad about the whole experience. In the NYPD, if you work in Internal Affairs, people looked at you as if you are a "rat." It's funny how criminals and cops both share the same code: rats are looked down upon in both cultures, which shows how we're on both sides of the same coin. I wasn't immune to that, either: even though I did the "right" thing, I didn't want it getting out about me that I ratted out a cop. But I couldn't turn down the order—it was my job.

But my job was soon to change.

You see, I was up to be transferred out of narcotics: that meant I'd finally be a detective. Once you get your gold detective shield, you're on your way out, like Lenny Bruce used to say. In law enforcement, that gold shield means you're the man. At this point, I'd been on the force four and a half years, two of those in Bronx Narcotics—it was my time. And of course, the new quotas didn't hurt. They don't tell you there are quotas, but there are. The mid-to-late '80s was at a time when the NYPD started seeing an influx of black and Hispanic sergeants; I got transferred because they needed black detectives in the squad. At last I get promoted in '86 to detective third-grade—gold shield and all, wearing a suit and tie like on *NYPD Blue*. I was happy, but if I thought the Bronx was tough, well, I learned I ain't seen nothing yet when I got my assignment.

After I found out I'd been promoted, me and my pals went out to celebrate. We hit all the hip-hop clubs—the Copa, Bentley's, Latin Quarter. I think we ended up at the Roxy to check out a new rap group called Boogie Down Productions. (I say "I think" because it was that kind of night; I'm not one for excess, but there are exceptions—I always say, "If you remember that night, you weren't really there.")

Boogie Down Productions were the hot street group at the time thanks to their charismatic, outspoken frontman named KRS-One, who used to be homeless on the same South Bronx streets I worked as an undercover narc. I loved Boogie Down Productions because I could relate to their music: even though he strongly criticized the police in his lyrics, "reality rapper" KRS-One rapped about what was really going on in the ghetto streets—BDP's first single was even called "Crack Attack." I knew the violent, desperate inner-city world Boogie Down Productions described, 'cause I was in it every day. Hearing KRS-One rhyme so vividly about it was strangely ther-apeutic. (The 1987 murder of Boogie Down Productions' D.J. and founding member Scott La Rock would be one of hip-hop crime's earliest tragedies.)

I wasn't the only one who could relate to Boogie Down Produc-tions' tragic tales of street life. In the nightclub's crowd, I noticed drug dealers who I'd been following in my work with Bronx Nar-cotics. These were the big ballers: the drug dealers themselves would adorn themselves in '80s-style bling, borrowing both from the style of pimps and hustlers exemplified in blaxploitation movies like *Superfly* and the roughneck "dookie rope" gold-chain look epit-omized by Run-DMC; soon rappers like Big Daddy Kane were bringing this playalistic look into hip-hop. What rappers and drug dealers shared, and began to respect in each other, is that they were always the brightest peacocks, the biggest Willie in the room. Natu-rally, they'd find their way to each other.

At the time, drug dealers would hit *all* the clubs, loudly letting their presence be known. Whether they were selling tins of coke in the bathroom or in the middle of the dance floor or just partying down off the clock, dealers were always the flyest in the room. Most of the time you could tell the drug dealers in the crowd—ballin' and blingin' was going on back then, too; bottle service wasn't like it is now at clubs, but drug dealers in those days could still be relied on to splash out and buy drinks for all the girls. The dealers would wear gold chains and shiny yellow suits, standing out in pimp-influenced style in outfits bought from the hip-hop haberdashers of the day—stores on Fulton Mall in Brooklyn, boutiques on Queens's Jamaica Avenue, or custom ghetto haberdashers like Dapper Dan's up in Harlem. Dapper Dan, a favorite clothier of Mike Tyson, was open twenty-four hours a day and could custom-make a faux Gucci or Louis Vuitton leather suit for real players ready to pony up the cash. And of course, every drug dealer had a gun back then—.357 and .44 magnums were the norm; it wasn't like now with AK-47 automatic machine guns, armor-piercing bullets, zip guns, and the like. But that era was close at hand.

Out on the town, I saw drugs were part of life; I had to remind myself I couldn't take it home with me. "I'm not working tonight," I would remind myself. But it got hard to ignore. Just like the crack-related murders coming straight outta Brooklyn, the next destination in my law-enforcement-sponsored grand tour of New York's crime capitals. I was going into the deadly world of the A-Team and the Supreme Team; unbeknownst to me, I was entering into a new, more lethal era of organized crime, the likes the NYPD had never seen before. And hip-hop was primed to get sucked in along with it.

WELCOME TO CROOKLYN:
Give Us Twenty-two Minutes,
and We'll Give You a Homicide . . .

I'm from the murder capital, where we murder for capital . . .
—Jay-Z, "Lucifer" (2004)

IT wasn't about the money so much. I mean, yeah, the money was better: I got something like $3,500 more a year—and back in the mid-'80s, three and half Gs actually *was* money. What it was really about, though, was the *respect*.

A regular cop is always a regular cop; a white shield is a white shield is a white shield, and that's it. But when you become a full detective, not only do you get better pay, you get a *gold* shield, homey. With a detective badge, you're *different*. A gold shield is respected everywhere. It's like the American Express card of the streets—when you flash the gold, everyone knows what's up: your fellow cops figure you probably have something on the ball, and those committing the crimes figure you're probably all up in their business already.

For me, a gold shield of my own felt like a big accomplishment. For one, it meant relief: I wasn't going to be stuck as a white-shield cop for twenty years. And it felt great to be one of the NYPD's few minority detectives: of the 38,000 cops on the force, there were fewer than 300 black detectives. I was fortunate: thanks to the good role models I had growing up, I always wanted to be the best I could be—my uncles, stepfather, neighbors, friends, and especially my father always pushed me out there. They gave me pride, and my shiny new gold shield confirmed it.

In my training at the Detective Bureau, I learned how detective work was different than narcotics: there was more paperwork, more typing, more situations where I was going to have to use my brain. But the hardest work was yet to come, as I found out one day back in February 1987, when I got handed the day's interdepartmental teletype. The teletype broadcasts description of wanted perps, citywide crime scenes, and department transfers. Looking over the transfers sent down, I was kind of surprised to find my name—not so much that I was being transferred, but about where I was going. The teletype read, "Derrick Parker, you are now transferred to the detective squad in the 75th Precinct." *Whoa!* I got a chill. The 75th meant East New York, Brooklyn. Or as both perps and po-po alike call it, *Crooklyn.*

"Crooklyn" was what the New York City borough of Brooklyn was called on the street long before Spike Lee made a movie with that title. The place deserves its nickname. At the age of twenty-four, I thought I'd seen it all: I'd started as foot cop in Times Square back in its dirtiest daze, when it was all about pimps, prostitutes, porno, and pushers; then I hit the slums and race riots of Far Rockaway, Queens, followed by an intense couple years on the wrong side of the bullet in Bronx Narcotics. But now . . . *Brooklyn?* Holy shit—that was the realest 'hood, the place where everything goes down. And now, that's where I'd be spending my days, going after the worst imaginable villains in the New York area.

Bronx people hated Brooklyn, and Brooklyn people hated the Bronx. Brooklyn was considered worse than the Bronx—way worse. The place was infamous for having the most homicides in New York. Detectives in the Bronx and Brooklyn would make bets on who had higher murder statistics; every year, Brooklyn won. Even the thugs in the Bronx considered Brooklyn New York's grimiest area, the final frontier, the furthest outpost where all the wildest wildcats stalked the boulevard, the place where you might really lose your life.

Indeed, East New York remains the epitome of urban claustrophobia: it's unbearably dense, with row houses smashed together and everybody living on top of each other. Here, in East New York's multicultural salad bowl of blacks, Dominicans, and other marginalized, brown-skinned minorities, industrial and residential areas blur grimly amidst forlorn empty lots tagged up with graffiti: the streets are pockmarked with man-size potholes, and everything seems to be boxed in with fences topped by coils of barbed wire. Back when I trawled these streets for killers, crime was everywhere, in plain sight. Fountain Avenue served as a dragstrip for street racing, and prostitution was rampant on even main drags—girls would sell their asses for twelve to fifteen dollars amidst the throngs milling the streets, either looking for trouble or just aimlessly hanging out outside drug spots posing as bodegas. Some days I'd find myself walking right into a shootout between neighbors. It was that kind of place.

My pals in Bronx Narcotics were like, "Derrick, what the hell are you going to Brooklyn for? If you thought the Bronx was bad, shit—in Brooklyn, you'll never go home." To be honest, I myself was like, "Why *am* I going to Brooklyn?" My NYPD bosses told me it was because it was closer to where I lived. I didn't believe them, but I wasn't going to argue. Brooklyn was a new frontier for me. I was excited, too; I didn't know what to expect.

What I learned was that Crooklyn is a great place to go if you want to learn to solve homicides; you sure get a lot of practice. If you've ever taken a cab in New York City, you've heard the tagline for 1010 WINS, the AM news station all cabbies have constantly blaring 24/7: "You give us twenty-two minutes, we'll give you the world." The first time I walked into the 75th Precinct's detective squad, I saw a sign on the wall that says, "Welcome to East New York's bloodiest precinct. You give us twenty-two minutes, we'll give you a homicide." That was typical Brooklyn humor. Except it wasn't really a joke.

The 75th Precinct had 250 cops for the 170,000-plus people living within its rotting borders. When I started there, the adrenaline and excitement was pumping at an all-time high: there were so many shootings and murders, and they were increasing exponentially thanks to the crack phenomenon. Before crack, the 75th might average maybe twenty-five to thirty murders a year in its five-and-a-half mile radius. After crack hit the block, those homicide numbers tripled, and sometimes quadrupled. It seemed like there were murders every single day; I remember one year in the '80s when we clocked *128 murders* alone. There's a saying in the streets: Manhattan makes it, but Brooklyn takes it. Soon I'd learn first-hand what that meant.

For my first day, I arrived at the 75th Precinct house on the corner of Sutter and Liberty avenues. Right away I met all the detectives, all done up in suits and ties like on *Law & Order*; the boss from the squad, Herbie Holman, a well-respected commander, made the introductions. At twenty-six, I was the youngest guy in the room, with just five and a half years on the force; most of the guys I was working with were already two-decade NYPD veterans. I had to learn the ropes, so they put me on as an extra man at first.

As the third guy on investigations, I was learning how to respond to cases, do cases, and most of all *close* cases. Cases have to be closed—that's always one's priority as a detective. I absorbed how detective work is all about the paper trail by writing up the official detective reports called "DD-5s." I also learned how to assign and rate cases. There are four such ratings. A case would get an "A" rating if there's an arrest that closes the case. "B" cases, meanwhile, are those where there's a clear explanation that clearly solves them—what looked like a homicide, say, is in fact certified by the medical examiner as death by natural causes, or a missing person thought to have been killed is in fact located and returned home. A "C" case is one where the crime is solved, but an arrest can't be made. For example, a "C-3" signifies that no positive identification of a suspect can be made. A "C-4," however, indicates an uncooperative complainant: the complainant might be able to identify the perpetrator, but refuses to press charges anyway. A "D" classification, meanwhile, implies that in such cases all leads have been exhausted, leading to a closure due to inconclusive evidence. "E" stands for "exceptional clearance," demarcating those cases where you have enough evidence to make an arrest and solve the case, but the authorities decline to prosecute for whatever reason. "Exceptional clearance" would be used, for example, in a circumstance where, say, the main suspect passes away, or if the suspect is incarcerated for twenty-five years to life and this conviction isn't the worth the resources. "C" and "E" cases are a detective's greatest problem; too many "C" cases can count against you. And some fifteen years after I joined the 75th, I would smell the stink of a potential "C" clearance wafting around the Jam Master Jay murder.

At the 75th, I found myself working at an alarmingly fast pace because of the sheer amount of homicides occurring in the precinct. Even on my first day, I had no time to settle in: I was catching cases immediately. The minute I walked into the squad room, Herbie Holman, the squad's very overweight German-Irish lieutenant, stops me and said, "Listen, kid, you're up for the next homicide." I was like, "I've never caught a homicide." Herbie rolled his eyes. "Now's the time," he said. "We had a guy killed on Sutter and Pitken Avenue—shot to death. Get over there."

My very first detective case set the tone for most of my work in the 75th; the crime scene was like a template for a nightmare I'd see over and over, day after day. I drove over to Sutter and Pitken with two more senior detectives with me. I stopped the car, however, at the sight of blood on concrete: there was a guy lying in the middle of the street who'd obviously been shot several times—I guessed at least ten rounds went into him. No doubt about it, he was dead, and it was pretty obvious that this homicide was drug related. Evidence was everywhere: numerous crack vials spilled next to him, and there were drugs in his pockets. After they removed the body, we took out the witnesses and notified the victim's family; all the while, we're trying to ascertain facts about how he got shot, canvassing the neighborhood and interviewing people for our DD-5s. When I got back, Lt. Herbie Holman was there smiling at me with a devilish grin: two more homicides were called in that I had to deal with. Welcome to the 75th, homey. Some homicides were the result of domestic violence, others came out of robbery and assaults, but a full *80 percent* were drug related. Solving such murders fascinated me—I had found my calling. I liked cases that were hard, that made you think;

then I would crack them. Working homicide didn't depress me; I was gung ho—I would've taken all the murders and solve every one of 'em if I could. I had a lot to occupy my mind in Brooklyn.

The lesson I learned early on trawling Crooklyn's mean streets for killers is this: if you want to solve a homicide, you're going to need informants. *Period*. Fuck DNA testing, fuck all the flashy, divorced-from-reality high-tech cop shows you see on TV: informants are the way most homicides are solved. Finding informants is not so different from being a door-to-door salesman: it's all about knocking on doors, sales pitches, and cultivation of mutually beneficial, long-term relationships.

Cultivating people is a crucial skill for any detective, yet not all of them get that. When it came to cultivating informants, my style proved different from most other cops I worked with, who had a distinct "us vs. them" attitude when it came to perps; intimidation was their preferred method. Me, I would go out on street and meet people, let them get to know me. If I stopped at a bodega to get a soda, I would stop and talk to the people standing on the corner outside. I would say, "Hey, man, what's your name? You're always at this store—what you doing?" I started to joke around with them, like, "I know you're out selling drugs—one of these days I'm going to catch you." They'd say, "Yo, man, you're not going to catch *me*."

Once the dudes on the corner realized I was part of the 'hood and not going anywhere, things got more friendly. To gain an informant's trust, you have to show them you're not always just looking to arrest them; you have to demonstrate that you can relate to them in a real way. To that end, I would talk to them in their lingo. I would talk to them as a minority would—because *I am a minority*; I knew their slang because that's how I spoke myself. I'd even joke around with them about what music they were listening to. If I saw a guy holding a cassette, I'd be like, "My man, Big Daddy Kane is hot—pimping *ain't* easy!" "How do you know Big Daddy Kane?" the guy would respond with a funny look, like I had just stepped out of a UFO. "You're a *cop*."

Inevitably, my street knowledge would pique their curiosity. "If you're so down, then who's your favorite rap group?" they'd ask, trying to trip me up. "Eric B. & Rakim are the best," I'd respond, "but Boogie Down Productions are hot, too." That usually shut them up right quick. I didn't talk down to them, see, and I would remember things, too: "Aren't you from Fairfield Towers? Yeah, you're Mrs. Jones's boy. I locked your brother up on an attempted murder charge last year." Homey's little friends would be like, "Yo, how does po-po know all that?" I made an effort to get to know everyone in my immediate orbit personally. This was where my undercover experience came in handy: as a narc, I had to get to know people, how they lived, because my life depended on it. Sure enough, after a while all the guys on the corner got to know my face, and then my name: if they saw me passing by, they'd say, "What's up, Parker?" And once in a while, they'd have a useful tidbit for whatever case I was working on.

It would be informants that would help take down East New York's most notorious gang, the urban death squad known as the A-Team. The 75th Precinct is lousy with housing projects: there are eight within its borders, all with folksy, phonily high-class names like "Pink Houses," "Unity Plaza," and "Fairfield Towers," which fail to disguise their crushing urban desolation. East New York projects are lessons in the architecture of oppression: each complex— monotonous tower compounds of red brick, white-framed windows, and the decaying amenities of an earlier era—sprawls over three or four city blocks.

It's not hard to see how these projects spawned some of New York's most notorious hustlers: living in them would make someone do anything and everything to get the hell out, even if it was illegal and risked jail. The thinking was, if you can do it there, you can do it anywhere. When I'd bust guys from East New York, I'd ask them why they didn't just get a job. "Yo, jail ain't any worse than the projects," was the typical response. And that the projects were all in such close proximity to each other created an ideal market for the crack trade, an open bazaar filled with a captive audience.

The most notorious housing project in the 75th was the clutch of buildings at Blake and Euclid avenues known as Cypress Hills. I learned that Cypress was ruled by a group of guys called A-Team around 1987 to 1988. True to the era, the A-Team used aliases that

were ghetto fabulous like the rapper names of the day—Bey-Bey,
Kool Aid, Unique. The A-Team was headed up by two charismatic,
but deadly, leaders: "Glaze" (real name: Brian Gibbs) and "King
Tut" (born Walter Johnson). They reigned over ghetto boulevards
with iron fists worthy of Stalin.

The Cypress projects were loaded with such characters trying to
make a name for themselves on the streets, but the A-Team were the
baddest of the bad. Glaze was a notorious killer, supposedly responsible for several murders; I think his body count totaled in the double digits. Once Glaze took one of the A-Team's female operatives
for a ride in his limo, then shot her and dumped her body out on the
street; she had been stealing and this was her punishment. Her
killing was meant as a *Godfather*-style message to underlings: do
not fuck around, or this will happen to *you*. King Tut, meanwhile,
already had a terrifying reputation from his many fearless escapades
that inspired respect on the streets. Tut would also play a key role in
hip-hop crime history, as a suspect in the 1994 Tupac shooting at the
Quad recording studio.

Everybody in East New York knew the A-Team were big in the
projects for drugs and shooting people, especially the residents that
lived there. Glaze and the A-Team controlled Cypress Hills with
fear, killing however many necessary to protect and ensure that their
drug operation would prosper and rule. For that reason, putting the
A-Team behind bars was an almost impossible task for those of us in
law enforcement. The crack epidemic was in full swing: dealers were
selling openly on the streets, and there were correspondingly many
homicides, but there were never any witnesses willing to testify.
They would either get murdered by Glaze and his crew or recant
their statements because they were afraid.

Citizens had good reason to be afraid. The .38 revolver pistols police carried were not the A-Team gun of choice—to them that was a
pussy gat. No, the A-Team represented a new school of organized
crime, far deadlier than the Italian Mafia ever was; these were the most
vicious criminals New York had ever seen. Glaze and his boys favored
military-grade weapons—Mac-10 submachine guns, 9mm Berettas,
Tek-9 semi-automatics—and military precision. The A-Team and

their ilk borrowed the paramilitary tactics of the Black Panthers—minus the revolutionary social consciousness; these new-style gangsters were as straight-up capitalist as the U.S. president of the day, Ronald Reagan, and had no problem gunning down their competitors. We got a lot of reports that guys were doing firearm training on Cypress's rooftops: for target practice, they'd throw cans in the air, or line up bottles and blow them away. Every night we could hear gunfire in the air as we did our rounds.

The A-Team was training so rigorously for two reasons—one, to outshoot the cops, and two, to gun down their rivals in the crack game. Each group controlled different corners, so these guys were training to protect their spot like their lives depended on it. The escalating profits from crack were raising the stakes to such levels, it was war on the streets: rival gangs were finding their territorial beefs over narcotics trade growing epic. Gangs got into shootouts with each other, or did "drive-bys" to take out their competitors, all of which led to an increase in the deaths of innocent civilians.

The game was on, and we had the cards stacked against us. The A-Team's firepower proved far superior to what the police had: they even used armor-piercing hollow-point shells and Black Talon bullets, specially designed to explode inside the body and tear apart one's insides. It became de rigueur to carry a backup weapon on the force. I would carry two guns, with two speed loaders to match: I even learned to reload while keeping one eye on my target. I was very confident that if something ever broke out, my skills were good enough. They had to be. As we were in a high-crime area, we had our guns out more than most. Stories circulated around the department about officers that were killed just because they weren't fast-enough shooters compared to the automatic weapons we started seeing on the streets. Soon enough, the A-Team would start going after the police themselves. In Brooklyn, cops were now as much a target as anybody.

If they knew you were a cop, that is. Me, I blended in more than most. Following the A-Team proved easy to me—they frequented the spots I frequented. A-Team partied at all the happening hip-hop clubs of the day. They hung out primarily at Bentley's, always the spot to go, and the Red Parrot, which took up a whole city block on Fifty-seventh Street; I'd also see them ballin' at joints like Silver Shadow, Latin Quarter, the Rooftop, Copacabana—any place that was hot. In particular, they followed this one D.J., Sugar Daddy, who was the most popular spinner of the day—at the time, he was way bigger than superstar D.J.s of today like Funkmaster Flex—and maybe checked out performances by, say, Heavy D and the Boyz, or whomever was big that moment.

The A-Team were always the flashiest customers in the club. These guys didn't have to wait in line—after their Mercedes and Cadillac stretch limos dumped out their ten-to-fifteen-man posse at the front door, someone would pay off the security with a fistful of twenties and go right in. Once inside, the finest champagne immediately arrived at their table—Moët was always the preferred brand, much like Cristal is today—and the coke was so prevalent, it was like a blizzard on the dance floor.

At the time, the A-Team was pushing big weight and dressing accordingly. The local macks were who they looked up to when they were growing up, so they took pimp style and updated it for the late-'80s era: they'd sport furs, silk suits, and Stacy Adams shoes, with big "rope" chains bearing lion's-head medallions and diamond-encrusted crosses hanging off your neck. These thugs were never what I would call inconspicuous. They'd have "high-top fade" haircuts with their names carved into their scalps, or rock giant gold nameplate necklaces. The cops would roll up and say, "What's up, Raheem?" They'd go, "Hey, how'd you know my name?"—when they were wearing it around their necks. Real smooth. We had a saying: if criminals weren't so dumb, we wouldn't catch 'em.

At the club, the A-Team didn't bring the violence and gunplay like they did in the 'hood. This was their off time, their moment to relax, to chill, and to enjoy the fruits of their ill-gotten gains; they were so bold they let their guard down, thinking they were safe, untouchable, that no one was watching. They were wrong—*I* was watching, and noting emerging patterns. I could see drug dealers were starting to align themselves with different celebrities. I saw well-known dealers at the kinds of parties and nightclubs where I might also see Mike Tyson, and R&B singers, and rappers like Freddie Foxx and Big Daddy Kane. Drug dealers would set up lush nighttime cruises where rappers would perform a few songs for a bagful of cash, no questions asked, as the boat circled around Manhattan.

The celebs respected drug dealers because they often grew up with them. Both Mike Tyson, who was the original hip-hop boxer, and rappers like Big Daddy Kane hailed from the same East New York streets as the A-Team. Some celebs even sold drugs before they made it in show business. And if a rapper or boxer had made it to the big time, they never forgot where they came from: to their homies from the 'hood, they were still that guy on corner. And back then, on the club scene, it wasn't the rappers that were the biggest celebrities—the drug dealers were. Narcotics heavies of the day like Kendu from Unity Plaza off Linden Boulevard in Brooklyn—when they went to the club, they were *bigger* than rappers. They had the clothes, the cars, the money, the women. At the time, the rappers looked up to the drug dealers for inspiration—the dealers were the guys that had "made it" first in their 'hood, that were always fly. So when rappers started to make big money, those were the guys they emulated. *Those* were their role models. But it was a two-way street: drug dealers coveted the official leather and wool baseball jackets that rap labels like Def Jam and Uptown gave to those in their inner circles.

It was an exciting and confusing time, indeed. By the late 1980s, hip-hop had entered what many consider its golden age. Rap had moved from old school to new school, and was more diverse than ever. Nimble tongued wordsmiths like Rakim and Big Daddy Kane were rewriting the M.C. rulebook, spitting out complex verses that left the old school rhymers in the dust. Smooth dudes on the mic like Heavy D were dressing classy and dropping jams for the ladies; meanwhile, uptown Harlem cats like Teddy Riley were redefining hip-hop with the futuristic, electronic, rump-shaking sound known as "new jack swing." LL Cool J was coming into his own as not just an arrogant young rapper with paramount skills, but a real superstar. Female rappers like MC Lyte, Salt-N-Pepa, and Roxanne Shanté were making inroads. Novelty songs like UTFO's "Roxanne, Rox-anne" were burning up rap-radio airwaves, while others—like Tone-Loc's "Wild Thing"—were reaching the top of the *pop* charts.

Most striking, however, was that social consciousness had entered hip-hop. Malcolm X was being rediscovered by a new generation of young African-Americans, and his messages of revolution started bubbling through pop culture. Groups like Public Enemy and Boo-gie Down Productions embraced the machine-gun rhetoric and raised-fist style of the Black Panthers; visionary M.C.s like Rakim espoused the lessons of a controversial black Islamic group; mean-while, new-school artists like De La Soul, A Tribe Called Quest, and the Jungle Brothers repped a back-to-Africa philosophy down to their Afrocentric fashions. Indeed, for a moment, the hip-hop street style of Avirex and Troop leather bomber jackets, British Knights sneakers, "doorknocker" gold earrings, and Gucci everything (Mike Tyson famously had his car seats reupholstered with Gucci-logoed leather) were replaced by *kente* cloth, *dashikis,* and wood medal-lions in the shape of the African motherland. But the message didn't always translate to the masses. I can't tell you how angry I'd get when I'd see crack dealers wearing Africa medallions—like they're uplifting the race. These scumbags were selling African-Americans into a new slavery of addiction, not unlike the way the Chinese fell victim to opium. The irony was lost on those fools, though. I became more and more determined to take down these thugs. Little did I know it at the time, but I was on my way to Mal-colm X Boulevard myself.

IT'S A HARD-KNOCK LIFE: TO LIVE AND DIE IN BED-STUY

Another day, another teletype: in the middle of my A-Team investi-gations, the order comes down: I was being transferred to the 81st Precinct—Bedford-Stuyvesvant, or as it's known on the streets, Bed-Stuy.

I have a special relationship to Bed-Stuy: it's where I was born—Halsey off Patchen Avenue is where I grew up for a spell before we moved to Queens. My roots in Bed-Stuy run deep—it's where my dad was born, where my grandparents lived when I was a kid; I'd come back every weekend to visit them, and every passing year I saw the area get worse and worse. Bed-Stuy is one of New York's long-standing African-American neighborhoods, which is made clear from local institutions like the Billie Holiday Theater—or just by looking up at the street signs, upon which you might find the name of a great free-thinking black man. One main thoroughfare is Malcolm X Boulevard, and another is named for Marcus Garvey. But by the time I returned there as a cop, though, too many residents weren't heeding Garvey's and Malcolm's call for empowerment; they were too busy being seduced by the siren song of crack.

By this point, it was a song I'd heard too many times before. Like East New York, Bed-Stuy was, and remains, one of New York's worst ghettos. This is the neighborhood where Spike Lee shot *Do The Right Thing*, and you can see why: it's the archetypal inner-city, in every direction. Bed-Stuy's gritty streets are always busy—they stay open 24/7. At midnight, the stores on Bed-Stuy's main drag, Lewis Avenue, lock their doors, but keep serving customers out of a small crack in their plate-glass windows; as well, stoops and corners are always crowded with young black men clutching forty ounce bottles of malt liquor. African hair-braiding salons collide with bakeries run by Hasidic Jews; meanwhile, boarded-up windows and "R.I.P." graffiti tags are omnipresent, and a giant mural celebrating "Brooklyn's Own Mike Tyson" is now as faded and washed out as the boxer's own reputation. Even police couldn't resist Bed-Stuy's nastiness: cops would often steal away between shifts for a quick blow job in Franklin Park with their local *goumada*.

Despite the area's devastation, a few flowers still managed to grow out of the cracks in Bed-Stuy's concrete. Out of this brutal urban crucible grew, inexplicably, some of hip-hop's greatest rappers—if not *the* greatest. Superstars like Biggie, Jay-Z, Lil' Kim, Fabolous, and Mos Def all claim "do-or-die Bed-Stuy" as their spawning grounds; the struggles of the neighborhood figure prominently in all their myths. Jay-Z hails from Bed-Stuy's Marcy housing projects over on Myrtle Avenue; Fabolous hails from "the Stuy's" Brevoort complex. Well before he ever gained the title as rap's greatest of all time, I would see Biggie and his crew hanging out and dealing at the local deli. Jay-Z has also extensively romanticized his days as a Bed-Stuy crack don in song.

The 81st was also home to some of the NYPD's greatest detectives—among them a number of African-Americans. I was happily surprised to see so many blacks with gold shields all in one place—seasoned veterans like Ernie Bostic, who had multiple decades on the job. I felt comfortable in this environment; finally, I had true role models on the force I could learn from. I even got partnered up with another black detective, a great guy named Robert Donowa, whom everybody called "Chink" due to his almond-shaped eyes.

Yeah, no one would ever say the 81st was a politically correct place to work, but there was real unity in the detective squad, regardless of race: Irish detectives like Tommy Fitzgerald, Jimmy McCabe, and Patrick Adams (whom we called the "blue-eyed devil") worked together with their African-American peers and even female investigators like Patty Kehoe. Then again, everybody had to get along—there was too much work not to.

Many of us barely ever went home: if we got off at 1:00 A.M., we had to be back in office by eight o'clock, so most guys would just sleep in these old, ripped-up bunk beds in the back of the squad room, which I'm guessing dated from the 1940s. The only problem was there were six detectives and only four beds, which meant you'd spend a lot of nights drinking coffee with old-timers. And if a homicide occurred at, say, three in the morning, you'd get rousted out of your bunk in your slippers and robe by a nightwatch detective you didn't know.

See, just as the Bed-Stuy streets ran 24/7, so did we. And around the 81st, the motto was always work hard, play hard, which only brought us closer. Around 1:00 A.M. each night after finishing the turnaround tour, the Irish would bust out the Scotch. I wasn't a big drinker, but I liked to have a good time, so me and Chink started throwing parties, hiring bands and D.J.s. It kept me in the music game, on the edge of the industry, which would prove to be an invaluable asset, as I'd soon find out.

Working Bed-Stuy, I started seeing celebrities associating with drug dealers again. In particular, there was a well-known Puerto Rican dealer named Angel who would hit the clubs and brag about his clout in the entertainment industry, his connections to big names. Angel was a real problem. Not only was he a big drug dealer, but he wasn't afraid to threaten cops.

"Hey, *cop,* I know what kind of car you drive," he'd say to our faces if we rolled by him on the avenue. "I'm going to rape your wife and kids—I'm going to blow up your house, pig." The next thing you knew, the cops would beat the shit out of him. Angel had to have a driver, because if cops saw him, they'd beat his ass. In no time the dealers had stepped up their attacks on the police. It was the homicide of a New York cop, in fact, that would seriously dent the A-Team's activities, as well as those of their Queens counterparts, the Supreme Team.

In fact, since I had left the 81st for Bed-Stuy, the A-Team had shamelessly stepped up their game, growing deadlier than ever; whispers on the street suggested they were spreading their empire, creating new affiliations and alliances across Brooklyn and even other boroughs like Queens. The A-Team had become a one-gang epidemic, so I wasn't surprised when in 1988, George Duke, one of my old squad commanders from the 75th, called me in for a new assignment. Working between the 75th and the 81st detective squads, I was to join up with a group of detectives from various Brooklyn precincts and create the A-Team Task Force, an elite cadre designed to bring these thugs down once and for all. There were such a pattern of homicides in our area associated with the A-Team, they had to be shut down.

Almost immediately, an A-Team-related homicide appeared on my radar. I caught a case involving a guy named Christopher Brothers: he was killed in front of a house on Herkimer Street between Saratoga and Howard avenues in Bed-Stuy. I was working on the Brothers case with a senior detective from the 81st named Terrence Murnane, a great investigator and hostage negotiator. Terry's nick-

name was "General Zod," after the powerful villain from the Super-
man comics. Terry would speak his mind so authoritatively, he
sound like a general. You didn't want to fuck with Terry.

Most cops were scared to go anywhere near the projects: they were
afraid they'd get shot. Me, I thrived on that kind of tension; I was so
crazy then, and Terry was just as fearless. We knocked on all the
doors in the block, just trying to figure out who Chris Brothers is,
where he lived, and what he was doing before he got shot.

Around midnight, General Zod and I stumbled onto something
interesting. We stopped at a house on the block where Brothers was
killed: after we rang the doorbell, four beautiful black women came
to the door in bathrobes and curlers—two sisters, Yolanda and
Raquel Thomas, their hot, young-looking mother, and a cousin. All
of the women denied knowing Christopher Brothers and declined
to give any further information.

When we left the house after interviewing those women, we still
felt there was more to the story. I said to General Zod, "This guy was
definitely coming from this house. How could four beautiful women
be up this late looking this fresh?" He agreed: I mean, *come on*—
with four women looking like that, I know that's where I'd be coming from.

The Brothers's homicide case got stranger still. When I interviewed Chris Brothers's mother, a church-going woman who cried so
hard when she learned her son was killed, she denied that her son
had any enemies. I noticed, however, that her apartment was completely furnished with expensive furniture and a brand-new washer
and dryer, which I found rather . . . *unusual* for an apartment in the
East New York projects.

As Zod and I delved deeper into Christopher Brothers's death, we
found out a lot of things that contradicted the interviews we'd done:
both Christopher and his brother Herman were in fact drug dealers.
Stranger still, we discovered Brothers's murder wasn't over drugs—
it was over a woman. Chris Brothers had been seeing one of the four
women from the house on Herkimer Street, Yolanda Thomas.
Yolanda proved to be the case's crucial link. I'd learn, in fact, that
she was an albatross, a ghetto femme fatale—seemingly everyone

she came in contact with would die a horrible death. Yolanda would later date three more guys that would be victims of brutal homicides, and Yolanda's beautiful, young mother would eventually get killed by her father. I felt sorry for her.

Not so sorry that I didn't want to get to the bottom of the case, however. I had become close with a girlfriend of Yolanda's who eventually gave me the clues I needed to piece the puzzle together. It took me some time to win this girl over; I followed her from place to place until she said, "Damn, Parker, you just don't give up." After much cajoling, this informant told me that Chris was killed because Yolanda had been seeing him on the side while her main boyfriend, K-Son, a drug dealer from Bed-Stuy's Tompkins Houses projects, was doing a prison bid. When K-Son was released from jail, he got wind of Christopher's undercover-lover routine and decided to kill him. After murdering Brothers, K-Son then threatened everyone in Yolanda's house, telling them that if they talk to the police, he'd kill them all. Now, I already knew something about the shooter. K-Son was notorious around Bed-Stuy. He lived in the Marcy projects (home of Jay-Z) and was notorious as a terror with a gun; he'd just gotten out of jail himself.

I knew I didn't have enough yet to charge K-Son with Brothers's homicide, but I was hot on his trail. Armed with all this new information, we did some additional background searching on Chris Brothers. We found that he lived in no other than East New York's Cypress Hill projects—home of the A-Team and my old 75th Precinct stomping grounds. I went over to Cypress one day to talk to the A-Team's number-one killer myself; it turns out Glaze was friends with Christopher Brothers. Inadvertently, I ended up giving K-Son his death sentence. Once I asked Glaze some questions about K-Son, the A-Teamer put two and two together immediately: when Glaze figured out who killed his friend, he was ready for vengeance.

"I hope you get K-Son before I get him," Glaze spat defiantly.

Glaze had real balls to say that to a cop, and apparently he made good on his word. K-Son was home one day in his Marcy projects apartment when a group of thugs put a gun to his girlfriend's head outside as she was returning home. Walking her up to the apartment she shared with K-Son, they made her open the door and rushed in. The intruders surprised K-Son, shooting him point-blank before he could get to his guns, which lay on his night table alongside his bulletproof vest. Terrified, K-Son's girlfriend ran out of the apartment, but as she started making her way down the stairs, the gunmen shot her in the head; she died en route to the hospital.

With the A-Team's ability to cause terror and fear like that— indeed, to erase anyone who might be a credible witness against them—it was hard to cultivate credible informants to take them; we had to be a little more creative. The only way to take down a group so organized, tight, and feared was to go to the people around them, starting at the gutter bottom. You go to their enemies, their girlfriends—maybe their neighbors are sick of putting up with their mayhem; there's always one disgruntled citizen in the bunch who's sick and tired and doesn't want to take the neighborhood bullies' shit anymore.

Me, I always found baby mommas to be the best informants. If the perp didn't pay his child support, if he's not taking care of his kids, if he's messing around with someone on the side, his baby momma will tell you anything and everything. Shit, she'll even show you where he hides his guns and drugs, and even the addresses of his other girlfriends—which is usually where he's hiding out.

Most of the informants who helped take down the A-Team came from arresting the people around them. As a result, the kind of people we were dealing with were not always the most trustworthy. Some of the guys from the A-Team's lower levels had been arrested for selling crack, or maybe they had a shooting or assault on their record. They'd be the losers of the bunch, often predicate felons; a predicate felon is someone who's convicted of two felonies or more. Some criminals are proud of their predicate-felon status, wearing it as a badge of honor—50 Cent's G-Unit homey Tony Yayo titled his debut album *Thoughts of a Predicate Felon*—but a lot of them didn't want to go back to prison. And if you have multiple felonies, it means you're going to start doing real time, which isn't fun as you get older. For a lot of these guys, when they're eighteen or nineteen, they can do their bid standing on their head. After a while, the novelty wears off.

Some of the lower-level A-Team members had grudges, too, that were easy for me to manipulate. It was inevitable: street gangs are a lot like regular business—there are those making bank at the top, but the kids on the corner, the ones who are exposed, the people doing the real work, they're the ones getting screwed. They're making the drug dealer equivalent of minimum wage, as notes a special report on "Blacks in America" from the August 6, 2005, edition of *The Economist*. "Contrary to popular belief, ghetto crime pays very badly. Sudhir Venkatesh, then of the University of Chicago, embedded himself with the Black Gangster Disciple Nation, a drug-dealing gang, and discovered that although a handful of bosses were pulling in $500,000 a year tax-free, their thousands of footsoldiers made only $3.30 an hour—less than the minimum wage. . . . [As well] each footsoldier had a one in four chance of being murdered."

It's not surprising, then, to learn that under such conditions, the crew's lowest level soldiers are treated like they're disposable, which only increases their rage when something goes wrong. I spoke to this one A-Team associated kid who had been picked up on a narcotics charge; I had actually been watching him for a minute, waiting for him to break. He was astonished that I knew who his baby momma was, what clubs he liked to party at, what ghetto Chinese restaurant he sold crack in front of—and that he had a growing beef with his superiors. One of the A-Team had shot him when he didn't return with the product he was supposed to, so he had a story to tell.

This was a young black guy who had nothing else but the street; it was incredible he'd made it to eighteen. He'd been busted first by a narcotics team, who allowed me to do a debriefing for the cases I was working on. This informant was very afraid—his life was literally in the balance: he knew he could be spending a serious chunk of his life in jail, and he knew what the A-Team could do to him. To his family. To his *kid*. He was sweating, nervous, reluctant at first. So instead of trying to intimidate him, which he expected, I got more personable. I got him a pack of cigarettes and whatever he wanted to eat. He wanted some "ghetto food"—a pack of chips and grape soda. Once he got comfortable, I hit him with the truth.

"I can't make you a deal, can't make no promises," I told him. "You've been brought in on a serious crime. This is what you're in for—you've got a couple felonies under your belt, so if you throw this latest thing in, it means you'll probably be up for some serious time behind bars. But if you talk, if you cooperate, I'll make a rec-ommendation to the D.A. that this infraction that brought you in here be overlooked." I wasn't bullshitting—nine times out of ten, the D.A. goes for it.

He thought about it for a second. "Going back to jail?" he said. "*Naw*. I'll tell you whatever you wanna know, money." He spilled a lot about A-Team activity, but in particular he told me how Chris and Herman Brothers were up-and-coming drug dealers. And there was a lot more.

We learned that the A-Team was involved in a lot of homicidal ac-tivity, and that the scale of it was bigger than we ever expected—drug trafficking, gun trafficking, money murders, territorial murders, drug-related murders, murders as punishment. If you sold drugs for the A-Team but smoked all your product up, you might get smoked yourself ("Never get high on your own supply": that's rule number four in Biggie's "Ten Crack Commandments"). Dealing and muscle—that was the A-Team's business. As we contin-ued our investigation, I got another witness who turned informant, placing one of the A-Team members in the killing of the owner of a Korean grocery store named Jung Dong Duk. The informant had been an actual member of the A-Team, and was in on a gun charge he hoped to get reduced: he was a mid-level guy, in his mid-twenties, and had a lot to lose. He didn't want to spend the rest of his adult years rotting in a penitentiary.

I don't like to have several people in a room when I interview a suspect. Other detectives bring in their own stupid shit, which makes the guy feel uncomfortable, and I never can get to my own agenda. So with this guy, I didn't want him getting nervous. I took him out of his cell to the 75th Precinct's activity room. It was basic:

benches, chairs, desk, two-way mirror. I sat down: after giving him a pack of cigarettes and some pizza, I started right in.

"You're already busted on a gun charge," I said, "but what you can tell me might help you in front of the D.A. when your case goes to trial. If you cooperate, the D.A. can make a recommendation, and maybe reduce your sentence. Without cooperation, what you're looking at is five years automatically for the gun; add in the two drug convictions, and it's *at least* ten years in jail."

All this made sense to him; shaken, he spilled the beans. He told me about the A-Team's activities in detail, the shootings they were involved with, who the members are, even what vehicles they drove. Best of all, he had witnessed the murder of the Korean grocer, and fingered an A-Team kingpin as the triggerman. This was the big score. The informant told me he witnessed in specific a guy named George, one of the A-Team's top dons, shooting the Korean grocer.

This time, with evidence this good, we were able to make an arrest stick, and a conviction: the informant agreed to testify in front of a grand jury. This proved to be a critical blow to the A-Team. By locking up George, one of the A-Team's head guys, the whole gang ended up losing power. When you cut the head off a gang, its infrastructure shatters: everyone's on their own, territories are lost, and the "organized" part of organized crime goes to shit.

It wasn't enough, though. Even though we significantly damaged the A-Team's activities, we were starting to realize the scale of their operation was greater than we thought: not only did their influence span across Brooklyn, but the A-Team had begun forging associations with equally criminally minded gangs in other boroughs, like Queens. In an A-Team Task Force meeting, I learned that Christopher Brothers's sibling Herman had ties to Howard "Pappy" Mason, Lorenzo "Fatcat" Nichols, Gerald "Prince" Miller, and Kenneth "Supreme" McGriff—the architects of the powerful Supreme Team organization. In the 75th, we looked at several surveillance photographs of Herman Brothers hanging out with Pappy Mason and others from the Supreme Team posse. I grew up in Queens, so I recognized the faces from the photos immediately—I knew all about

Supreme Team. You'd see them driving around the boulevard in their late-model expensive cars; in the neighborhood, I'd hear guys talking about the Supreme Team's reputation—homicides they supposedly committed, how and where they were selling drugs, where the bodies might be buried. They were the bad dudes in my 'hood—the heroic villains of urban folklore, the first hip-hop-styled *gangsta* conglomerate to hit the big time. Their legend was so potent among boys in the 'hood, it still reverberates in hip-hop rhymes of today: "See, 'Preme was a business man and Prince was the killer" raps 50 Cent on "Ghetto Qu'ran."

The Supreme Team were the best in their field—the premier criminal organization of the day. McGriff was the gang's financial mastermind: under his watch, the Supreme Team reportedly brought in $10 million annually from their crack-cocaine activity alone. Operating out of the Baisley House projects in Jamaica, Queens, the Supreme Team's enormous enterprise would move *tens of thousands* of crack vials each week.

Meanwhile, the Supreme Team's homicidal instincts knew no bounds, and were growing bolder by the week. They appeared untouchable. In 1985, McGriff was sentenced to nine years on gun and drug charges, but got off with under two years in prison due to a problem with a search warrant used in his case. But what had really stoked the NYPD's ire was the Supreme Team's deathly impulses toward the police. Most criminals don't go after cops as a general rule: it's bad for business, as it raises the bloodlust in the boys in blue to unacceptable levels. But the Supreme Team felt they were above the law, with a license to kill. These guys made *The Sopranos* look like pussies—in the Supreme Team's eyes, anything with a badge was a target.

The NYPD was particularly heated about two such incidents. Fatcat Nichols had put out a hit on his parole officer. And, in an even more brutal move, Pappy Mason ordered the murder of Edward Byrne, a twenty-two-year-old NYPD officer barely out of the Police Academy. Early in the morning on February 26, 1988, Byrne was shot five times in the head while sitting in his patrol car in Queens's 103rd Precinct. The reason behind Byrne's killing? He was protecting a witness who, sick of seeing his neighborhood devolve into a narcotics zoo, was willing to take a stand and testify against the Supreme Team.

To NYPD top brass, Byrne's killing was a throwing down of the gauntlet that had to be punished. Typically, detectives had severe rivalries with investigators from other boroughs: most detectives in Brooklyn I knew hated Queens detectives. But with two law-enforcement officers killed, this was no time for a territorial fight. A line had been crossed, so everyone pitched in to bring these cop killers down. "This was an order, not for the murder of a particular police officer, but of any officer, for the sole purpose of delivering a message of death to anyone who opposed Nichols," Lt. Phillip Panzarella, former head of the Queens Homicide Squad, told the *Queens Tribune* in 1998.

From my informants within Bed-Stuy and East New York, a lot of new information became available. I learned that at least two of Byrne's shooters had been recruited from Brooklyn, in particular the Cypress Hills projects, despite it being a Supreme Team–ordered hit. That a trusted A-Team worker like Herman Brothers had ties to Supreme Team heavies like Fatcat and Pappy clarified the connection even more. Violence and drug trafficking is what linked the two gangs from different boroughs. The association was made clear when Brothers appeared in surveillance photos taken of Supreme Team activity by Queens's narcotics squads. Another benefit to the connection between the Supreme Team and the A-Team was that the latter were far less notorious within the NYPD; the A-Team operated more under the radar, and could get away with certain things Supreme couldn't. Regardless, the evidence was piling up, and it couldn't be ignored any longer. Our mandate was clear: we had to deal with both the A-Team and the Supreme Team and dismantle them for good.

My colleagues and I teamed up and ran all over East New York and Bed-Stuy gathering information, photographs, and criminal histories of everyone we thought might be involved, all the while cultivating informants; as well, Queens detectives were simultaneously running with the Supreme Team angle. There was so much to unravel, sometimes our investigations led to other investigations. To the NYPD, this case was bigger than that of Nicky Barnes, the multi-millionaire "heroin king of Harlem" and self-proclaimed "Mr. Untouchable."

Barnes felt so above the law, he posed for the cover of *The New York Times Magazine* before he was finally sentenced to life in prison in 1978. Barnes had been the forefather of the African-American organized crime gangs that had replaced the traditional Italian Mafia in black neighborhoods and eventually ran the New York area's drug trade. But while Nicky Barnes provided the proto-type and inspiration for the likes of the Supreme Team and the A-Team, he still represented the older, increasingly obsolete '70s model; the Supreme Team, on the other hand, were retrofitted to '80s excess, and significantly raised the stakes in the process. As a re-sult, the A-Team and Supreme Team had to be prosecuted accord-ingly. With all the information we had acquired about their activities, the A-Team could not be prosecuted at a local level: this was racketeering of the highest order—at this point, the Feds had to step in and finish the job. I had done what I could to take down the A-Team on the state level; now one of my key partners, Det. Richard Sullivan, along with Joseph Ponzi, chief of investigations in the Brooklyn D.A.'s office, were going to run the investigations on a federal level. I knew this case would be closed very soon.

Both brilliant in their fields, Richie Sullivan and Joe Ponzi would do a Major RICO investigation on Glaze and the A-Team's racue-teering activities and succeed. In court, however, it was Leslie Cald-well that put these gangs to bed. At the time, Leslie was an assistant U.S. attorney in Brooklyn with just two years' experience on the job. Us cops loved Leslie—she wasn't afraid of anyone. To her, a crimi-nal was a criminal, regardless of what they looked like and how much money they had. Leslie succeeded in shutting down the A-Team, and getting murder convictions for most of the Supreme Team heavies—Fatcat, Pappy, Prince. "We were very aggressive with them—including arresting [some of] their mothers, [who were] intimately involved in their drug operations," Caldwell explained to the *Houston Chronicle*. There was one key exception to the

Supreme Team convictions, however: the gang's mastermind, Kenneth "Supreme" McGriff, an exception that would come to haunt hip-hop in the post-millennial era. It was a small setback for Leslie Caldwell, who would become one of New York's greatest prosecutors: she would later gain fame as the U.S. attorney that led the charge to take down Enron.

The A-Team and Supreme Team—that was how I spent the late '80s. By 1991, I was a veteran detective, with nine years on job. And I was still doing murders—and still noting the emerging patterns in the confluence of hip-hop and criminal activity.

One case in particular stuck out to me: two guys got killed in a Bed-Stuy shootout. I interviewed one of my street informants from the neighborhood about it: he identified the perps by showing me a Big Daddy Kane album—the shooters are pictured posing on the album's back cover photograph! That wasn't Big Daddy Kane's only brush with illegality—he was almost turned into a victim. A thug who variously went by the street aliases Infinite and Infinity was looking to rob and kidnap Kane; back then, kidnapping was common—they'd hold notable hostages for ransom, but the police would never know, because no one ever reported these kidnappings to the police out of fear. Infinite had the ability to get to even a celebrity like Big Daddy Kane: he was big in the streets, rode around in fancy limos, and knew the right people in the music industry. Thankfully, Kane managed to avoid Infinite's abduction attempts, but they foreshadowed future trends in hip-hop crime that I'd find myself exploring nearly a decade later, in incidents affecting rap artists like Busta Rhymes, Foxy Brown, and Ol' Dirty Bastard. As well, it's on the streets of early-'90s Brooklyn where I encounter another hip-hop-styled smooth criminal, Killer Ben. Killer Ben had already been immortalized in hip-hop rhyme by the greatest rapper of the day, Rakim, on the 1990 song "What's On Your Mind" ("Next stop was mine, a familiar scene/I was meeting my friend Killer Ben in Fort Greene"), and had hosted mixtapes by the likes of superstar D.J.s like Kid Capri; later, Killer Ben would figure in the 1994 shooting of Tupac at Manhattan's Quad recording studios. And Kenneth "Supreme" McGriff would play a continuing role in the darker side of hip-hop history, eventually becoming the linchpin in the government's effort that almost took down the mighty Murder Inc. empire in 2005.

Ah, Manhattan makes it, but Brooklyn takes it. At this point in my career, I was intrigued: I'd seen both hip-hop and crime evolve and interweave right before my eyes. The '90s would serve as a new era for both: hip-hop would rise to cultural dominance while crime attached to its underbelly like a barnacle, drawn to the allure of rap's bling-bling, high-rolling lifestyle. Meanwhile, law enforcement would find itself on the sidelines, trying to make sense of it all. And the man who would embody all these contradictions is one Sean Combs, aka Puff Daddy, aka P. Diddy. Combs would go on to shape '90s hip-hop in his own ghetto fabulous image, but he wasn't always as famous as he is today.

The night that shot his name into popular culture for the first time was, in fact, also the first time he would be linked to death and tragedy. I remember it well. On December 28, 1991, I was working late on a murder in the 81st Detective Squad when a report came over the citywide scanner: an oversold celebrity charity basketball game organized by Puff Daddy and rap star Heavy D and featuring superstars like LL Cool J and Run-DMC ended gruesomely when nine people were trampled to death by a crowd stampede. Recognizing the names of those involved, immediately I wanted to find out for myself what was really going on. I turned excitedly to my supervising officer on duty.

"Lieutenant, we've got to go up to City College in Manhattan," I implored him. "People are dying at this charity basketball game organized by Puff Daddy."

"No, Parker, forget it," my lieutenant responded. "They got enough guys up there already, I'm sure. And besides, who's this 'Puff Daddy' character anyway?"

Welcome to the '90s, where things weren't going to get better, but worse . . .

JACKING THE RAPPER:
The "Puff Daddy" Era—Rap Legends
Born into Blood

It's all about the Benjamins, baby . . .
—Puff Daddy

THE next day, December 29, 1991, I woke up to see headlines as big as billboards on the Sunday papers:

RAMPAGE!

NINE DEAD!

RAP STARS IN DEADLY STAMPEDE!

The tragedy was all over the news: the local twenty-four-hour news channel New York One ran updates constantly. The charity basketball game at Harlem's City College, organized as an AIDS benefit, had turned into a slaughterhouse: nine kids dead, crushed in a stairwell.

In retrospect, it seemed the disaster could've been avoided. Hyped on local hip-hop radio for weeks, the event drew 5,000 fans attempting to push into a gymnasium that seated little more than 2,700. On top of that, the event was assigned only *seven* security guards—who shared just two walkie-talkies between them. The building featured eleven doors, with only one entryway into the event area; however, of those, nine were closed. As the event's co-organizer, Sean "Puff Daddy" Combs found himself enduring endless scrutiny. New York City's then-mayor, David Dinkins, appointed a special investigation into the incident. Lawsuits dragged on well into the decade. And, of course, the media had a field day laying blame.

What sent the media into frenzy over this tragic event, however, were two words joined by a hyphen: *hip-hop*. What had drawn such a huge crowd to CCNY's Jeremiah Mahoney Hall at 138th Street and Convent Avenue was the presence of rap stars like LL Cool J, Run-DMC, and Heavy D. The media saw the CCNY incident as confirmation of rap as a Pied Piper of violence and death: to the major news outlets and grandstanding politicians, rap was the light, and violence was the moth. Run-DMC in particular had been haunted by the specter of violence—a gang fight between Bloods and Crips during a 1987 Run-DMC concert at the Long Beach Arena left some forty attendees injured, and the theatrical release of the group's movie *Tougher Than Leather* a year later found violent incidents following screenings of the film. But the CCNY incident provided the media a new figurehead around which to demonize rap: Sean Combs, or, as he was known back then, "Puff Daddy." For years to come, he wouldn't disappoint: tragedy and Combs would find themselves frequent bedfellows.

Even then, at the dawn of '90s, the media loved seeing this funny name, *Puff Daddy*, in headlines. He was barely twenty-two years old at the time of the City College incident, yet from then on Combs's name would be linked to hip-hop violence. In a way, the CCNY incident had gruesomely jumpstarted Combs's celebrity, which would multiply exponentially in coming years. As Puff Daddy, and later, as P. Diddy, Combs would become the epitome of fame during the 1990s: the best-dressed man, the thrower of the biggest parties, the lover of the most beautiful women—the essence of ghetto-fabulous bling-bling.

Combs has likened himself to a Frank Sinatra retrofitted for contemporary times, and it's actually a pretty apt comparison. Puffy could always be counted on for newsworthy spectacle—a gossip item, a scandalous headline. Combs would be on hand for many of the top exhibits in the Hip-Hop Tragedy Hall of Fame. The City College tragedy. The Club New York shooting involving his then-girlfriend, Jennifer Lopez, and rap protégé Shyne. And most tragically, the East Coast–West Coast rap war, which would claim hip-hop's greatest stars, Tupac and Biggie, among its victims.

Even before the CCNY disaster, well before he was a tabloid fixture, I had became aware of Puffy. He was hard to miss as he gallivanted around early '90s hip-hop clubs and up the ladder of the music industry, right from the bottom rung. At the time, Puffy was little known outside music biz circles: he wasn't even a performer yet, but a rising A&R executive at Uptown Records who threw crazy, notoriously raucous parties at a midtown club called Red Zone. I knew about Puffy even then because I'd always kept one foot in the music world. I'd been promoting parties and hitting the clubs, as well as performing and recording demos as an R&B singer. What really kept my knowledge of music industry inner workings fresh, however, was my repeated attendance at the annual "Jack the Rapper" convention.

Jack the Rapper was named for its founder, Jack Gibson. Gibson wasn't a rapper in the sense that the term is used today; he got his distinctive nickname working as a radio D.J. where between songs he would talk (or "rap") about current events, the music he was playing, or whatever crossed his mind. A titanic figure in African-American music, Gibson was arguably the first black D.J. in the United States; he also started the first black radio station, WERD, in Atlanta, Georgia, back in 1949, and served as a key executive for Motown Records.

Gibson had started his namesake conventions as a way for black-music industry folks to network; these confabs offered seminars in music-business practices and allowed up-and-comers to showcase their demos, among other services. As well, with a captive audience of radio, promotions, and marketing executives brought together from regional scenes all over the country, Jack the Rapper became *the* place to promote up-and-coming urban releases—as well as have lots of crazy sex, drugs, and booze-filled parties. As a result, those in attendance at Jack the Rapper typically read like a who's-who of the black music industry.

As hip-hop rose to dominate the urban-music biz, Jack the Rapper followed right along, embracing the excitement around the

growth of this new African-American musical form. It's not so surprising in retrospect, but the Jack the Rapper conventions inadvertently gave me a front-row perch to watch the emerging phenomenon
of hip-hop-related crime. My attendance there had nothing to do
with police work: I would go as a civilian, strictly for my own musical interests. But that didn't mean I didn't have my eyes open. And
it was at the 1992 Jack the Rapper that I started seeing crime and
hip-hop becoming truly intertwined for the first time.

Nineteen ninety-two was a big year at Jack the Rapper. For one,
the convention was being held at Disney World in Orlando, Florida—
the first time it took place outside of its original home of Atlanta,
Georgia. And the celebrities were out in full force. On hand was a
young Will Smith back when he was still the "Fresh Prince": rocking multicolored overalls, he enthusiastically promoted his come-
back single "Summertime" to Jack's industry folk. Then there was
the original "super freak" himself, Rick James, long before anyone
had heard of Dave Chappelle. All the urban music stars and moguls
of the day were there—Ice Cube, Boyz II Men, Babyface, original
Yo! MTV Raps host Fab 5 Freddy, Def Jam founder and burgeoning socialite Russell Simmons, MC Lyte, KRS-One, Daddy-O of
Stetsasonic, even revered black-music icons like Isaac Hayes. Sports
stars like boxers Evander Holyfield and Tommy "Hitman" Hearns
and basketball great Charles Oakley made appearances alongside actors like Tommy Lister and Bill Bellamy and comedian Sinbad.

That year, however, the most buzz at Jack stemmed from a couple
of little-known crews. Recently fired from his Uptown Records post,
Puff Daddy was on the premises hyping up his new enterprise, Bad
Boy Records, even before he had a label deal. Meanwhile, that year's
festivities would also include showcasing the industry's real coming-
out party for Death Row Records, a then-burgeoning partnership
between former N.W.A. producer Dr. Dre and thug-mogul-in-the-
making Suge Knight.

It was just a few years before Bad Boy and Death Row's deadly rivalry would go nuclear, claiming the lives of Biggie and Tupac,
among others; longer still the national media would wait to learn
that Death Row was initially funded by drug money via Los Angeles

cocaine don, O.G. gangster, and convicted murderer Michael "Harry O" Harris (although Suge Knight never hid his affiliation with the notorious Los Angeles gang known as the Bloods). But at Jack the Rapper way back when, for the most part both Death Row and Bad Boy were just trying to make some noise and get noticed. They made a lot of noise, let me tell you—everyone at Jack the Rapper that year brought their A-game when it came to going buck wild. That weekend, so many black people descended on Disney World that people got scared—white people got *really* scared. Shit, *black people* were terrified.

My friend Stanley, who lived in Orlando, picked me up from the airport. Stanley's preppy, about five feet six inches with glasses—a nerdy "Urkel" type—and he was not prepared for Jack the Rapper. Then again, who could be? The first thing we saw as we drove up to Disney World is Mickey Mouse waving his hands and greeting guests with his permanent grin: "Hi, boys and girls!" The next thing you knew, Mickey had a gun in his face: the world's most famous cartoon character was getting stuck up by couple of b-boy thugs from out of town.

Observing Mickey's mugging, Stanley turned to me, slackjawed. "What the hell is going on?," he implored. I just shrugged. When I first saw the guy with the gun, I wanted to run out of the car and scream, "Police—you're under arrest!" But I reminded myself I'm not in New York, I'm not in Brooklyn, but in another city. I wasn't a cop in Florida: I couldn't travel with guns, so that weekend I was a total civilian. But *man* . . . Mickey Mouse getting jacked by a couple of out-of-town stick-up kids? *Classic.* That surreal sight set the tone for the whole weekend, in fact.

As we pulled into the parking lot, we were greeted by a blast of full-on gangsta rap at full volume. Once inside, we saw guys dressed in full on pimp outfits, complete with rollers in their hair, sitting in customized low-rider '64 Chevys and old Buicks tricked out with spoke rims—and seriously ghetto-blasting speakers. It was a contest: these dudes were battling to see whose car had the most powerful sound system! Our walk to hotel reception proved equally colorful. Stanley was horrified by the sight of so many African-

Americans openly acting the fool. Open bottles of liquor were everywhere and marijuana permeated the atmosphere at this so-called family resort, so there was no shortage of fucked-up black men endlessly crashing motorboats and jet skis into the onshore reeds. I won't even talk about the pool scene we stumbled upon—that's definitely not for the family. Stanley had never seen anything like it.

"Why did you bring all these *black* people here?" Stanley said to me angrily—conveniently forgetting the fact that *he himself* is African-American.

"*I* didn't bring them," I responded.

"Well, having all these black people here is not good—something's gonna happen," Stanley snapped. He was nervous, and he wasn't alone. At the hotel's check-in desk, there was a white couple in front of us asking if there are any rooms available. The concierge, an older white lady looking a bit shellshocked, leaned in conspiratorially to them.

"I don't think you want to stay here," she hissed in an exasperated stage whisper. "These people are *animals*! And they are tearing up the hotel! Look around you!" The couple, after a 360-degree ogle, grabbed their luggage and quickly made for the nearest exit as advised. When we got to the head of the line, the concierge looked at me and groaned. "These people are savages!" she grumbled accusatorily.

"Hey lady, why are you looking at *me*? I have nothing to do with this!" I shot right back, giving her my credit card and a flash of my NYPD badge, which shut her right up.

Still, the carnage continued—the scene inside the hotel played like an African-American stage production of *Caligula,* but with a beat you can dance to. As we walked toward the elevator, Stanley and I passed the hotel bar, where we saw a thug snatch the cash register, and casually scoot away with it under his arm as if nothing has happened. If that's not enough, as we entered the elevator, we discovered the floor was covered in blood. "Yo, man, I don't like this," Stanley said, freaking out. "You've got all these *niggers* down here, and they're tearing Disney World apart! Orlando is not prepared for all these black people. Call me chicken, but as soon we drop off your bags I'm getting out of here!"

At that moment, as if on cue, six of the finest young black women I've ever seen entered the elevator—wearing next to nothing. Stanley shut up real quick. His eyes bulged out so much, they almost pushed his glasses off his nose.

Everywhere I went at Jack the Rapper, I found myself running into big names. It was the kind of event where you'd discover Erick Sermon from the rap group EPMD just hanging out at McDonald's; I'd turn a corner, and there would be Andre Harrell, the grand poobah of Uptown Records, chilling by the pool, surrounded by an entourage of classy ladies, artists, and employees having a ghetto-fab good ol' time. And then I saw a lot of craziness, too—at seemingly every event, every party, it was straight-up sex, drugs, rap and roll, from morning 'til night and back again. Artists were taking two and three girls to rooms at a time—if they made it to the room: one guy was so drunk, he was banging a girl in the hallway. There were fistfights everywhere, and shots fired outside the hotel more than a few times. Partiers would wipe their asses with towels and just leave them wherever, so the hotel stopped providing towels to guests. I was having fun, just observing the chaos, but it got to be a little much for my weak-stomached pal Stanley.

I can't lie—it *was* a volatile situation. Everywhere I looked, there were "crews" roaming the premises, sometimes twenty, maybe thirty guys deep. The biggest crews were the ones from New York and Los Angeles. Representing the East Coast was Puff Daddy and his Bad Boy posse, who made for an intimidating sight. Everyone in the Bad Boy entourage dressed identically in black, and held up enormous placards bearing the black-and-white Bad Boy logo. Biggie wasn't even fully in the Bad Boy picture yet, and Puffy's flagship rapper Craig Mack had only appeared on some remixes. Mack's break-through single, "Flava In Your Ear," the hit that would begin Bad Boy's triumphant assault on the charts, hadn't even been officially released.

The award for most thugged-out crew at '92's Jack the Rapper definitely went to Death Row Records, however. At this point, Death Row was on the verge of exploding. The label had already popped off a hot single with "Deep Cover," Dr. Dre's 1992 collaboration with a young rapper from Long Beach, California, named Snoop Doggy Dogg; "Deep Cover" was Snoop Dogg's recorded debut, and on it he didn't hide his affiliation with the deadly Los Angeles gang the Crips.

At the time, Death Row was about to unleash Dre's genre-defining masterpiece album known as *The Chronic,* which was named after a particularly potent strain of pot favored by Southern California rappers. There was certainly a lot of "chronic" smoke, and a lot of gangbangers, around the Death Row crew at Jack the Rapper at all times. Making the Death Row crew even more ominous was the way its members wore black hoods over their heads as if they were about to be executed. When it came to thuggin' out, Death Row definitely put their money where their mouth was, even in its early days, as their behavior at one Jack the Rapper event made clear.

Midway through the convention weekend, Stanley and I were leaving a seminar when we saw all these S.W.A.T. trucks roll up, with police exiting in full riot gear. I overheard from one of the cops talking on a walkie-talkie that they were going into one of the concert areas: because I understood police code, I knew from his conversation that a performance by Snoop Doggy Dogg had been interrupted by thugs pulling guns and knives on each other. When I rushed inside the concert area, it was a full-on mêleé—yet despite the chaos, all the crews were still keeping up their promotional duties, pushing their Death Row and Bad Boy signs in the air and passing out flyers as fights erupted all around them.

On the stage was a full-on replica of an electric chair: it was as if those of us that were there were actually prisoners on death row ourselves, waiting for that final shock. It was all a little too . . . *authentic* for Stanley. He took one look at that electric chair, then turned to me in a panic. "Derrick, if I were you I'd get on a fucking plane *now,*" he said before hightailing it out of there to his car. I didn't see Stanley again the entire rest of the weekend.

There were plenty of other familiar faces to occupy my attention, though, as I soon discovered. I was surprised to see big drug dealers from Brooklyn whom I've been watching for a while, making the scene at all the big Jack the Rapper parties. They were moving major weight back at home, kilo after kilo of cocaine, and now they appeared to be expanding their world.

Everywhere I went, in fact, I saw faces that were all too familiar: criminals I recognized from working the Bed-Stuy streets. Among them were corner crack dealers, credit-card scammers, shooters, robbers, and known murderers who had never been convicted because witnesses were too scared to testify; you name it, every facet of the criminal element was there in force at Jack the Rapper. Puffy's camp had a few Brooklyn hard rocks in it with reps for violent crime on the street. In particular, I noticed a lot of cats from the Sumner and Marcus Garvey housing projects hoisting those Bad Boy picket signs.

As well, I met up with my friend named Troy at Jack the Rapper. Troy's from the West Coast: he knew all the L.A. gang-bangers and pointed them out to me. Troy noted whom amongst the convention-eers was a "real" Blood or Crip (like Suge and Snoop) and who was a mere "studio gangster"—that is, a rapper who wore the colors of a gang and rhymed about his thuggish gang exploits, but whom had never really been affiliated with a "set" in his life. Alas, the "studio gangsters" were few and far between. I was shocked at the amount of real hard-core criminals attending Jack the Rapper, making inroads in the music industry—I've never seen them in these concentrations before at the convention. But then again, these patterns confirmed what I was already seeing on the streets of New York.

Once my Florida vacation concluded, I went back to work at the 81st detective squad—back to murder and mayhem, Brooklyn style. My experiences at the Jack the Rapper convention made clear I was leading a double life between my activities in both law enforcement and music, and the worlds were beginning to cross over. When I went out, I was always in the cut—there, but not there. I was busy chasing down the new breed of Brooklyn gangsters—drug dealers, murderers, stick-up kids: all more ruthless than their predecessors, more renegade than their counterparts in the other boroughs. These

were the new jacks, the hip-hop gangstas—young, fly, and flashy, the
ghetto-fabulous parasites of the projects. Some Brooklyn cocaine
kingpins were making so much money—sometimes $200,000 a
day—that they saw themselves as just another branch of New York's
wealthy elite. Crack became a stealth, efficient industry: New York
City's shadow economy.

Brooklyn's new-jack hustlers had funny names, which showed
they either read too many comic books or spent too much time
boosting at Macy's department store. Of the former, there was
Supreme Magneto. Magneto (who also went by "Supreme Mag-
netic") was in the drug game; he was very respected in his Fort
Greene 'hood, knew many people in the music industry, and no one
dared fuck with him. Of the latter, you had drug figures calling
themselves "Bill Blass" and "Calvin Klein," lifting their street
monikers from high-end fashion designers. Bed-Stuy–based Klein
was a big name on the street, one of the most powerful drug lords
Brooklyn had ever seen, and well respected within the music biz.

In Brooklyn, there were two kinds of criminals. On the one hand,
guys like Calvin "Klein" Bacote were businessmen above all else.
These guys weren't big shooters: they were tough, yeah, but smart
first. They didn't want the heat that violence brings to affect their
day-to-day business. Their lessons didn't get lost on the new generation of rappers coming up out of Brooklyn, though, who modeled
themselves after charismatic, smooth criminals. In fact, hip-hop
uber-businessman Jay-Z has lionized Calvin "Klein" Bacote in his
rhymes, praising his acumen and style as an influence on Jay-Z's
own empire building. "I never felt more alive than ridin' shotgun in
Klein's green five," Jay-Z rapped nostalgically on his 2004 song "Allure," referring to Bacote.

However, the other, and more common, Brooklyn bad guy typically *just did not give a fuck*. If you had something they wanted,
they would kill you and take it; if you came between them and their
money, they would kill you; if you offended them in some way, they
would just . . . kill you. These guys were my homicide team's bread-
and-butter—they lived out the murderous tales described in the

gangsta rap lyrics of the day, and sometimes inspired them with true stories.

Sequan from the Lafayette Gardens crew, Kendu from East New York, D-Nice (not related to the Bronx rapper associated with Boogie Down Productions who shares the same name), Wiz, JuJu from Bed-Stuy: these were the real bad guys, the top echelon of drug-dealing's murderous elite. Karma has spared some of the baddest guys I used to investigate: a dude named Chaka Raysor is still wanted, still a fugitive on the streets, and surely up to no good. He was part of a major crew known for narcotics trafficking and homicide who were responsible for the deaths of several people; his name still crops up on the occasional *America's Most Wanted* episode to this day. But Raysor is the exception.

The thing is, when you rule through death, death has a funny way of coming back to you. JuJu moved a lot of weight and was a well-known dude, but that didn't keep him from getting killed one night. JuJu's homicide was a scenario straight out of Kool G Rap's classic document of New York crime time, "Streets of New York"— "Three men slain inside an apartment/All you could see was the sparks when it darkened." Juju had a safe-house apartment in Fort Greene, where he was surprised by a gang of guys wearing masks. His assailants tied him up, made him give up the combination to the safe, then shot him point-blank.

Brooklyn bad boys back then were more bloodthirsty than the Italian Mafia ever was, but they still put the "organized" in organized crime; they were moving too much money, running too much game, to be anything but. These were real businesses, run like corporations, their names recognizable brands on the streets for mayhem. The Black Guerilla Family, from Fort Greene, were responsible for a lot of murders. The Mayo Family, from Bed-Stuy's 81st Precinct, were alleged to have run a *massive* drug operation.

This was the moment when I saw the connection of crews and stick-up-kids to the music industry. All the bad guys in our precinct had ties to other bad guys in Brooklyn, ties to East New York, Brownsville, Marcy Houses, Fort Greene, Lafayette Gardens, Brevoort. These

'hoods and housing projects would produce rapper after rapper, like
they were rap factories: some would become famous, boldfaced
named, others would never blow up, but all felt like it was their time
to get on. After N.W.A. and Eazy-E turned tales of L.A. gang culture and street life into the stuff of platinum record sales, every kid
with a rep on the streets figured he could get on rapping on the microphone. New York was fiending for a rapper who could put the
East Coast gangsta legacy on wax the way the West Coast rappers
did, and every thug on the street thought it was *he* who was up next.
They lived the stories, they figured, so why not get paid legit money
to tell them in rhyme?

At this point, I knew something was up, so I cultivated informants that played in both the rap game and the crime on the streets.
These informants traveled all over New York City embedded within
rap camps, rolling to recording-studio sessions and working inside
record labels like Puff Daddy's Bad Boy or Andre Harrell's Uptown
Records. They provided me with critical intelligence on individual
dudes that I had my eye on—who were big in both music and the
streets. Deadly stick-up kid Killer Ben from the Fort Greene area in
the 88th Precinct had been shouted-out in songs by Eric B. &
Rakim—and was known as a wild, uncontrollable shooter; his reputation included murders and other acts of violence. Hip-hop hit pro-
ducer/performer Teddy Riley—the innovator of "new-jack swing"
responsible for jams by Big Daddy Kane, Guy, Blackstreet, Keith
Sweat, Mary J. Blige, and even Michael Jackson—was partnered
with Gene Griffin, a former muscle guy feared in the streets and self-
professed hustler who had notched up some serious prison time before committing himself to his legit music-biz activities.

Then there was Jacques Agnant, aka "Haitian Jack," a Harlem-
based music manager/executive as well as an infamous thug who
aligned himself with a lot of people, and was very feared on the
streets. In fact, what Jack was famed for—and remains so—was his
fearlessness: he wasn't afraid to run up on *anyone*. He ran a good
business this way, with an underlying logic behind it to boot: "My
thing is robbing drug dealers. The drug dealer, see, he isn't going to

call the police," Haitian Jack told me years later, in an interrogation conducted by myself and F.B.I. agent Kendall Hobson involving a case where Jack allegedly took merchandise by force from a Los Angeles jeweler arising from an earlier dispute between the merchant and Jack's pal, rapper Wyclef Jean (who's also of Haitian descent).

Haitian Jack was a flamboyant type guy—still is—adorning himself with gold chains and furs and always driving the finest Mercedes sedans. Above all, Jack flaunted his close relationships with rappers like Tupac, hit all the celebrity parties, and was reputed to be friendly with Madonna. Jack's music-biz contacts and activities (he's also managed various rappers at times) give him an additional outlet for his criminal pursuits.

Jack continues his one-man assault wave right up to today: in months past, he allegedly shot a patron at a L.A. nightclub. Jack was also rumored to have stepped to Jay-Z in public and pinned him to wall after the rapper supposedly disrespected him in some way— with no retribution. As well, the Feds recently brought Jack back to New York for further questioning about Tupac's 1994 shooting incident at New York's Quad recording studio.

Sometimes the connections between rappers and criminals take years to come out; but when they do, the connections are Byzantine and layered like a web. Take the case of Ivory "Peanut" Davis, who got killed outside a Manhattan club called NV years later on August 10, 2000: at around four in the morning, Peanut was shot in the back while sitting in his idling car; wounded but not yet dead, Peanut sped off from the scene, his car killing an innocent pedestrian. The shooter in Peanut's homicide was allegedly a man named Damion "World" Hardy, who was indicted for the crime along with two associates in July 2005 by the Brooklyn U.S. attorney's office. According to an official press release from the United States attorney's office, Hardy was a member of a Brooklyn gang called the Cash Money Brothers, "a violent Brooklyn street gang responsible for five murders, the attempted murder of a witness, the kidnapping and attempted robbery of a drug dealer, assault, and illegal firearms possession. The government's investigation revealed that for more than ten years, CMB members, led by Damion Hardy, controlled narcotics trafficking in the Lafayette Gardens Houses in the Bedford-Stuyvesant section of Brooklyn through violence and intimidation directed against their drug-trafficking competitors, innocent civilians, and potential witnesses." In my time in Brooklyn, I had my eye on Hardy and CMB, but I could never make anything stick. Thankfully the Feds were patient and could do what I couldn't, successfully bringing them down on racketeering, murder, and other charges.

Hardy's Cash Money Brothers took their name from the fictional drug gang of the same moniker in the classic early '90s "hip-hop crime" movie *New Jack City*. That wasn't the only instance of life imitating art, and vice versa. What the press release leaves out is, at the time of Peanut's killing, "World" was also the boyfriend of rapper, Biggie protégée/lover and future prison-bound perjurer Lil' Kim.

Biggie was known for his criminal associations himself. His manager and partner in the "Undeas" record label that released albums by Kim and Big's crew Junior M.A.F.I.A. was Lance "Un" Rivera. Rivera's name was often mentioned around the neighborhood by my informants as a bad dude; he was later stabbed by Jay-Z at midtown Manhattan's Kit Kat Klub in 2000, supposedly in retaliation for bootlegging Jay's albums in advance of their release date. Jay-Z received three years' probation; according to news reports, Jay-Z paid out somewhere between $300,000 and $600,000 to halt Rivera's cooperation in the case.

Big and Jay-Z weren't, er, *big* like these dudes were. They didn't have that kind of rep. Biggie for one wasn't superpowerful in the streets. He was there, sure, but from what I saw he was more of a dealer selling on the corner than someone really pushing serious weight. Jay-Z's place in Brooklyn's drug-dealing hierarchy remains hazier, more enigmatic. In songs and interviews, Jay-Z claims an extensive history as a cocaine kingpin, and shouts out authentic drug players like Calvin "Klein" Bacote in his rhymes; yet as far as I knew, though, even though he was from the right 'hood for it, he was never in that picture. I can't say for certain whether Jay-Z was a big dealer or not, but if he was, I'm pretty sure I would've heard about it.

Bouncing between hip-hop and law enforcement, I heard about most things happening on the street; I was immersed simultaneously in two antithetical, antagonistic worlds. But I wasn't the only one in the NYPD leading a double life. Back at the 81st Precinct, I learned that one of my colleagues in the detective squad, a guy we'll call Kraken, was developing a cocaine problem that was affecting his work. This became clear when one of my informants, a streetwalking prostitute we'll call Shy-Shy, came in to the precinct house and told me Kraken had something she needed.

"I don't like you coming up to the office like this," I told her. I didn't want people on the street to see her talking to the police. I had Shy-Shy informing in an investigation with a major local drug dealer named Cesar Gonzales; at this point, she was giving info to the Feds about Gonzales, and if anyone saw her voluntarily going into the precinct house, it could endanger her life.

"But I'm here for services rendered," Shy-Shy protested as I tried to lead her out. I stopped and pulled her over into a corner.

"What do you mean, 'services rendered'?" I whispered pointedly. "To whom?"

"I gave Detective Kraken a blow job last night," Shy-Shy mentioned blithely, "and he promised to pay me."

She continued to describe how she had smoked crack with Kraken and then performed fellatio on him. Shy-Shy said Kraken gave her his ATM card to get money, but when she went to withdraw what she was owed, she discovered there was no money in Kraken's account—that was because his crack addiction was burning through it. I knew she was telling the truth because she had Kraken's PIN number. Meanwhile, she was describing Kraken's house accurately; I'd been there myself.

My heart fell in my lap. I couldn't believe Kraken exposed himself like that. And for what? I mean, Shy-Shy was so cracked out, her front teeth were missing! I decided to confront Kraken before tak-

ing further action, but before I could do so, Shy-Shy went and
squealed to the district attorney, who commenced a federal investigation into the 81st's detective squad.

Kraken's partners came under suspicion, and the case became
even more complicated when the D.A.'s brother came under investigation from the Bureau of Alcohol, Tobacco, and Firearms—and
was caught on a wire selling guns. In the end, Kraken was doled,
tested positive for coke, and fired. The whole experience of this federal investigation left a bad taste in my mouth. It hurt all of us.

Kraken wasn't the only corrupt cop to fall under my watch in
those days, however. By the summer of 1992, I had been placed by
the supervising lieutenant into a special team devoted strictly to investigating homicides in the 81st Precinct. The team was made up
of three detectives: me, Richie Sullivan, and Terry Murnane. We
were a young group of guys—still gung ho, but with a lot of experience between us. Together, we'd track emerging patterns of violence
from the criminals in our area. We were innovative: we knew what
bad guys to go after, who was in what crew, even what cars the crews
drove—down to the license plates.

We made a good team, as each of us played our own roles: I was
more the interrogator, Richie was the hunter, and Terry was the guy
who took care of paperwork. Richie was very good at getting info on
bad guys in other precincts—criminals in Fort Greene, Lafayette
Gardens, Marcy Houses, or Queens that may play into our caseload.
We would have different cases, Richie liked to do what are known as
RICO cases. Congress passed the Racketeer Influenced and Corrupt
Organizations (or RICO) Act in 1970, largely to take down the traditional Mafia groupings; we found, in the crack-driven '80s and '90s,
that RICO had application far beyond the Italians and the other expected, well-known organized crime groups. We liked RICO because
it got the federal government involved, which gave us more latitude
under the law, more power under the law, and more juice. We'd also
get more mileage out of the Brooklyn D.A.'s office: they'd give us
search warrants, and team us up with federal agents.

Together, our team used to hunt the worst of the worst—just the
three of us in a blue Chevy Impala with no hubcaps, cruising the

night looking for bad guys. We never had to look too far; in fact, one of the worst was one of our own, right there under our noses. One day a case comes across my desk that involves hunting down a perp named Jeffrey Marshall, known on the street as "Big Born." This guy was bad news, and *massive*—at six feet three inches and 250 pounds, Big Born *was* big—allegedly linked to several robberies and at least one murder within the confines of the 81st Precinct; in addition to stickups and home invasions, he was doing muscle-man work and contract murders for drug dealers. Feared by some, respected by others, Marshall was above all a *predator*, a piece of garbage from the streets of Bed-Stuy—the projects at 99 Tompkins Avenue, to be exact.

I started fixating on Big Born; he was a menace to society, and I wanted to shut him down. Despite his constant activity, however, it wasn't easy getting a hold on him. The thing was, Jeffrey Marshall was above all an intimidator. With every case we got involving Big Born, witnesses never wanted to get involved, or they'd claim they couldn't ID him. Even the numerous people I interviewed who said Marshall was conclusively involved in something didn't want to to testify.

Big Born's luck turned when he was alleged to have murdered a pimp named Leon Cromer. Apparently Cromer had come over to see a girl who lived on Lewis Avenue in the 81st Precinct. Cromer pulled up in a gold Acura, went up to the girl's apartment, then left. As he got in his car, someone blew his brains out. When I got to the scene, no one was able to identify the body, it was so torn apart. Finally, Cromer's girlfriend was located, and she was able to identify him.

Soon after, I tied Marshall to the armed heist of a Long Island jewelry store and the robbery of a butcher. I'd had enough of Big Born. I had to make a move. I was going to put Marshall in custody; there was enough on him to pull him in and stop him for the moment. But I didn't have the witness to keep him locked up for good. Time was working against me. But then I found that witness; it was going to require delicate handling, and some stealth moves, but I was going to bring Big Born down.

One day Pete Sloan and I went over to Marshall's house. He lived with some girl in Bushwick, Brooklyn, in a two-family house. We knocked on the door, and a girl answered. At first she told us Big Born wasn't there, but we told her we knew otherwise, and that we'd wait until he showed up, anyway.

After a minute, Marshall appeared at the top of the stairs shirtless, wearing only sweatpants and a bad attitude. He was on to us: people had told him the cops were asking around about him on the streets, and he knew we were homicide detectives. Therefore, it was no surprise that he wasn't happy to see us.

"I'm tired of you guys harassing me," he said as he walked down the stairs towards us. "Parker, I'm getting tired of *you*."

"Shut your fat ass up and put some clothes on, or I'll drag you to the precinct half naked," I barked back. After pulling on a shirt, Big Born came with us voluntarily. I didn't put the handcuffs on him—I wanted to get him identified by a witness first, before I arrested him. Besides, I wanted to see what he was going to say.

Once we reached the precinct, I brought Marshall into the interview room. "You know why you're here," I said, sitting him down. "I've got you here for the murders and the robberies." I was bluffing him; he had no clue what I had on him.

"I know you've been on to me, but I didn't do nothing," Marshall shot back.

"I'm not in a mood for bullshitting," I told him, "so wipe that smile off your face because I'm putting you in a lineup."

Marshall was feeling cocky; as usual, he figured anyone would be too scared to ID him. But I'd convinced a witness to come in, a female from Big Born's neighborhood who had seen the Cromer killing. It took me almost a year to get through to her. First I became friends with her—I'd give her money when she was facing life difficulties, maybe buy her food sometimes. And I had to assure her that when Marshall was in custody, I would be there, and that I would recommend to the D.A.'s office that she get protection. Sure enough, when we brought Marshall in for the lineup, she picked him right away.

Marshall was naturally upset that his jig was up, so I let him stew in the interrogation room for a spell while I drove my star witness home; when I came back, he'd been marinating in his own paranoia for over an hour. In other words, he was perfectly vulnerable enough to start dishing up the real goods. For one, Marshall needed his insulin. He was diabetic, so we allowed him to take his medicine; after that, we informed him that he was arrested, and we locked him in a cell. As we walked away, he called out to me, an edge of panic in his voice.

"Parker, you guys do your homework, don't you?" Marshall yelled from behind the cell bars. "Let's talk—I want to make a deal with you."

"What kind?" I asked. Now I was interested.

"I want to give you a bad cop," he said.

"Yeah, *right*." I figured Big Born was just grasping at straws. But then Marshall threw me a bone with some meat on it.

"Yo, Parker, your police ID card, is it red and white?" Marshall asked.

"Yeah," I responded, turning back around. "What of it?"

"Well, this dirty cop I know," Marshall continued, "his ID card is all perforated and punched with holes." This information stopped me in my tracks: a perforated NYPD ID card means an officer is on modified assignment—like if he's not allowed to carry a gun because of some violation, or that he's under investigation by Internal Affairs. What strikes me is that there's no way Marshall would know what a modified assignment ID looked like if he hadn't actually seen it. Something *was* up, something bigger than the murder of a pimp.

Intrigued, I led Big Born out of his cell and into the interview room. We started talking, and he mentioned he had something on a cop named "Cabeza"—that means "head" in Spanish. Supposedly Marshall, this guy Cabeza, and some other accomplices robbed a liquor store on Tompkins Avenue; in the process, someone shot the Korean owner to death. Also present at the scene was a black guy from the neighborhood who worked at the store. According to Marshall, Cabeza said, "That dude saw my face; he's gotta go, too"—so he shot the black guy. The thing is, the black guy lived. He was paralyzed by the bullet, but he was still alive.

I was trying to keep my cool around Marshall, but hearing his tale
of a cop involved with him in a double robbery-homicide made my
jaw drop; this was *huge.* I immediately notified the three bodies I
was certain would be interested in Marshall's revelations—the
Brooklyn district attorney's office, which was starting a cop corruption unit; Internal Affairs, of course; and the 79th Precinct Detective Squad, which was already investigating the liquor store case.
Usually the Brookyn D.A. doesn't get involved in cases that involve
just one witness, but because a cop was involved, they were happy to
take it on.

I discovered that Cabeza was indeed on modified assignment: after he discharged his NYPD-issued gun in the air at party while off-
duty, the weapon was taken away from him. As well, while he was
supposedly out on sick leave, he was actually committing robberies
with Marshall. I also learned that on the night of the liquor store
robbery-murder, he went to the scene of the crime while walking his
dog. He'd identified himself as a cop to the officers on the scene,
then asked what happened. What a scumbag: I thought, "Yeah, I'm
going to put this guy away *forever.*"

We did a lineup with Marshall and Cabeza: sure enough, the black
guy who was paralyzed during the robbery identified both of them.
Alas, we weren't as lucky when we put Marshall on trial for the
Cromer murder, which we lost. But the D.A.'s office was more interested in successfully prosecuting a case involving a corrupt, homicidal cop than one where some pimp got shot. Either way, Marshall
was going away for a long time.

Marshall plead out twelve to twenty-five years, with the agreement
that he would testify against Cabeza. If it accepted plea, the D.A.'s
office would drop the other cases pending against him. Cabeza ends
up getting thirty-three plus years to life for homicide and robbery.
When you pile a felony on top of another felony, it's a double
whammy, and the judge was all-too-happy to lower the boom on
Cabeza.

As well, the boom bap of hip-hop was never too far out of my
senses, however, even as I busied myself taking down dirty cops. I,
and the world, would have no trouble hearing about the next major

milestone in hip-hop crime: the 1994 Tupac shooting. It was a shot heard 'round the world, but I remember hearing about it immediately, around 1:00 A.M.—less than an hour after it happened—as soon as the first police reports came in on the NYPD's citywide band radio. The reports said that detectives from Midtown North had already responded to the scene. The case was out of my precinct's jurisdiction, but I knew I'd find my way inside, anyway. After all, most bad things can usually be traced back to Crooklyn somehow.

RIDE OR DIE:
The Rise and Fall of Tupac Shakur

*The government found Saddam Hussein in a hole. But they can't find out
who killed Tupac. And Tupac was shot in front of Circus Circus!*
—*Chris Rock*

THIS first Tupac shooting has been analyzed and mytholo-
gized into legend. Here are the basics: the incident occurred on
November 30, 1994, at a time when Tupac Shakur's life was already
in turmoil. In the year before he was shot, Tupac had had a smash album with *Strictly For My N.I.G.G.A.Z.*, with hits like "I Get
Around" and "Keep Ya Head Up." But by November 30, 1994, he'd
been indicted for the rape of a nineteen-year-old woman, whom he'd
met twelve days earlier on the dance floor of the downtown Manhattan nightclub Nell's. Just a day earlier, on November 29, in fact, the
jury had started deliberating the case. The charges included gun
possession, sexual assault, and sodomy; if convicted of any of the
charges, which was nearly a certainty, Tupac was looking at serious
time behind bars. It was 'Pac's second close call—in early October,
he had been acquitted of assault charges involves in the shooting of
two Georgia police officers—and he probably wouldn't be so lucky
this time.

In fact, Tupac's luck had run out. He had agreed to do a cameo
rap on a song for a Brooklyn rapper named Little Shawn, who was
known mostly for a minor hit called "Hickeys on Your Chest"; in a
way, this was a comedown for Tupac, as Shawn was in many ways his
inferior as an artist. The nighttime session for Tupac's guest verse
was being held at Quad Studios, a recording-studio complex in an

office building on Seventh Avenue in New York City's Times
Square. In the Quad building recording at the same time was Notorious B.I.G. and his Junior M.A.F.I.A. posse, along with Puff
Daddy. Uptown Records founder Andre Harrell, meanwhile, was
overseeing the Little Shawn session that Tupac was to perform on.

When Tupac and his three-person entourage—manager Freddie
Moore, Randy Walker (aka "Stretch" of the rap group Live Squad,
who had collaborated with 'Pac on . . . *N.I.G.G.A.Z.*'s "The Streetz
R Deathrow"), and his sister's boyfriend—arrived at Quad, they
were assaulted at gunpoint at the entrance. Their assailants, three
men wearing combat camouflage, demanded the group's jewelry.
When Tupac refused, they shot him five times, resulting in injuries
to his head, leg, and testicles. According to sources of mine within
the police department, Tupac's own gun went off and shot him in
the balls; however, in Nick Broomfield's documentary film *Biggie &
Tupac*, 'Pac's father Michael Garland claims Tupac exposed himself
to show him physical proof that his genitalia was actually un-
harmed. "That's when I knew he was my son," Garland laughs.
Shockingly, despite being hit by so many bullets, Tupac survived his
injuries.

I came in to work next day, and the Tupac shooting was all over the
news—headlines in the *New York Post*, the *Daily News*, even *The
New York Times*; it was the scandal du jour. As a major Tupac fan, I
was stunned. I wasn't like all those other police, who immediately
hated Tupac because of his rebellious attitude toward law enforcement. To this day, I think Tupac was a genius, a soulful, powerful
renegade; in 1994, he wasn't just the hot rapper on the streets, but an
instant icon. It was like his songs were stories, and he was the character in the stories: they focused the rage, the passion, the contradictions of being a young black male. And they had hot beats, too.

I had heard of Tupac's legacy long before he ever put out a
record—that's because my old sergeant, Richie Bushrod, and I had
talked about Afeni Shakur, Tupac's mother, when I was at Bronx
Narcotics. Richie had worked NYPD Intel back in the '70s, where
he was a team leader. He used to tell me about going after the Black
Liberation Army (BLA) radical organization as an undercover. It

was an incredibly dangerous assignment. Two cops had been killed in Queens following the BLA when Richie got the job. It was the '70s, a time of radical black activism, violence, civil-rights tumult, and terrorist threats.

Richie's job involved surveillance of different BLA members, as well as infiltrating and monitoring the organization—Richie had to follow BLA perps on subways, through parks, all around the country, monitoring them. Out of all of Richie's stories, one name that rang a bell to me was Afeni Shakur; she and her husband were both associated with the Black Panthers. Later, when I first started seeing the name "Tupac Shakur," it all started to come together.

The '60s was a turbulent era percolating with conspiracy theories; in the wake of Tupac's shooting at Quad, it was like déjà vu. Not that the NYPD had any particular theories about the incident—when it came to rap, back then law enforcement was totally out to sea, even more than they are now. As soon as I heard about the Tupac shooting, I immediately called Joe Babnick, the detective assigned to the Quad investigation. Babnick was part of the Midtown North's Robbery Identification Program; he got the Tupac case because it was a robbery. But Babnick didn't know who shot Tupac; he didn't know what was going on—he wasn't a rap guy. He was always a good person, and a good detective, but I knew he wouldn't get anywhere with this case.

I visited him at the Midtown North precinct house, where Joe told me he wasn't learning much from Little Shawn, the people at studio—or anyone that was involved, really. After his assault case in Georgia, and his family's history of being persecuted by law enforcement, Tupac certainly wasn't going to talk the cops; it was the code of the streets keeping him silent, ghetto *omerta*. Meanwhile, everyone else got "lawyered up": Puffy wasn't going to talk to anyone—he had his attorneys protect him.

I went through some of Babnick's reports and, yeah, he didn't have much to go on. It was the same old story; just like in the 81st, nobody wanted to talk. I told Babnick that I would try to help him in any way I could. I knew the streets would start whispering. Soon enough, they did.

Tupac himself, and others, had theories about who was behind the Quad incident. In particular, Haitian Jack's name surfaced as a possible suspect. Babnick wanted to talk to Haitian Jack: he had learned that Jack knew Tupac—supposedly Jack was portraying himself as Tupac's manager. Jack had also been Tupac's codefendant in the sexual assault trial; before the indictment came down, Tupac and Jack had become fast friends, but the assault trial had split them apart; ultimately, Jack pleaded guilty to misdemeanor charges, but the more serious assault charges were dismissed. What I heard from the streets was that Tupac felt Jack was a snitch—there was talk that he was talking to the D.A.'s office, rumors that he was informing to police. According to Ronin Ro's book *Have Gun Will Travel*, speculation abounded that Haitian Jack was one of 'Pac's shooters. Ro also notes that the person who arranged the Little Shawn session with Tupac, a music-business insider named "Booker," had ties to Jack.

Tupac's head began to burst with conspiracy theories. One thing feeding his paranoia was the fact that the same three NYPD cops—Joseph Kelly, William Kelly, and Craig McKernan—that had responded to (and testified for the prosecution in) 'Pac's sexual-assault case had been the first to arrive at the Quad scene. It *was* an eerie coincidence, I can't lie. But then Tupac decided that it was his former friend Biggie that was behind the shooting. For 'Pac, it was too much of a coincidence that Biggie and Puff and Junior M.A.F.I.A. were at the studio. And 'Pac recognized the camouflage gear the shooters were wearing as the uniform of Brooklyn street thugs—the kind of dudes Biggie hung with.

To my mind, Tupac was correct in his assessment that the perps were from Brooklyn. Brooklyn guys *did* wear army fatigues. Street recognizes street—if a street guy sees two individuals wearing fatigues, he knows that they're Brooklyn soldiers. But there had to be more than he knew as to why he thought they were from Brooklyn.

Why would Tupac go to Quad and get shot? Who would know he was there? Who did he have beef with? For one, I knew that this first Tupac shooting was planned; it was totally deliberate. Someone had to let the shooters in, or they had to know how to get in there. They had to know when Tupac was coming or going. This shooting didn't "just happen." For one, the circumstances were odd; the robbery aspect of it seemed like an afterthought, a ruse to throw the scent off the real intent. Indeed, the real intent appeared to be to kill Tupac above all else.

Then I got the call that convinced me.

With a case like this, if you want to know the truth, often it's best to let a little time go by. With all the press sensationalizing going on, you have to let everything die down a bit; then the real story starts floating to the surface. After almost a year passed, I got a call at the 81st Precinct from a confidential informant. This C.I. was an informant I had been working with in Brooklyn, in the streets, on my A-Team investigations. Everything this informant had ever told me turned out to be true; I wasn't about to start doubting him now.

"Hey, Parker," the familiar voice on the other end of the line said. "Yo, man, I wasn't there, but this is who I heard was down with that Tupac shooting. The talk is that it was King Tut and Nubbs. They were the shooters."

Whoa—this information was making the case even more personal for me. King Tut was an O.G. of the A-Team posse; somehow, though, he had actually avoided being successfully prosecuted in Leslie Caldwell's federal sting of the gang. Tut was a mastermind—they called him that because he planned things like this brilliantly; his muscle was more effective because his mind knew what to do with it.

Nubbs was supposedly Tut's second guy. I didn't know much about Nubbs. I'd heard he was called Nubbs because he'd lost the tips of his fingers in a motorcycle accident, leaving only nubs on his hand. What I did know was that Nubbs was from Flatbush, Brooklyn's south side, and that he and Tut were somehow connected.

According to the C.I., the Quad incident was a contract shooting coming from Biggie. I suspect that's true because Tupac and Biggie had a war brewing. Biggie and Tupac had been friends—they had even recorded a song together—but Tupac had seen Haitian Jack hanging out with Biggie, which could have upset him. Either way, the streets were saying that Biggie and Tupac had had a falling out, that the two didn't like each other that much anymore, even before the media got wind of any beef; I had heard such chatter even before Tupac got shot.

There were a bunch of theories floating around, but after putting together all the information I'd received, the most plausible one for me was that the order came from Biggie; the streets were talking, and word was that it was him. Biggie surely knew Tut because of his Brooklyn ties. Furthermore, Biggie associates like manager Lance "Un" Rivera themselves hailed from Brooklyn's criminal underworld, so it's clear the rapper could've accessed figures like Tut and Nubbs without much difficulty; everybody knows everyone in Brooklyn, especially those in the street life. I believed this theory— I thought this might be the key to solving the case. I did everything I could to verify the information was true.

Next I called Babnick. I told him "I think I can help you—I think guys from Brooklyn are involved in your investigation." He thanked me for the help, but told me he was going to close the case out because Tupac was an uncooperative complainant; the case was coded either C-3 (no suspect, because the witness won't cooperate) or C-4 (the witness can't make an identification). In the end, the perps identified by the informant were taken out of the picture, brought down by their own violent tendencies. A detective in the 63rd Precinct told me that Nubbs had been killed in the Brooklyn South area, supposedly over a romantic dispute.

Tut himself had been put away by New York's "three strikes" rule. Soon after the Tupac shooting, he'd been caught on his third felony robbery offense. That meant the Feds were now involved, and Tut was going to be spending some real time behind bars.

Ultimately, Tupac's Quad shooting case didn't mean much to the NYPD—they weren't concerned about rap music back then. To them, it was just an entertainer that got shot, and a black one at that, no big deal. There wasn't much interest from the D.A., I could tell you that. They didn't see it as a burgeoning pattern or trend. They had no intricate knowledge that there was a dispute or a conspiracy, or a war brewing. Little did they know what was coming.

In all fairness, at the end of the day, there was nothing that the NYPD could do about the Quad shooting—it wasn't a murder, and

Tupac never liked the police. He was a rebel, invincible, on a mission. Cooperating with the police wasn't his code, even if he knew who did it. He was going to take care of it himself. Maybe he did. Tupac suspected Randy "Stretch" Walker was more involved than he let on. Exactly one year to the day after Tupac's Quad shooting, on November 30, 1995, Stretch was shot to death in Queens. A coincidence? Yeah, *right* . . .

The year 1995 was in fact when hip-hop crime started to spike—the moment when rap took a turn to the murderous that would leave a permanent scar on pop culture. It was the year when the East Coast–West Coast rap war went into overdrive. Hip-hop's deadly coastal rivalry had its roots in the competition between Los Angeles's Death Row Records and New York's Bad Boy label.

Since 1992, when Dr. Dre had released his landmark G-funk gangsta-rap masterpiece *The Chronic* on Death Row, the Left Coast label had dominated hip-hop with its charismatic superstars like Snoop Dogg. Death Row's only real competition came from the aggressive hustle of Puff Daddy's upstart startup imprint Bad Boy; Combs had a breakout hit with the label's first artist Craig Mack, but it was Notorious B.I.G. who posed the real threat on the charts. Since he appeared on the scene, Biggie's charisma and myth proved irresistible. The first-generation son of West Indian immigrants, he was an unlikely New York gangsta remix of the American dream: an overweight kid with a lazy eye who went from low-level street thug to rap's Michael Jordan seemingly overnight. Big's 1994 debut *Ready to Die* was an instant classic—suddenly there was a new candidate for the greatest M.C. in hip-hop.

Ironically, Death Row and Bad Boy had a lot in common. Both were guided by young, brash hustlers like Sean "Puffy" Combs and Suge Knight, who would do anything, and I mean *anything*, to see their acts succeed; both had grown out of earlier label entanglements that would eventually be left in the dust by the new jack's success. Bad Boy Puffy had been unceremoniously fired from Andre Harrell's Uptown Records after delivering numerous hits, while Death Row sonic surgeon Dr. Dre had to escape the contractual grip of former N.W.A. bandmate Eazy-E's Ruthless Records. Each featured the hottest, state-of-the-art production hip-hop had heard yet; and as for mic talent, each label was spearheaded by the most hard-core, gangsta, yet lyrically dextrous M.V.P.s on the mic, each of whom authentically represented their 'hood (Snoop Dogg had authentic Crip gang credentials via Long Beach, California, while Biggie was a crack-dealing Brooklyn hustler). It was almost like hip-hop wasn't big enough for both Bad Boy and Death Row; their beef along regional lines was social Darwinism driven by funky-ass beats.

The tensions between Death Row and Bad Boy would explode at the 1995 Source Awards. The Source Awards are like hip-hop's Academy Awards: sponsored by *The Source* magazine, the Source Awards honor rap's greatest artists and achievements of the year, and feature numerous appearances and performances from hip-hop celebrities. Naturally, the Source Awards have proven somewhat raucous, but 1995's edition would set the standard for tension. Competition between East Coast and West Coast rappers was fierce, and their grand poobahs stoked the fires.

"Any artist out there that want to be an artist and want to stay a star and don't want to worry about the executive producer all up in the videos, all on the records dancing, come to Death Row," Suge Knight exclaimed upon hitting the Source Awards stage. Suge's words were a barely concealed dis of rival Puffy, who was indeed known for hogging the spotlight in music videos (so many that MTV one year ran a countdown of "the best videos featuring Puff Daddy") and spiking his productions with his own ad-libs long before he made a solo record of his own. Snoop Doggy Dogg, meanwhile, continued the hate, telling the crowd "we got no love for the East Coast"; Snoop's Death Row labelmate and Dogg Pound homey Daz instructed the audience that they "can eat this dick."

The East Coast–West Coast rivalry was what made the headlines, but the 1995 Source Awards also featured some gangsta business— real street shit, that managed to elude the radar of law enforcement.

Late that night, I got a call from one of my C.I.s: "Yo, did you hear what happened at the Source Awards?"

"I had heard Suge and Death Row were talking shit about the East Coast," I said.

"That's old news, man," the C.I. responded. "What I'm saying is, did you hear about Killer Ben and Biggie?"

According to this C.I., there was a robbery at the Source Awards in Manhattan that never got reported to the police: a guy named Zack with Biggie and the Bad Boy camp had his gold chain stolen. I received word that Ben O'Gara—aka Killer Ben, the notorious gunman from Myrtle Avenue in North Brooklyn—had something to do with that. Not soon after, Killer Ben was shot with a .40-caliber handgun while talking at a pay phone in his Myrtle Avenue stomping grounds.

Informants in the street tell me Ben's death was payback for that robbery, with Biggie commissioning the hit. To this day, there's a mural next to where Killer Ben was killed commemorating his short life—although it leaves out the bloody stuff. Next to a kitschy portrait of the killer as a young man, posing him against a blue, palm-tree laden background, is a sentimental eulogy from his wife that reads thus: "Benjamin C. O'Gara, Nov. 5, 1968–August 17, 1995: You remain in our hearts and you'll never be forgotten ever as you continue to watch over us and guide us!"

It's unclear who was watching over Killer Ben; his life expectancy was never going to be very long, alas. Ben finally messed with someone heavier than him—there's always somebody out there that's heavier, and if your job is being a stick-up kid like Ben, then inevitably you'll find that person. Stick-up kids, especially ones from Brooklyn, feel like they can rob anybody they want. Anyone can get tapped, even other guys from Brooklyn; athletes, rappers, drug dealers, and other thugs are all fair game—a stick-up kid like Killer Ben isn't scared of anyone. Killer Ben had a rep because he had killed a lot of people; he was fearless on the streets, which made him feared.

Killer Ben had a reputation that was similar to that of the "real" 50 Cent. The rapper 50 Cent of today took his name in homage to an actual criminal named 50 Cent, who was a street legend. While the rapping 50 Cent of G-Unit fame is from Queens, the original 50 was a Brooklyn stick-up kid infamous for his straight-up *I-don't-give-a-fuck* fearlessness. He would rob anyone anytime, then go right past his victim like nothing happened; as he would drive around the neighborhood in his blue Audi, people would say, "I know you robbed this guy," and he'd be like, "So what?" That was the mentality of Brooklyn guys—but there's always someone bigger.

The original 50, tough as he was, got killed in a setup. That's the key difference between stick-up kids and killers: the killer will set you up. Despite his name, Killer Ben wasn't a killer like that—but he messed with some, and got shot in cold blood.

It would be another cold-blooded killing that year that would continue to stoke East Coast–West Coast tensions. On September 24, 1995, Jermaine Dupri, a well-known hit producer and founder of the So So Def label, threw a birthday party at the Platinum City nightclub in his hometown of Atlanta, Georgia. Despite the heightened tension between the camps, posses from both Bad Boy and Death Row attended Dupri's gala, headed up by their respective honchos, Sean "Puff Daddy" Combs and Suge Knight. Almost inevitably, the night ended in confrontation, and even more sadly, death: a dispute broke out between Puffy's longtime bodyguard, alleged cousin, and known street dude Anthony "Wolf" Jones and Suge's right-hand man Jake Robles, a tough guy in his own right.

When the dispute moved outside, Robles ended up shot, with eyewitnesses fingering Wolf as the shooter—although Wolf would never be prosecuted because, in by now typical fashion, the witnesses refused to testify. Robles would die days later due to injuries from the incident. Although Puff Daddy claimed he was not involved in Robles's death in any way (and no charges were ever brought against him), Suge Knight never forgave him for the death of his trusted lieutenant Robles; this would solidify the bloody divide between East and West Coast rap camps even further.

The antipathy between Death Row and Bad Boy reached its apex when Suge Knight signed Tupac just a few weeks later after Jake Robles's homicide. Suge Knight even violated the terms of his house arrest by going out of state to visit 'Pac to seal the deal at upstate New York's brutal Dannemora prison, where the rapper was serving out his sentence for sexual assault. The union was not just musical: Tupac and Suge had complementary beefs, with 'Pac's newfound hatred of Biggie fitting in perfectly with Knight's disdain for

Puff Daddy. From a distance, I started watching Suge Knight closely at this time, tracking his movements through my contacts and informants. His presence was like a time bomb: he could go off at any time, with casualties a certainty.

THE CASE GOES COLD: TUPAC SHAKUR, R.I.P.

As eventful as 1995 was in terms of hip-hop related criminal activity, the following year would make good on its threats, resulting in the death of hip-hop's greatest icons. In 1996, everything fell into place. Both Tupac and Biggie would be murdered publicly and tragically. And in January of that year, my police work would take on a new evolution: that's when I would join the NYPD's newly formed, controversial Cold Case Squad—an elite unit devoted to solving unsolved crimes across all boroughs.

My involvement with Cold Case stems back from December 1995, when we got a new Lieutenant Commander in the 81st detective squad office, a good-looking, sharply dressed Italian guy named Joe Pollini who fancied himself after Al Pacino. A thirty-year department vet, Pollini had actually gotten a lateral demotion by getting sent to Brooklyn from the Major Case Squad, where he had been coping with bank robbers, kidnappings, and the like.

Pollini was gung ho: he wasn't the type of boss to sit around and wait for things to happen—he made things happen. With all the investigations we did, Pollini was always first out the door. If we had a hostage situation, Pollini would be the first guy to respond—he was a hostage negotiator, and very good.

Pollini wanted to close cases with arrests, and he pushed hard. One thing about Joe: he didn't mind telling a boss, a captain, or an inspector that he was going to do things against the grain. For example, when there was a spike in burglaries in the precinct, Pollini changed the detective tours to midnight shifts. Several old-timers were opposed to this—they'd say, "You can't change union procedures—that's for night watch." But Pollini did it anyway.

Pollini liked me so much, he would assign me homicides that

other people couldn't solve. I would always tell him, "Don't complain about the overtime, because if you want to catch murderers, it's going to cost money."

The thing was, you could tell that while Pollini liked his work, he didn't like being stuck in the Brooklyn ghetto; after all, he had come from working in *Manhattan*. Manhattan had the glory, the nightlife, and, most importantly, great restaurants (that's a crucial thing for all detectives—we love to eat, and to eat well). He was about to be saved from outer-borough hell, though, and so was I. It was the beginning of the Bill Bratton era for all of us in the NYPD, and our world was gonna change, like it or not.

In January 1996, Pollini got a phone call from headquarters: Bill Bratton, our new police commissioner, and Bratton's deputy commissioner, Jack Maple, wanted to talk. Bratton was Mayor Rudy Giuliani's first commish, and he was ready to shake things *up*. Giuliani wanted to see instant results in getting crime off the streets, and Bill Bratton was prepared to do anything to accomplish that goal.

Bratton came into the NYPD as a law-enforcement innovator, which meant big changes were in store: new computers, automatic firearms, new technology, new ways of doing things. Bratton turned the infrastructure of police department inside out. For example, to cut red tape, he merged the Transit Police into the NYPD so they could better work together; he also went after a lot of quality-of-life crimes, figuring you might catch a few murderers just by being stricter about fare jumping in the subway, or jaywalking. Above all, Bratton wanted to modernize the NYPD, and did so with the introduction of innovations like COMPSTAT, a computer program that monitored and analyzed criminal activity across the department.

At first, Giuliani encouraged Bratton's initiatives—the ideas didn't come from Giuliani but really from Bratton and Maple. However, after Bratton started taking too much credit in the media, Giuliani got competitive with him and eventually forced him out. But not before Bratton created Cold Case. Bratton figured if we could solve these cases, we could get even more dangerous criminals off the street who remained at large. He was right, but what Bratton didn't bank on was how hostile the rest of NYPD was to this new division: most cops figured Cold Case would expose their laziness on the job, corruption, or both, and they were loath to cooperate.

Bratton and Maple were grooming Pollini to become bigger with a new squad. We got wind they were going to create a team called the Cold Case Squad. When the orders came down, I was quite surprised and honored that Pollini chose me to go with him to Cold Case—he could've chosen a hundred other guys. At this point, I was a detective, third grade, and ready to rise up the ranks.

On the day we were transferred, we reported to 300 Gold Street, a building opposite the 84th Precinct in the Flatbush area of Brooklyn, near the courts. I found I already knew some of my new colleagues, like Willie Ceberello, with whom I'd worked undercover narcotics back in 1984.

At the first meeting of the Cold Case Squad, Commissioner Ed Norris introduced himself and explained our new mission. "We're creating this squad to solve all the unsolved and open murder cases in the city of New York," Norris explained. Cold Case was born out of the new administration's innovations: when they started getting results from the COMPSTAT system, Bratton, Jack Maple, and chief of the department Louis Anemone noticed that there were a lot of murder cases that weren't getting solved, and with the advent of "Giuliani Time"—a period of the mayor's intensive, extreme law-enforcement crackdown felt in everyday life throughout New York—this spike had to be dealt with: closing out a lot of murder cases would most likely help reduce crime rates overall.

To achieve all this, this new unit had to make an impact: we were the heavy hitters, the Mark McGwires and Sammy Sosas of solving homicides. As long as a case was older than six months and remained unsolved, we had authority to take it. Norris told us we would be assigned to separate boroughs and there would also be an all-borough special projects team. We would be traveling everywhere to solve cases—we could go to different cities and even different *countries* to pursue perps. I was put on the Brooklyn team; Pollini's explanation was they didn't have anybody that knew Brooklyn like I knew it. I'd been there over ten years and I knew homicides—and Brooklyn—all too well.

I thrived in Cold Case, becoming a machine—some weeks I'd close three, maybe four homicide cases. But it wasn't easy, and it certainly didn't make me popular. At first, Cold Case was not liked by the old-timers: you were going in and grabbing their cases, and they didn't want to be embarrassed and made to look like they weren't doing their jobs. For example, I took a case out of the 83rd Precinct's detective squad, where an investigator put in twenty detective division reports (DD-5s) labeled "Nothing to report." That indicated that the detective was lazy: a homicide victim got shot, and the case hit a standstill after just the investigation's third day. Norris wanted to present this case at the next strategy meeting because he wanted to show the police commissioner and Jack Maple that Cold Case was making progress. But in the process, we were also making enemies.

I became a bit innovative when I got into Cold Case. I hooked up with an ATF agent named Howie Stern. Me and Howie started working on some good old murder cases. Together, we had the ability to merge with federal agencies. I'd done Fed cases before, so I was open to that: for one, they had better resources and money.

One of my early investigations in Cold Case turned on the ever-expanding web linking the urban music business and the crime figures coming out of New York City's ghettos. I had told Norris that there was an unsolved homicide involving a bodyguard for Teddy Riley's group, Guy, that I was interested in solving. The homicide had occurred at a club at Forty-eighth Street and Lexington Avenue, and I sensed there was something bigger going on because of who was involved. I had told Norris that I thought I could solve this murder because I had intricate knowledge of the music industry and the people that attended this party. I was still out in the nightlife every night, gaining information after hours in the clubs, and this case was perfect for me to unite my knowledge of both music and murder-solving skills.

Indeed, when I looked through the photographs in the case folder, I realized that there were several people that I knew involved in the case—people I knew from hanging out at Chas & Wilson's, a place I used to go to on Seventy-second Street and Amsterdam Avenue. Sunday nights there meant R&B night, and everybody and their mother wanted to get in because it was *the* hot scene. There were celebrities there, of course—rappers like Salt-N-Pepa, Teddy Riley's new-jack-swing group Guy, and basketball players Rod Strickland and Anthony Mason from the Knicks, Then there were the "street" celebrities—the upscale, hard-partying, hip-hop era criminals I'd gotten to know throughout my investigations in the 81st.

Haitian Jack liked to hang out at Chas & Wilson's, as did Peter Shue, a big drug dealer from Harlem who was a real character: he was light-skinned, half Chinese and half black, and flamboyant, favoring furs and blinged-out jewelry. Shue was known for supplying celebs.

Several celebrities, meanwhile, were at the event where the unsolved homicide of Guy's bodyguard took place. On the one hand, famous actors and athletes were in attendance; on the other, so was Peter Shue and "Alpo." Alpo was a drug dealer from Harlem who ran the city's largest drug operations. Alpo was the Nicky Barnes for the '90s; the film *Paid In Full* is supposedly based on his notorious exploits as an Uptown hustler. I explained to Norris I could handle this case in a delicate way and get results without embarrassing people—the police *and* the boldfaced names—without too much press coverage. Norris agreed and told me to run with the case.

I started interviewing people very secretly, quickly getting results. The squad originally on the case from the 17th Precinct didn't know how to handle this type of murder; of course, those detectives didn't get any cooperation because they didn't know how to deal with the music industry. With a music-related case, you have to deal with the people involved in a different way. You can't approach a case like that as a "conventional" homicide—you have to know what steps you can take, who you can contact that will give you pertinent information, who the players are. You have to know about what you're investigating, in particular the circumstances surrounding the death and why they got killed. The detectives from the 17th didn't know what questions to ask.

I begin having much success with this case. Most helpful was my interrogation of a pimp named Frank; he was at the party and had a lot of girls working for him there. Frank explained that the incident with Guy's bodyguard involved a physical dispute, a detail that had never come up previously. He said the bodyguard was pushy and liked to throw his weight around a lot—and pushed the wrong dude. And the dude shot him. He told me the shooter was from uptown Harlem—he believed it was either Alpo or someone affiliated with Alpo. He then told me I really needed to speak to Peter Shue, who was also at the club when the homicide occurred.

The problem was, Peter Shue was going on trial for selling kilos to undercovers in Nassau County, Long Island. The U.S. Attorney had already lost the first two rounds prosecuting him in mistrials and he didn't want anybody talking to Shue until he was convicted, which made sense. The prosecutor, however, gave me the wrong sentencing date, which blew it. Once he was convicted, there was no way I could negotiate to get information out of him: if he had spoken to me, it might've given him a bargaining chip in his case, but now it wasn't worth it. His sentence was already passed down, so I wasn't going to get any more out of Shue.

This put the case into tailspin. When I reached out to the victim's family, the bodyguard's mother told me she thought a well-known African-American comedian and movie actor who had been at the party killed her son. I asked her why, and she said she was told that the comedian was standing next to son when he was shot. *Oy.* "In no way does [this comedian] have anything to do with this," I assured her. I was probably going to have to interview this superstar eventually, but it was going to be difficult because of his stature. This case was starting to unravel just as it got interesting.

I called the comedian's uncle, whom I knew via my ties in the music industry. I told the uncle what the victim's mother said, and he got very upset about it, threatening to sue. I told him there was no need for all that, but would like to talk to his nephew and whoever was at the party with him.

"He's not going to talk to the police," the uncle said flatly before hanging up the phone. I left it alone. The Guy bodyguard case ultimately went nowhere, thanks to the bungling of a U.S. Attorney and the reluctance of celebrities to testify. I was pissed—this case could've been closed, but it ended up back in the Cold Case freezer, never solved. Still, it alerted my superiors in the NYPD about the growing ties between the entertainment industry and the organized crime gangs coming out of the 'hood that I'd been following for some time.

In the meantime, I went back and started closing murder cases. We were solving a good majority of cases in Cold Case—and I was among the squad's top three in solving murders. I was partnered with a new federal agent, Mike Santory, so I could do bigger and bigger cases.

Together, me and Mike commenced a series of investigations into a pair of drug-dealing brothers with the last name of Ortiz: at the time, the Ortiz brothers controlled a majority chunk of the crack sales in Brooklyn's Bushwick and East New York neighborhoods. The Ortiz brothers were making approximately half a million to a million dollars a month, all the while engaging their competitors in a bloody turf war—literally bloody: the Ortiz brothers would hire hit men to eliminate the competition.

One of the Ortiz's contract killers was a short little monster named Franklin Frias: he'd killed at least ten people in his lifetime. One day, he went up to 139th Street and Broadway to negotiate with a guy about money due for a kilo of cocaine. Franklin thought he wasn't going to get paid, so he just killed the guy in middle of street. This time, Franklin's brazenness not only got him caught, but he was convicted of murder, too. Still, no one thought to see what he was really into beyond this one case. It turned out to be a lot.

After all, Franklin Frias was a hit man, and he worked for a number of major drug dealers. When they needed someone killed, they called Franklin. As I delved deeper into the case, I discovered Frias linked to murders spanning precincts in Brooklyn, Queens, and Manhattan.

At first, getting Frias to admit his crimes wasn't so easy. When we went to go see Franklin in prison at first, he told us to go fuck ourselves. When he realized we'd locked up his old bosses, the Ortiz brothers, on a separate charge—they'd admitted to five murders—

Frias started giving up everything. Frias was mad when he found out the Ortiz brothers only got such a small sentence compared to his.

"Why do they get fifteen years when they did five murders when I only got convicted for one murder and got twenty-five years?" he asked. Franklin wanted to cut a deal for early release. I told him the government wasn't interested in retrying him for other murders. Upset, he unloaded and told me about all the murders he did.

I located most of the unsolved murder cases Frias was confessing to, which led me into the middle of a big drug war in New York's Dominican community. There was a big organization of Dominicans who came to New York from Santo Domingo and were killing competitors at an alarming rate. The war involved Bushwick, Brooklyn, along with parts of Queens and northern Manhattan. Thanks to Frias's jailhouse confession, I end up wrapping up twenty murders that were unsolved almost instantaneously. This kind of success is why the Cold Case Squad was formed in the first place.

Being in Cold Case, where I had access to citywide homicide info, gave me the ability to start seeing crime patterns in the music and entertainment industry. From our working together on the first Tupac case, Joe Babnick was telling people throughout the department that I was knowledgeable about music industry–related crimes; as a result, I was getting known as the guy to call in the NYPD whenever a case involving a rapper or someone from the entertainment industry came up.

I had ties to detectives and informants in Queens, Brooklyn, and the Bronx who were feeding me all this info about robberies and homicides in the music industry. I was hearing about record producers being stabbed, promoters being kidnapped, shootings at clubs, rappers in possession of firearms. For example, I remember getting a call around this time regarding an arrest involving rapper Ghostface Killah. Ghostface and three associates had their vehicle stopped by police in East Harlem's 25th Precinct. The officers at the scene alleged that the Wu-Tang Clan member was in possession of a concealed, unregistered, loaded gun and wearing a bulletproof vest, both of which are extremely forbidden for known felons convicted of violent crimes.

As such, my superiors in the NYPD were getting more interested in the rap music industry because of incidents like this and the Guy bodyguard case; it was clear these felonious characters were aligning themselves with different celebs. But none of it compared with what next fell across my plate: the 1996 killing of Tupac Shakur in Las Vegas.

Cliché though it may be, it seemed like Tupac was hip-hop's cat with nine lives. After surviving the Quad shooting and his various ordeals, it appeared Tupac was invincible. But his 1996 murder proved otherwise. It was one of the coldest-blooded murders in recent memory—in full view of the public, right out in the open, one of the most famous men in America was killed. Looking back over what led up to Tupac's death, I suppose it seemed inevitable in retrospect.

I had been following the East Coast–West Coast feud that had been developing between New York and Los Angeles rappers since the Source Awards. I had been calling around the country talking to different detectives, like Ken Knox from the Los Angeles Police Department: much of what was happening wasn't in my jurisdiction, but I knew the East Coast–West Coast animosity could come back to New York in an ugly way. The dialogue was already getting ugly on wax. On Tupac's most poisonous diatribe ever, "Hit 'Em Up," Death Row's superstar insults Biggie with murderous intent—even claiming biblical relations with Big's wife, R&B singer Faith Evans, also a Bad Boy recording artist. "That's why I fucked your bitch, you fat mutha-fucka/West Side Bad Boy killers, you know who the realest is," Tupac spits on the track with fury. (Faith Evans has repeatedly denied Tupac's claim of a sexual relationship.)

After such bloodlust being expressed on both sides, it's hard to think Tupac's killing couldn't have been avoided. In a nutshell, what happened is this:

On September 7, 1996, Tupac traveled to the MGM Grand in Las Vegas to attend a boxing match between Mike Tyson and Bruce Seldon. He was rolling with the full Death Row entourage, Suge Knight right by his side.

After the fight, as Tupac's posse made its way through the MGM's lobby, a Death Row associate saw a rival gang member, Orlando "Baby Lane" Anderson of the Crips, across the room. Allegedly, Anderson had been involved in the humiliating theft of the associate's gold Death Row chain in a previous assault; that Suge Knight and his crew are affiliated with the Bloods gang, the Crips' deadliest opponents, intensified the animosity. Tupac confronted Anderson, and a mêlée ensued; the Death Row camp is caught on security tape giving Anderson a beatdown.

After security broke up the fight, Anderson refused to press charges, and the Death Row camp exited the MGM Grand. Following the fight, Tupac returned to his hotel, the Luxor, to change before going out again. After a brief pit stop at Suge Knight's Las Vegas mansion, the Death Row entourage began a fifteen-car convoy down Las Vegas's strip toward Knight's Vegas nightclub, the 662 Club. Tupac rode in the front passenger seat in Knight's BMW four-door sedan, which was second in the caravan, with Knight at the wheel.

Just before reaching 662, a white Cadillac pulled up at a stoplight next to Knight's car. In full view of a large crowd on the Vegas Strip, a gunman inside the Caddy fired four bullets from a .223 rifle into Tupac; one bullet ended up grazing Suge Knight's head. After a convoluted escape attempt, Tupac was taken to the University Medical Center hospital. Following a number of intensive surgeries, Tupac died there some two days later.

Those are the nuts and bolts of Tupac's murder; the emotional truth is more complicated. Despite tensions with their West Coast counterparts, when Tupac got killed, the New York rap community showed Tupac a lot of love and mourning. New York Hot 97 radio personality Angie Martinez cried on the radio after hearing the news, and it was truly moving. She had just interviewed Tupac recently, and her response showed that this was something that affected everyone across the nation, regardless of regional beef.

Immediately, the conspiracy theories started percolating about who killed Tupac; in fact, they're still percolating. Many such theories fixate on the fact that Tupac wasn't wearing a bulletproof vest, and that there were inconsistencies in his security detail. There's been chatter about how Tupac was planning on leaving Death Row, and Suge Knight might've been involved in his killing to make sure that never happened. Tupac *had* previously replaced Death Row lawyer David Kenner as his legal counsel and started a separate entertainment company of his own called Euphanasia; much has been made about the fact that the night he was killed, Tupac was wearing a Euphanasia pendant instead of his Death Row chain. Some say that the fight with Orlando Anderson was a staged ruse to throw the scent off the real killer. Also curious is the fact that Tupac's cousin Yafa Fula, the only eyewitness who offered to testify to law enforcement, was killed before he could offer up his testimony.

The most outlandish theory, however, came from Pulitzer Prize–winning journalist Chuck Philips of the *Los Angeles Times*. Now, Chuck's a friend of mine, but I had doubts about his conclusion on who killed Tupac and why. In a series of articles for the *Los Angeles Times,* Phillips spelled out a lurid scenario that placed Biggie in Las Vegas, where he allegedly paid a Crip hit man a million dollars *in cash* to assassinate Tupac—but only if the Crip used Big's own gun.

If only. This imagining has all the drama of a *Sopranos* episode, but to my homicide detective mind it doesn't sound very realistic. Neither Biggie nor any of his crew were checked into any local hotels, as room records have demonstrated; for a celebrity of Biggie's stature to be in Las Vegas and have nobody notice also seems hard to swallow. And to use a gun potentially traceable to him seems unlikely: as Biggie once rapped memorably, "Bad boys move in silence," and that would be a pretty loud mistake for even a common hoodlum. Regardless of the manifold theories surrounding Tupac's death, I knew that the investigation was being mishandled. Soon I would see for myself just how badly.

In the days following the Tupac homicide, I went to Las Vegas because I knew Tupac homicide had nothing to do with the East Coast—it was West Coast guys that did it. I was sure of it. I was monitoring the East-West feud very hard: even before Tupac had been killed, I had been in contact with LAPD officer Ken Knox because I was following people from my jurisdiction traveling to Los Angeles.

A middle-aged white guy, Ken Knox was the LAPD's community affairs guy in Tarzana, California. During my monitoring of the East-West situation, we had become friends and had developed a productive relationship where we're sharing information, sending each other stuff through department mail. Fortuitously, Tarzana was where Death Row's recording studio complex, Can-Am, was located. Can-Am had been a repeated problem in the Tarzana community, with many disturbances involving Death Row; Knox had kept me abreast of all of Can-Am's comings and going, as well as any unusual activity that was happening around the studio.

Knox would send me lists of names, saying "I don't know these people—maybe they ring a bell with you?" They rang loud and clear: Knox had documented that rap bigshots like MC Hammer and Eric B. of Eric B. & Rakim hung out at Can-Am, along with Quincy Jones's son; he had the sign-in sheets of the studio, as well as the license-plate numbers of the cars in Can-Am's parking lot. Knox sent me surveillance photos of Suge's office highlighting its crimson carpet, which signifies membership in the Bloods' gang (red is the Bloods' trademark color; red's contrasting color, blue, represents their rivals, the Crips). He'd even send me search warrants and lists of people affiliated with Suge.

What was most interesting was that he sent me photos of a painting hanging in Death Row's office: in one painting, Puffy and Biggie are depicted wearing ballet tutus while looking on as Dr. Dre is being sodomized by a blonde transvestite. If those images aren't proof of a beef, I don't know what is. But what happened in Vegas confirmed my worst fears.

To me, it's clear who Tupac's killer is. Everyone I've talked to on the street knows who it is, too: Orlando Anderson. So much points to this hypothesis.

For one, the MGM Grand where Tupac was with Suge Knight before he got killed had a clear videotape of the incident that led to Tupac's death. The tape clearly shows Suge and Tupac stomping Anderson out. Additionally, Ken Knox and I pooled our street informants from various gangs: all not only placed Orlando Anderson

inside the white Cadillac, but fingered him as one of the shooters—
or *the* shooter.

To my seasoned perspective as a homicide investigator, unlike
Biggie's murder, or even Jam Master Jay's homicide years later, Tupac's murder resembles an unplanned crime of passion and revenge,
with Anderson exacting payback for his beatdown. Personally, I
doubt that Tupac's murder involved Biggie, although I did get one
piece of information that suggested a potential link. Some informants indicated that also riding in the white Caddy was a man by the
name of Dwayne Davis (aka "Keefee D"), Orlando Anderson's uncle and a gang heavy himself with the Southside Crips. Keefee D, I
would later learn, was allegedly central in getting the Crips to provide protection for Biggie, Puffy, and the Bad Boy crew in the midst
of the East Coast–West Coast beef; his name would also surface in
the investigation around Biggie's homicide.

Regardless, Anderson's Crip status would've certainly provoked
the Bloods in Death Row's entourage; after such a humiliation, all
that remains is a blood feud. In the immediate aftermath of Tupac's
death, there were numerous killings of Crips vs. Bloods and vice
versa in Southern California's gang territory. That means only one
thing: retaliation. The Bloods were punishing the Crips for their involvement in Tupac's murder, and the Crips were fighting back.
"The theory that the Crips were responsible for Tupac's murder was
most strongly backed by the bloody gang war that broke out in the
[Los Angeles ghetto suburb] Compton in the immediate aftermath
of Shakur's shooting in Las Vegas," wrote Randall Sullivan in
LAbyrinth, his epic, brilliant investigative tome on LAPD corruption and rap wars.

As well, Anderson was killed under mysterious circumstances
two years later at a car wash in South Central Los Angeles; as an admitted gang member, Anderson was most likely up to no good, but
the coincidence of this homicide was too much to bear. Whether
Anderson can ever be proven to be Tupac's killer beyond a shadow
of a doubt is debatable, however, due to missteps in the investigation
of Tupac's murder from the beginning.

From my point of view, all the steps undertaken by the Las Vegas Police Department were incorrect. I saw this when I went to Las Vegas right after Tupac's murder. I was there to assist: there I met with the officer who was in charge of LVPD's investigation in Vegas.

Even though Tupac was on a respirator and close to death, Sergeant Manning didn't find much sympathy for his cause among 'Pac's inner circle. "Tupac got the same treatment as any other homicide here," Manning told journalist Chuck Philips in a September 7, 2002, *Los Angeles Times* article entitled, "How Vegas Police Probe Foundered." "But you know what? We can't do it alone. We rely on cooperative citizens to step forward and help us solve crimes. And in Tupac's case, we got no cooperation whatsoever."

It's not like Suge and his Death Row cronies would cooperate, but with that attitude, who ever would? The paranoia surrounding Tupac's murder soon extended to Las Vegas's relationship with Los Angeles law enforcement, as Philips further clarified in his article:

> To identify those responsible, police would have to take their investigation to Compton and develop informants within the gangs.
>
> The Vegas cops were ill-suited to do that. They had little experience with gang investigations or gang culture. The Compton Police Department did have entree to the gang underworld. Its investigators had known many gang members since they were babies. They took their first mug shots. They testified at their trials. They visited them in jail. In return, they often got valuable information.
>
> But Las Vegas police worried that the Compton investigators were too close to the gangs and their rap-industry patrons and might leak information. The Vegas detectives kept their distance from the gang squad, and their investigation quickly hit a dead end.

It was us against them all over again. The classic law-enforcement hard-charging attitude toward hip-hop artists had now infected the Tupac case, and the disease was full blown. Once I got to Vegas, I was seeing it with my own eyes.

Once LVPD heard I was in Vegas, I was sought out by Paul Paige,

the detective from LVPD's Organized Crime Control Division assigned to the Tupac case. Later Paul would come to New York because the LVPD wanted to investigate Suge Knight's connection to
Tupac's killing—in particular any link to the feud between Puffy
and Suge that made sense from the Vegas side. LVPD really wanted
to investigate Suge and find something—*anything*. Las Vegas was
very upset that Suge Knight wasn't cooperating in the Tupac case,
so they began an enormous investigation into his background. Paul
spent a week in New York City, where I educated him in the details
of Suge and Death Row's criminal associations.

LVPD brass were eager to take Knight down on a federal level—
to get him to "flip." Vegas po-po was looking to shut down his businesses to get leverage and to force him to cooperate in the Tupac
investigation; it's a classic move by the Feds in such investigations,
one that would show up in the indictment of the principals of the
Murder Inc. label almost a decade later. When LVPD heard the dis-
puted rumor that Suge had hung Vanilla Ice over a hotel balcony
and threatened to drop him if he didn't sign over his publishing
rights to a Suge-affiliated artist, as well as his ties to the notorious,
imprisoned drug dealer Harry O, they figured they might be able to
build some kind of RICO case against the mogul. Paul and the
LVPD were also investigating Suge's 662 Club.

I went out to Vegas to look at how to possibly assist in shutting
662 down, which even in its name suggested Suge's ties to criminal
activity. As Ronin Ro notes in his book *Have Gun Will Travel*, the
numbers "662" spell out "M-O-B" on a telephone pad (beyond the
obvious gangster association, "m-o-b" is an acronym for "Men of
Bloods" which Knight also sports on a ring worn by him and close
associates); as well, Ro points out 662 is California penal code for
"death row." It's no surprise, then, that 662 was in LVPD's sights:
they had gathered evidence of all Suge's assets in Vegas, all his
files—they were ready to run him out of town, using all legal means.

I told Paul that, while potentially effective down the line, such
hostile moves weren't the right approach to take with the rap community regarding Tupac. "Suge's not going to talk to you because he
doesn't like cops, period," I said. "The first thing I would've tried to

do was to get other witnesses. I would've spent time talking to all of Suge's associates out there that I could, even if it took me a year to cultivate those relationships." I am almost positive I would've gotten someone who would've cooperated. The LVPD confirmed it: the problem in solving such cases was that police everywhere don't know how to approach the rap industry. These rap guys had money, power, the best lawyers money could buy—and the only law they obeyed was the code of the streets. True bad boys do move in silence, and that's why none of these cases get solved. It takes patience and empathy to smash the deafening quiet.

Furthermore, I told Paul that LVPD should've seen this all coming—from my standpoint, Tupac's murder was *preventable*. The only way you could know whether Suge was coming to town was to talk to good, reliable informants both from the street and the music industry—and once you have the info, prepare security accordingly. LVPD should've been educated about the East vs. West beef, about who hung out in Tupac and Suge's Death Row entourage. They should've had an active database shared with other cities that lists known gang members, and their own gang specialists should've been attending any and all big boxing events like the Seldon-Tyson showdown.

The criminal world and the legit music industry unfortunately go hand in hand, especially in a sin city like Vegas; law enforcement needs to be able to see the shades of gray. Violence in the rap industry was very prevalent at the time, yet LVPD didn't see any pattern—they didn't see it coming. I did. The street is always where you get info from—that's just basic police work, whether you're the hip-hop cop or not.

Back in New York City, I had to keep tabs on what was going down on *all* coasts; it was all interconnected. I was keeping my ears open, going to clubs, picking up reports on certain murders and disputes at concerts, reading the newspapers, listening to the news from both the radio and the street. Paul Paige, Ken Knox, and I maintained constant contact, keeping each other abreast of developments in our cities that could affect the others' investigations.

At one point, LVPD asked me to come out to Vegas again. There was another Tyson fight at the MGM, this time against Evander Holyfield. Vegas was doing everything in its power to prevent a repeat of September 7, 1996; besides, history has proven that when a homicide occurs at a boxing match, it's usually at a Tyson fight. Mike Tyson is from Brooklyn, and you know Brooklyn . . .

When I got to Vegas on the day before the fight, I spent the afternoon working with LVPD on preparations for the fight. After that, I led a big seminar in the conference room at the MGM Grand, educating representatives from all over the country in hip-hop crime— and how to avoid incidents like the Tupac homicide in the future.

When we got down to the MGM's conference room, I met with representatives from Oakland ATF, Washington, D.C.'s, homicide squad, LAPD's Gang Unit, and others. We began with a briefing about the Holyfield-Tyson fight. This time LVPD had done their homework: they'd prepared a list of all the people staying in Vegas hotels, down to who was staying where and in what room. The list was broken down geographically as well, noting specifically who was attending from New York, New Jersey, Detroit, Washington, D.C., Los Angeles, Oakland, Miami, Atlanta, Chicago, and other major cities.

The breakdown by region proved very useful. As a group we discussed intelligence reports about what potential troublemakers were staying in which hotel. We turned up one guy, reportedly a onetime employee of Mike Tyson who was wanted for federal violations. Meanwhile, a hotel maid found firearms in one room rented to two guys from Washington, D.C. Several lists that LVPD and LAPD ran through exposed gang members. As a matter of fact, LVPD made a master list that they gave to all of us attending this meeting of all people wanted for homicides in other cities that were attending this fight.

For the fight itself, we sectioned off into teams. Each LVPD guy paired up with someone from out of state. I was paired up with Oakland ATF; Paul Paige from Vegas hung with the LAPD gang guy. The night of the fight, any incidents that happened we were prepared to respond to. For example, if something major like a shooting or robbery happened, I was to respond; I was from New York City, so I knew those players more than the other guys.

Even before the fight started, there were a lot of people there. As the crowd started taking its seats, I was placed in the area where all the celebs were coming in: in the "green room" reserved for V.I.P.s, I saw Star Jones (whom I knew back when she was a lawyer in the Brooklyn D.A.'s office) and James McDaniel, better known as Lieutenant Fancy on *NYPD Blue.* I wanted to be upstairs to see who's coming in, too. Soon enough, I got my chance.

We got a call on police radio from one of the Oakland ATF guys: "We've stopped the actor Steven Seagal with a firearm. Come to the main entrance." We ran over there to find a ponytailed Seagal wearing a three-quarter-length multicolored Native American–style fur coat with black jeans and boots, flanked by an off-duty LAPD cop as his security detail. "What's going on?" I asked. It turned out Seagal *did* have a gun.

Seagal showed us his gun license, which was from a Louisiana judge. The ATF agent told him, "This is invalid. You can't have that firearm." Oakland ATF was ready to lock him up. I told Oakland, "Let's see what's really going on first—we don't want an incident for nothing." Meanwhile, Seagal was getting really pissed. I told the ATF guys, "Look, we're not really here to lock up *Steven Seagal.* This may cause a bigger incident, and he does have an LAPD guy with him."

Seagal, meanwhile, was asking everybody what city they're from. When he got to me, I told him I represented the NYPD. "Let me talk to you alone, then," Seagal said. With the firearm secured by Oakland for the moment, we moved into a corner to chat.

"So, NYPD, what's the big deal here?" Seagal asked me. He was genuinely curious about all the heat that's around. "Why are all you different jurisdictions here? Why's NYPD in Las Vegas?"

"Mr. Seagal, what happened was there was a homicide at the last fight," I said.

"I know, the Tupac homicide," he responded.

"We're down here conducting an investigation, monitoring the people at the fight," I continued, "and we don't want weapons in the building."

Seagal gives me a funny look. "Do you know Ralph Cefarello?" he asked.

"Yeah, I know Ralph," I said. Cefarello's a detective in the NYPD's Major Case Squad.

"Right—well, Ralphie is my security when I'm in New York City, and I'm asking for a little courtesy here," Seagal continued. He was pleading a little now, dropping the tough-guy act.

I told him that, jurisdictionally, there was a problem with his gun license. Seagal's face fell. I figured out a solution, however: if his LAPD companion took possession of the firearm and secured it, then the problem would be solved, and we could send Mr. "Above the Law" on to his seat. Almost immediately after squashing the Seagal situation, we got a call about another firearm. A criminal out of Detroit had come in and tried to check his firearm. When asked if he had a license, he said no, so he was arrested by LVPD. The other units were keeping busy, too: the reps from L.A.'s Gang Unit were identifying gang members in the crowd, patrolling to stem any incidents that could arise. Meanwhile, Washington, D.C., homicide didn't catch the perps from their area because gang members got wind that the police were snooping around.

The night of the Holyfield-Tyson fight went remarkably smoothly, and for a moment I thought that maybe there was hope for law enforcement in dealing sensibly with hip-hop crime. Then, soon after I returned to New York, I find out that LVPD was no longer cooperating with any other law-enforcement agencies about the Tupac case. LVPD was afraid of leaks; it had determined that some off-duty LAPD officers were providing security to Suge, and as a consequence Vegas cut off communication with the LAPD. I thought the LVPD's shutout of the LAPD was a major mistake: for one, the perps are all *from Los Angeles.* LVPD's mistrust of their fellow police officers was almost as huge as their mistrust of Suge Knight himself. The paranoia became so thick, it seemed impossible that any useful investigative work could be done in such an atmosphere. Of course, I wasn't expecting I'd run into similar problems in New York. If only I knew what I was in for . . .

I learn, however, that what happens in Vegas apparently doesn't stay in Vegas. Soon I would discover that the Tupac homicide was only the beginning of the end.

7

READY TO DIE:
Inside the Tragic Slaying of the Notorious B.I.G.

I swear to God, I feel like death is fuckin' callin' me.
—Notorious B.I.G., "Suicidal Thoughts"

Hip-hop itself is at a pit stop itself
Seeing Big die, I wish the shit would stop itself.
—The Lox, "We'll Always Love Big Poppa"

MARCH 8, 1997, was just another Saturday night, or so I thought. I actually had the night off this one particular Saturday, which made it unusual. But otherwise, same old, same old . . . I met up with a girl I'd met at a party the week before. We had dinner, came home, watched a little TV, then went to bed.

Any postcoital reverie, however, was shattered the next morning come 7:00 A.M. when my clock radio went off. I'd left my alarm set, forgetting that I didn't have to work the next day.

Grumpily, I reached across my bedmate to switch the radio off when I heard Ice-T's raspy voice bellowing out of the tinny speakers. Ice sounded a little uncharacteristically shook. The half-asleep girl next to me murmured for me to turn it off, but I was intrigued and kept listening.

"This is a shame, man—now no one is going to be safe," Ice-T was telling an interviewer on Hot 97, New York City's premier urban radio station. Wiping the sleep from my eyes, I gradually comprehended what he was going on about: the night before, the greatest rapper in the world had been shot. Biggie was dead. Shot to death in Los Angeles at the midnight hour, little more than a half hour past the time when Saturday night officially turned into Sunday morning. Even more eerie, Biggie's murder occurred exactly six months to the day from Tupac's homicide.

Hearing the news, the girl beside me sat up shocked, tears streaming down her face. Me, I'd stopped paying attention to her already. "Holy shit," I said to myself, "this is huge news." Not only had the greatest rapper in the world been killed just hours before; his homicide was the latest salvo in a deadly war that showed no sign of stopping.

Notorious B.I.G. held many monikers in his abbreviated life. He was born Christopher Wallace in 1972; as a fledgling rapper he took on the stage name Biggie Smalls until another rapper claimed he had it first, causing Wallace to become known as Notorious B.I.G. until his death by the gun in 1997. Wallace also took on other aliases—he was fond of calling himself "the black Frank White," taking the name of Christopher Walken's righteous gangster character from the film *King of New York*. But everyone, from family to fans, knew Wallace as "Biggie" or just plain "Big." And eventually, he was the king of New York.

Biggie's story put a particularly ghetto twist on the American dream. A gifted "A" student as a child, Big grew up on tree-lined, residential St. James Street off Fulton Avenue in downtown Brooklyn, but he preferred to claim nearby Bed-Stuy as the 'hood that made him. Biggie dropped out of high school to become a crack dealer working street corners in Bedford-Stuyvesant. But Biggie would come to be known as the greatest rapper in the world, a Michael Jordan on the mic, his only challenger to his throne his former friend and eventual deadly rival Tupac Shakur. When it came to album sales, Big lived up to his name. His 1994 album debut *Ready to Die* would sell over four million copies in the United States alone; *Life After Death*, his spookily titled swan song, would move over ten million copies following its posthumous release in 1997.

With Big's death, especially as it came so soon after Tupac's, I knew the NYPD had to leap into action. Even if my colleagues didn't agree, I had to wake them up, just as I had been so abruptly awakened by the news of Big's death. If the NYPD wasn't prepared for the aftermath, the ghettos could end up burned down. If there was a riot goin' on, it would be there, and the NYPD would shoulder some of the blame.

Immediately, I called my captain, Ray Ferrari, the commanding officer of Cold Case. "Derrick, please," he said groggily. "It's Sunday morning, and you're calling me about a guy getting killed in *Los Angeles*. What does that have to do with New York?"

"Captain, this is a big deal," I implored him. "I don't think you understand what's happening here." I insisted we had an immediate conference call with Inspector Paul Admundsen, the commanding officer of the NYPD's Fugitive Enforcement Division, or F.E.D., the umbrella under which the Cold Case, Warrants, and Juvenile Crime divisions all belonged.

We caught Admundsen at home in a three-way conference call; he wasn't happy to hear from me early on a Sunday morning, either. I tried to explain to him what relevance Biggie Smalls's murder had to do with New York City. Not only was he the number-one-selling rap artist, Biggie was also, along with Tupac, America's most beloved rapper. A regional rap war had claimed the two most massive icons in the music industry at this time. I was sure that Big's murder was definitely related to Tupac's homicide in some way. And the war was just about to explode on our front lines.

"Inspector, Biggie Smalls was killed in L.A., and it's all going to come back to New York City," I said. "It's going to affect New York."

"How?" Admundsen wasn't buying it.

"There's going to be riots on the streets of Brooklyn if the NYPD doesn't get its shit together pronto," I responded. "Look, Biggie's *from* Brooklyn. His death will create a ripple effect and intensify the East Coast–West Coast feud. Tupac was one of theirs, and Biggie was one of ours. Do you know the violence that's going to go down because of this man's murder? Between here and L.A., we'd better get on the ball."

I heard a loud sigh on the other end of the line. "Derrick, these guys are just *animals*," Inspector Admundsen said. That was his exact word—*animals*. I'll never forget it: animals, criminals, who cares? Let the savages all kill each other—that was his attitude. I was annoyed. He didn't want to recognize the problem; I could practically hear him rolling his eyes over the phone.

After Admundsen hung up, Captain Ferrari stayed on the line. "Derrick, you're not involved," he said. "That's an order. I want you to stay out of it."

"Captain, do you know the ramifications this murder is going to have around the country?" I was desperate now, but he wasn't hearing it. I tried one last time: "Captain, you heard it from me first: it's all coming back to New York." It was no use, so I hung up the phone. Two or three days later, the chickens came home to roost.

I got the word that Biggie's body was coming back to New York to be buried. It was going to be a service fit for a king, one of the biggest funerals New York City would ever see—and one of the scariest. This was life during wartime on the streets of New York, and Biggie was the latest, most significant casualty.

Biggie's celebrity was so huge that, when he was killed in Los Angeles under mysterious circumstances, it created a whole new set of problems for the NYPD. It was the beginning of the second week of March 1997, when I got the call from the NYPD's big-boss Deputy Commissioner of Operations Edward Norris, and Louis Anemone, the four-star chief of the entire NYPD.

"Derrick, you've got to come down to headquarters right away," Norris said. I knew what was up.

"This is about the Notorious B.I.G. homicide, right?" I ask.

"Yes, it is," Anemone responded gravely. My predictions were coming true; even the NYPD's top brass had heard the streets rumbling. We barely had time to get it together before Biggie's funeral. If we got it wrong, it could mean hundreds, maybe thousands, dead.

I hauled my ass downtown to One Police Plaza right away. The meeting was on the thirteenth floor, where all the chiefs have their offices. There was a lot of power in the conference room that day: Anemone and Norris were there, along with Chief Nicholas Estavillo, borough commander of Manhattan North, who had also brought a special-ops lieutenant with him. They were a bunch of colorful, tough guys who'd operated their way to the top of the NYPD.

Louis Anemone was hated by a lot of big bosses on the job. Just over six feet tall, Anemone was a middle-aged Italian-American with salt-and-pepper hair. He always wore glasses and kept his uniform neat, four stars shining off his lapels. Anemone spoke intelligently, but yelled a lot. He wasn't afraid to embarrass an officer in front of his subordinates if he thought he wasn't doing his job. He was one of Bratton's main guys, and the NYPD really changed on Anemone's watch—because he was feared. He was tearing commanders *down* on a regular basis.

Edward Norris, on the other hand, was in his late thirties, Irish, a bit portly; he was Anemone's confidant, but more of a quiet, suit-wearing boss. Norris was smart, so he ascended the ranks very fast—his rise to the NYPD's upper echelon was the fastest that I'd ever heard of. He was easygoing, educated, and liked across the department—younger guys on the force especially identified with him.

Norris saw the police department needed to change, and he wasn't afraid to do the job himself. But sometimes even the big bosses caught a case. After Norris left the NYPD for a commissioner job with Baltimore law enforcement, the F.B.I. indicted him for misappropriating funds; he was allegedly chasing women on business trips, misusing funds, the whole scandalous bit. Norris had just recently came out of prison, after doing six months federal jail time. I never thought Norris would be *that* guy.

Estavillo, meanwhile, was the two-star chief of all patrol officers from Fifty-ninth Street all the way up to Dyckman Heights, where Manhattan ends. He stands about five feet eight inches, a silver-haired Latino who many people thought was Italian. Estavillo was very pleasant, but also very competent. He didn't take shit, and he knew his territory like none other.

Once everyone collected in the room, I began explaining to the group about the whole East Coast–West Coast beef involving Puffy, Biggie, Tupac, and Death Row. More than anything, I conveyed to them how massive an undertaking Biggie's funeral was going to be, and what we needed to be ready for.

It had already begun, actually: Estavillo mentioned he'd received reports of bomb threats at the Frank E. Campbell Funeral Home on

Ninety-third Street and Madison Avenue, where Biggie's body was arriving the next day. Threats to Puff Daddy's life had been pouring in as well. "A lot of people are very upset that Biggie got killed," I explained, "and we could have a Mafia-style war. This is something that you haven't seen before—people are going to get killed in the streets if we don't prepare for it."

Chief Estavillo assigned me to the funeral home as his eyes and ears; he was worried about those threats to Puff Daddy. I told them that Puffy's only the beginning—the entire rap-music industry will be at this funeral, meaning there would be a lot more targets than just Puffy to worry about.

At this point, Biggie's wake was two or three days away; his funeral would take place a day or two later, toward the end of the week. Biggie's corpse was already en route to arrive in the city via plane. I ended up being among the very first people in New York to see Biggie's dead body. It was me, Estavillo, a female sergeant that worked for him, and two very nice detectives from the 19th Precinct that were present when his coffin arrived in New York from Los Angeles. We went to the funeral home's basement to look at the body, which had just arrived from the airport. It was something else—Biggie was six feet three inches and 400 pounds when he died; his eyes were closed, his hands at his side, and he was dressed in an elegant yet elegiac black suit. Even the assistant funeral director was shocked.

"Wow, this guy is *massive*," he exclaimed as he opened the casket. "But Derrick, this guy's from Brooklyn—why are they burying him in Manhattan on the Upper East Side? Shouldn't he be buried in Brooklyn?"

"Don't all the big celebs get buried here?" I asked.

"You got a point," the assistant funeral director said as he inspected Big's luxurious, opulent coffin: according to him, the casket alone cost nearly twenty thousand dollars. However, it already needed to be replaced because Big's body fluids had contaminated it; therefore, it couldn't be used for public viewing.

The public might've been in greater danger from other things, though. As we left the funeral home, Estavillo told me we needed a plan because of the bomb threats. Now this thing was becoming *big*.

Meanwhile, the LAPD was coming along for the ride: two detectives from the Los Angeles Police Department flew in and met me in my office. They were in town to interview witnesses in the case and associates like Biggie's mother Voletta Wallace, Lil' Kim, and Lil' Cease. Lil' Cease was Biggie's right-hand associate in their "Junior M.A.F.I.A." crew—and an eyewitness to his murder. I was to attend all of these interrogations: with the LAPD I learned many things about the Biggie homicide that hadn't been made public, including how an NYPD detective had been tailing Big for two to three weeks in Los Angeles prior to his killing.

Meanwhile, other units wanted to horn in on Biggie's funeral plan. The Feds were poking around—even the division concentrating on Chinese gangs wanted to do surveillance. NYPD homicide detectives figured some wanted murder suspects might also show up, for the ceremony; Brooklyn North was looking for a wanted perp they thought would most likely show up at the service. I wasn't gonna stand for that: I made it very clear that *in no way* were there to be arrests at the funeral home. If that happened, I was sure we'd have a riot on our hands. "No," I said, "let the people grieve. If they don't get their mourning out, there'll be even bigger problems."

At Biggie's wake at the funeral home a couple days later, well, *everyone* was there—it was more like the Grammy Awards than a funeral. Biggie's mother presided over the ceremony, greeting a crowd that included the R&B star Faith Evans (who is Biggie's widow and mother to some of his children), Puff Daddy, Fat Joe, Jay-Z, Busta Rhymes, Big Pun, Mary J. Blige, and Russell Simmons alongside politicians and black-community leaders like Al Sharpton.

This all proved to be a very sad, emotional, timeless moment: everyone was crying over Big's body in the casket, who was now wearing dark black sunglasses to cover his dead eyes. Lil' Cease and Faith seemed particularly upset. Faith kept her distance tastefully from Lil' Kim, who'd been openly carrying on an affair with Big. Uniform cops patrolled outside, where steel barricades guaranteed no one would be able to park in front of the funeral home. There was a lot of police presence that day, but it was nothing compared to how we had prepared for the funeral.

For the funeral, we had a tactical attack plan in place in case something, *anything* happened. A truck sat across the street from the funeral, housing a surveillance team. Highway cars, the kind used for
funeral escorts and dignitary processions, were to lead the escape
route if necessary. If someone required medical assistance, we'd des-
ignated a hospital car. S.W.A.T. teams, Emergency Services, and the
New York Fire Department were all on hand, at the ready. In the procession, I was to drive a civilian unmarked Ford Taurus with the detectives from the LAPD riding with me. It was going to be a long day.

On the day of the funeral, we set up the actual procession, with
everyone maintaining communication via cell phones and walkie-
talkies. Biggie's procession was to move through Manhattan and
drive through Brooklyn. Even at the start of the journey, at least
10,000 to 20,000 people, not to mention hundreds of photographers
and media representatives, jammed the pavement all around us. We
had to block streets from almost two miles away so the nearly forty-
car procession could move at a crawl. After Brooklyn, the caravan
was to move to a crematory in Queens. Puffy was going to attend
Biggie's cremation alongside Mrs. Wallace, Lil' Kim, Big's Junior
M.A.F.I.A. homies, and close family members.

Once we arrived at the beginning of the funeral ceremonies on
the actual day, I couldn't even see who all was there, it was so
packed. The LAPD detectives, who were accompanying me in my
car, couldn't believe their eyes: "Holy cow, this is crazy," they kept
murmuring, eyes pressed to the windows.

"You ain't seen nothing yet," I tell them. "Wait'll we get to *Brooklyn.*"

I wasn't wrong—Brooklyn didn't disappoint; Biggie's fans in his
hometown borough came out in *throngs.* When we got to Brooklyn,
crowds had surged upwards to 50,000 people. Ultimately, 10,000
cops—*one-third of the entire NYPD*—were on hand just to keep
the peace. And the crowds don't stop cheering as they surged toward
the procession. Once we hit the Fulton Mall, spectators started rush-
ing to the vehicle that held Biggie's coffin. The police had to physi-
cally hold the crowd back; there were definitely arrests made that
day for disorderly conduct.

After hours spent creeping through Brooklyn, the procession finally got Biggie's body to the cremation site. In a private ceremony, everybody there stopped to say a prayer and a last farewell over Biggie before he was put in a box and stuck into a furnace to be cremated.

It was the end of a crazy, crazy day, and the end of an era. Thankfully, there were no major problems because we'd prepared exhaustively: I'd made sure everyone in the NYPD knew who the players were enough in advance to make a difference. All the chiefs, in fact, were happy that the funeral went off with no problems.

Biggie's funeral was in fact a shining example of what happened when the NYPD did its job *right* when it came to hip-hop. That didn't mean they were going to get it right all the time. But now the NYPD was starting to comprehend how big this hip-hop thing really was. The president of the United States doesn't even attract the kind of crowds that Biggie's funeral did; still, that didn't mean the NYPD knew how to deal with the phenomenon. That dichotomy became my cross to bear.

Indeed, Biggie's funeral brought out the growing paranoia in NYPD around hip-hop. The Chinese Gangs unit made a surveillance tape of the funeral, yet they refused to share it with other departments; the Brooklyn North precinct did the same thing. How did the NYPD expect to solve rap-related investigations if there wasn't even cooperation within the department? I would find out later that there were other renegade forces working within the NYPD, including a detective who may have seen Biggie's murder. This was war all right—war on the streets, and war within the NYPD.

Now that Biggie's funeral was over, I had to deal with the two LAPD detectives and make sure they got what they came to New York for. In the process, I hoped that I would find some answers for myself; my chiefs, however, were just relieved that Biggie's investigation wasn't the jurisdictional responsibility of the NYPD—thank God this happened in someone else's backyard, that was their attitude.

I discovered quickly that the two visiting LAPD detectives, Edwards and Jackson, weren't exactly sure what they're looking for, though. They came from the Wilshire Divison, a relatively small L.A. precinct that doesn't see that much action, let alone cases of this magnitude and complexity. Wilshire got assigned the case because Biggie was shot in the precinct area, but already it was clear they were a little out of their league.

The LAPD guys were both black detectives, and very nice gentlemen, but I felt the odds were stacked against them actually solving the case. For one, Jackson and Edwards weren't up on the rap music industry; they didn't have the rap playbook; they couldn't tell difference between the heroes and villains involved.

"Hey, we just got assigned this case," they told me. "We don't listen to rappers, but our kids do." They didn't know about the East Coast–West Coast War, or who was in Junior M.A.F.I.A.; they were so out of touch, they barely knew who Suge Knight was, even though he was a notorious figure in their own hometown. As a result, my LAPD friends didn't really have a grasp of the players in the Biggie homicide; therefore, they weren't really sure who they considered to be the murder suspect in their investigation. I had to sit them down and explain just what this whole investigation was about.

Edwards and Jackson met me around 10:00 A.M. the next day in my office at Cold Case. I debriefed them, giving up everything I knew about their investigation. The LAPD detectives told me they had a six pack—and they weren't talking about beer: the LAPD calls their photo arrays of possible suspects that they show witnesses "six packs." Their six pack featured the main guy the detectives were looking for, along with five other guys that fit the perp's description. They wanted to show their six pack to various witnesses and persons of interest in the case who were based in New York and New Jersey.

In particular, Edwards and Jackson wanted to speak with Biggie's mother, Mrs. Voletta Wallace, along with members of Big's entourage and Junior M.A.F.I.A. posse, including Lil' Kim. They were especially interested, though, in meeting with two eyewitnesses to the shooting—Big's rap protégé Lil' Cease and Biggie's bodyguard, Gregory "G" Young.

We set up the interviews to take place the next day at Biggie's condo out in Teaneck, New Jersey. In advance, I spoke with Teaneck Police Lieutenant Dean Kuzinski. Lieutenant Kuzinski had raided Biggie's Teaneck home before, which had resulted in gun and marijuana charges for the rapper in 1994, and had come to the funeral home to work with us on the day of Big's funeral. With Kuzinski's presence alongside me and the LAPD investigators, we made up a mini-task force that spanned police departments from three states—California, New Jersey, and New York. Other than Kuzinski, we were all black detectives.

We make our way to Biggie's house in Teaneck, New Jersey, which was located in a gated, suburban apartment complex—a far cry from the rugged city blocks of his beloved Bed-Stuy Brooklyn. Biggie's mother greeted us at the front door; she was very nice and mild-mannered, but obviously swimming in the depths of grief.

I let the LAPD guys do the interviews themselves. I wanted to gain their trust; I didn't want them to think I was trying to take over their investigation. It was hard not to stick my two cents in, though. After Mrs. Wallace, we met with Lil' Kim. The L.A. guys didn't know who Lil' Kim was—they had no idea what she looked like. Kim looked and acted nothing like her performing persona, however, she was dressed casually in a sweatsuit. It was clear she was quite upset, yet she was very quiet.

Kim talked to the LAPD freely—Edwards and Jackson found her cooperative: it was clear she wanted to help in the investigation, and was desperate for Biggie's killer to be brought to justice. Lil' Cease was the most important interview of the day, though. His was the crucial eyewitness account, since he had been sitting right there next to Big in the car at the time of the homicide.

We spoke to Cease in Mrs. Wallace's kitchen, where he broke down the circumstances of Biggie's homicide in depth. It goes a little something like this:

Biggie and his Junior M.A.F.I.A. posse, along with mentor Puff Daddy, were out in Los Angeles for the Soul Train Awards. On the night of March 8, 1997, they attended a *VIBE* magazine party being thrown at the Petersen Automotive Museum located on L.A.'s "museum row" at the corner of Wilshire Boulevard and Fairfax Avenue.

Due to overcrowding, the Fire Marshal shut down the *VIBE* party just a few minutes after 12:30 A.M. Biggie and his entourage then piled into two rented Chevrolet Suburban sport-utility vehicles. Puffy led the way in a white Suburban filled with him and three bodyguards. Biggie's ride, a green Suburban, went second: inside, Big's bodyguard Gregory "G" Young was at the wheel, with Biggie seated beside him in the front passenger seat. Lil' Cease sat behind Biggie in the right rear passenger seat next to Big's longtime friend and associate Damion "D-Roc" Butler (after Big was killed, Butler would eventually become Lil' Kim's boyfriend; as well, D-Roc would figure heavily in a 2001 shooting at the Hot 97 radio station that would result in Lil' Kim's conviction for perjury in 2005). Following up the rear was a black Chevrolet Blazer driven by longtime Bad Boy security guy Paul Offord, with an off-duty cop moonlighting from the LAPD riding shotgun alongside him.

Big's car had barely moved but a couple blocks when it stopped at a red light on Fairfax. A black Chevy Impala SS pulled up on the right; Cease looked over at the driver directly to see who it was, thinking it might be a friend or fan. In the process, he noticed that the driver had a gun, but Cease couldn't react quickly enough. Almost immediately, the Impala's driver unloaded seven shots from his automatic weapon in Biggie's direction, then sped away. Biggie was the only one injured, and he was hurt badly: his chest and stomach area were torn apart by bullets and was gushing blood. The entourage sped him to nearby Cedar-Sinai Hospital, but it was too late.

By 1:15 A.M., forty minutes after the party ended, Christopher Wallace, aka Notorious B.I.G., aka Biggie Smalls, aka Biggie, aka Big, was dead. At just twenty-four years old, he was on the verge of releasing his second masterpiece, the prophetically titled *Life After Death* album.

Once Cease finished his eyewitness account, the LAPD guys questioned him about any possible motive he thought might be behind the murder: was there anything suspicious at the party, any problems that night, any disputes that might have led to this?

"Big had hurt his leg and couldn't walk much," Cease explained, "but it was all love at the party. I don't know who shot my friend, or why."

LAPD also showed Cease their six pack, but he didn't identify any of the suspects' photos within it. Cease did offer up his own detailed description of the shooter, though, saying he was a black male with a large forehead, maybe in his late thirties or early forties. Furthermore, Cease said Biggie's killer looked "like a Muslim"—meaning he wore the suit-and-bow tie uniform of the Fruit of Islam (F.O.I.), the security wing of Louis Farrakhan's Nation of Islam sect.

At the time, it was very fashionable for rappers to use Fruit of Islam security: Snoop Dogg, for example, surrounded himself with Fruit of Islam after he left Suge Knight and Death Row Records under bad terms. However, this information also opened up more questions: in particular, a key component of Fruit of Islam's security approach is that they do not carry weapons. If Biggie's wasn't F.O.I., then who was he?

The LAPD detectives were ecstatic about Cease's information, in particular his detailed description of the perp. They asked me if I knew a "composite artist"—someone who could create a detailed drawing of a suspect from a "composite" of witnesses' descriptions. I did, so they scheduled Cease to meet with the artist. The resulting composite drawing was the one that subsequently appeared everywhere in the media as the definitive image of Big's at-large killer.

After the interviews are completed, the LAPD guys and I went to dinner, where we really got into it regarding their investigation into Biggie's homicide. For one, I knew they were not telling me everything: while Edwards and Jackson were perfectly friendly to me, they were also being secretive amongst themselves, sneaking off to make phone calls to their commander whenever they landed a juicy lead. I confronted them about this.

"Guys, what's really going on with this case?" I asked. "I mean, what's *really* going on?" Edwards and Jackson came clean with me, even though they were nervous to open up to anyone in the NYPD because of potential leaks. They were concerned in particular because they had information that Biggie was being tailed by a NYPD detective for maybe two weeks or more before his death. LAPD thought this detective might've even been present at Biggie's homicide.

Hearing this, I had a suspicion about who was following Biggie in Los Angeles. "Was it Bill Oldham?" I asked. Bill Oldham was a detective in the NYPD's Major Case Squad. I knew Oldham because he had a case with King Tut—the "three strikes" one that eventually brought him down; later, Oldham had became involved in the first Tupac shooting case. But Oldham wasn't one to cooperate with my investigations.

Oldham's investigation into the Tupac shooting at the Quad recording studios focused in particular on what Biggie's involvement might've been. Two or three weeks prior to Biggie's murder, I called Oldham and told him that I could probably help with his investigations. His response was tellingly abrupt, and cold as ice: "What's it to you?" I said, "Have a good day" and hung up.

Oldham was cagey: someone, an informant probably, was giving him new information and he didn't want to share. He wanted to solve cases his own way, even though Chief Anemone had sent down through the commands that I was supposed to be notified about all rap investigations. I was, after all, the NYPD's hip-hop industry specialist. However, these rap cases that once only I cared about were suddenly big game to select individuals within NYPD—a trend I would only see increase. I was starting to have some competition on the hip-hop beat inside the department, when what was needed was *cooperation.*

LAPD had had a similarly frustrating experience with Oldham. Oldham had definitely been investigating Big in Los Angeles. He had registered with the LAPD, as all outside law enforcement is required to do, but wasn't sharing a lot of information with his hosts. Apparently Oldham had some kind of investigation going on involving Biggie before he was murdered, and was probably with working with a federal agent; even Anemone didn't know about it. As a result of Oldham's activities, Edwards told me he and his partner were initially reluctant to open up to me.

When I told Edwards and Jackson that I hadn't spoken to Oldham and I didn't get along with him, they respected that gesture and started opening up. LAPD were afraid that Oldham was withholding information; they were anxious to solve Biggie's murder, so we concluded we'd work together. Additionally, they confirmed to me that there were LAPD police officers doing security for the Bad Boy crew the night Biggie was killed, but they had fled the scene of the crime. That sounded very strange to me—a car full of cops is right there, and yet they take off the minute a violent crime is committed? Mrs. Wallace had said in her interview with us that she knew cops were following her son, so why didn't they see who shot him?

I learned that the majority of the cops moonlighting as Bad Boy security officers were in fact with the Compton, California, police department. When they saw the Biggie homicide going down, they probably didn't want to get involved in the investigation—LAPD had enough scandal already because some rogue LAPD cops had been revealed to be on Suge's Death Row Records payroll. It also eventually came out that the son of Lieutenant Richard Wright, the Commanding Officer of Compton PD's homicide division, was the head of security company that employed the Compton officers— and that his family had ties to Suge Knight and Death Row.

Yup, this case was going in a bad direction for everyone involved; everyone seemed to have their fingers stuck where they shouldn't be. The NYPD was covertly investigating Biggie about King Tut and Tupac; the Compton PD were behaving strangely while moonlighting; LAPD officers were caught working for Suge. LAPD was also touchy because of what became known as the "Rampart" scandal, where L.A.'s finest were found to be involved in the very gang activity they were supposed to be fighting.

Three of the LAPD officers involved in the Rampart scandal, Kevin Gaines, David Mack, and Rafael Perez, not only were covert members of the Bloods street gang, but they had even deeper ties to Suge Knight and Death Row. Even before he became a central figure in the civil lawsuit brought by Notorious B.I.G.'s family against the city of Los Angeles, David Mack would eventually be sent to prison for his activities moonlighting as a bank robber (he was convicted as a participant in a 1997 Bank of America looting that netted $722,000). Mack had also been placed at the Petersen Automotive Museum the night of Biggie's death by members of Biggie's entourage and others. Kevin Gaines's name would surface as well: before his death in a shoot-out with a fellow LAPD officer, Gaines had even become romantically involved with Sharitha Knight, an ex-wife of Suge's (the film *Training Day*, which garnered Denzel Washington an Academy Award for his portrayal of a corrupt cop, was reportedly based partly on Gaines's infamous history).

I stayed in touch with LAPD on the Biggie front. Eventually, Edwards and Jackson informed me that they were leaving the case: the LAPD's Robbery/Homicide division was taking over from the Wilshire Precinct, having assigned a detective named Russell Poole and his superior officer, Fred Miller, to the investigation.

These new guys didn't seem quite as forthcoming as the Wilshire detectives. I called Russell Poole once, and he never called me back (Poole's story has become urban legend—Randall Sullivan's great book *LAbyrinth* details Poole's struggle with the many-tentacled Biggie case and his reluctant LAPD superiors). I thought I was making more headway with Miller, however, or so I thought. Miller and I had a short conversation about a person of interest in the Biggie homicide investigation named "Zip." "If you get Zip, let me know," Miller told me. "I'll come out to New York to interrogate him."

This Zip was an interesting guy. His government name was Vaughn Williams, but everyone on the street knew him as Zip. Zip was most respected on the street, a true "O.G" (a slang acronym for "original gangstas") from uptown Harlem. I knew Zip was tied to a lot of drug dealing and that he traveled throughout the country to pursue his business activities, legit and otherwise.

I was also aware of Zip's ties to people in the sports and entertainment fields. Zip knew Mike Tyson, and when I finally caught up with him, he was in the car of basketball player Albert King, a former member of the New Jersey Nets and brother of Bernard King of the New York Knicks. Yeah, Zip knew people, but he was especially tied in with Sean "Puff Daddy" Combs.

According to Cheo Hodari Coker's brilliant book, *Unbelievable:*

The Life, Death, and Afterlife of The Notorious B.I.G., Zip was a dear friend and associate of Puffy's criminally connected father and was considered "the Yoda to Puffy's Luke." Biggie also was apparently close to Zip, crediting him on his first two albums as "Uncle Zip—The Spiritual Advisor."

Even though Puffy has repeatedly denied ever using gang members for security purposes, Zip was also reportedly Bad Boy's security advisor when it came to dealing with street-gang culture. For one, I myself knew from my police work that Zip had connections to O.G.s in other cities, and had traveled from New York to Los Angeles; in fact, Zip had lived out in Los Angeles, which we at NYPD knew from surveillance and running his driver's licenses. Zip knew everybody—gangs, street people, celebs; he could reach out and connect with anyone that Biggie or Puffy couldn't themselves. In particular, Zip was reportedly tight with the Crips gang—and may have very well been one himself. In Coker's book, he quotes a source who states, "The nigga that's a major figure that's a Crip is named Zip. That's like Puff's right-hand man. But he would never go out and expose that shit."

Coker's reporting confirms much of what I already knew about Zip at the time from informants: Zip was deeply involved in activities that had potential reverberations involving both Biggie's and Tupac's homicide cases. For one, Coker claims that Zip was tight with Keefee D, the Los Angeles–area Crip O.G. who was questioned by police in connection with Tupac's homicide.

Coker also refers to an LAPD interrogation with Davis regarding Big's homicide, where Davis allegedly owned up to attending a meeting in Anaheim, California, with Puffy, Biggie, Zip, and members of the Southside Crips. "I was in a room full of Crip killers," says another of Coker's sources. "Puff said they were going to be doing security for us [on the West Coast]."

In the lyrics of Bad Boy–affiliated artists, there appeared to be references to the Crips as well. On Notorious B.I.G.'s "Long Kiss Goodnight," Big mentions his "team in the marine blue"; meanwhile, on the posthumous tribute cut "Biggie," Lil' Cease raps that he likes "marine blue, marine green, roll with a mean team." In such instances, "marine blue" is thought to refer to the identifying blue color worn to signify Crip membership.

In fact, an informant of mine had let me know that Zip *was* in Los Angeles around the time of the Biggie homicide. This was actually not an informant per se—a C.I. (confidential informant) is someone who's officially registered with the NYPD. No, this guy was too hot, too close to the action to be registered, where he could potentially be found out; he was rather a "law enforcement source" on the street. This source was very close to the rap industry, and had worked with many high-profile rappers and artists, so I trusted implicitly what he told me.

I explained to my source that I'd heard the theory that there was a financial arrangement made by Bad Boy in exchange for protection by the Crips. "That's right," he explained. "Zip is one of the guys who brokered this deal." But was Zip's security deal about protecting the Bad Boy camp from retaliation from Death Row? Did it have something to do with Tupac's murder? Sometimes it's best to make potential enemies your friends, but those friends can always turn on you. There were whispers on the street that Bad Boy or Biggie owed the Crips money, anywhere from $10,000 to $100,000; when the Bad Boy camp reneged, the rumor went, the Crips took out Biggie. Or did Bad Boy hire the Crips to assassinate Tupac and then back out of payment, angering and humiliating the gang in the process?

There were other intriguing links as well: Coker notes in *Unbelievable* that Dwayne "Keefee D" Davis "owned a black SS Impala matching the description of the car seen leaving [the scene of Biggie's homicide]. [LAPD] confiscated the vehicle and hauled in Davis for questioning. Soon after both Davis and his car were released, and the police later declared that he was not a suspect. But the streets kept talking."

Yes, they did—and I thought Zip could be just the person to say who exactly the Crips were protecting Biggie from. At the time, Zip was out of my jurisdiction: he was in New Jersey, so I had to have the FBI bring him in. I got in contact with an old friend of mine from Bronx Narcotics named Kevin Aquinas, who was now on a joint FBI/NYPD task force. Kevin knew a lot about Zip and told me,

"I can help you get this guy if you want him." Kevin had a case in New Jersey involving some guys Zip knew anyway, so he was more than eager to do it.

Aquinas found Zip with little hassle. Once he was in custody, I met Zip in an interrogation room in the Southern District headquarters at One St. Andrews Plaza, in lower Manhattan near the court buildings. Zip was stunned, and a little nervous, about the surroundings he'd found himself in: "Man, this is not a police station—this is *federal*. Hey, man, where are you from?" he asked me. "And what is this all about?"

I explained to Zip why he'd been picked up: he had an old outstanding warrant for an assault involving a hospital cop, as well pending crimes that he'd never returned to court for. That wasn't why I needed to talk to him, though.

First, however, Zip and I got acquainted. I took his handcuffs off and told him everything I knew about his activities—and it was a lot. I knew he'd been gambling in Atlantic City recently, where he drove around with two girls in a black Lincoln Navigator. I knew how Zip had traveled often to Washington, D.C.; I knew the names of all the businesses he owned, and the kind of woman he liked to have on his arm.

"One thing I have to compliment you about—you always travel with a lot of beautiful women," I said.

Zip laughed, but he was puzzled. "Wow—you know *everything* about me," he said. "And yet you are the nicest detective I've ever met. You have treated me with respect, and not like a scumbag criminal."

I told Zip I wasn't really interested in the bullshit outstandings I pulled him in for. Instead, I wanted to learn what he knew about the Biggie murder.

"I knew you've been down there in L.A. dealing with it," I told him. "I'm not saying you pulled the trigger, but I want to know if you were behind the deal between Big and the Crips. I heard through the grapevine that you brokered a deal a couple weeks before the Soul Train Awards. Why? What's up? Why does Biggie need the Crips? Can you help me?"

I talked with Zip for hours that day. He danced around my queries like a pro, making sure that I learned certain things but protecting himself from a legal standpoint. Zip was being as honest as he could be with me—as honest as any real child of the streets could ever be to a *cop*, even if he was the "nicest detective [he'd] ever met." Zip made it clear enough that he might know something, but that he also might be killed if he let it out in a way that could expose him. It was the code of the streets that he could not let go. "Parker, as a gentleman, I can't tell you anything," he shrugged. "I can't get involved with this."

That was cool with me—I wanted him to tell me what he knew about the Biggie homicide honestly. I didn't want there to be animosity if I'd forced the information out of him; I might've needed him in the future, and I thought I could gain more of his trust over time. In a sense, he'd told me enough. Even though Zip didn't fully disclose anything, it was clear from what he implied between the lines that there was more to the story if I wanted to look for it.

As well, I figured LAPD could get more mileage out of him, anyway. I didn't want to empty Zip's gas tank immediately, especially as Biggie's murder really was the responsibility of Los Angeles law enforcement. After all, Fred Miller would certainly be coming to New York with such a valuable perp to the Big homicide investigation in custody. He'd told me so.

Alas, I soon learned LAPD were no longer interested in coming eastward for Zip, or anything. Russell Poole should've come out to New York if he really wanted to find out who killed Biggie; that was the major flaw in his handling of the case. It was almost like the regional animosity of the East Coast–West Coast rap war of the streets had carried over to law enforcement. While the NYPD and LAPD weren't at war per se, my interactions suggested that we were not to work together openly, and were perhaps in fact adversaries. Meanwhile, Poole's partner Fred Miller was blasé, which I found out when I called him about picking up Zip.

Miller was so hot to speak to Zip when we first spoke, but when I told him I'd actually gotten the suspect he requested in custody, Miller brushed off my news with a joke. "You know what, tell Zip I say 'hi.' " *Tell Zip I say "hi."* That was it. I hung up the phone immediately.

Now I was livid. I was now seeing directly how the Biggie case—as it traveled around the LAPD, passed like a hot potato from division to division, detective to detective—was losing momentum at each new stop. Of course, the LAPD would pass the Biggie baton yet again, slowing it down further. The next LAPD investigator to pick up's Big's homicide was a detective named Steven Katz, who, despite his Jewish last name, was in fact a light-skinned black of Southern descent.

Unlike his LAPD predecessors Poole and Miller, Katz actually deigned to come to New York to continue the investigation. Katz's East Coast journey involved interviewing me and following up on suspects and persons of interest around New York. We went out to interrogate some people together, and I took him and his partner to a Yankees game.

Katz admitted he hated Russell Poole, who had been all but shut out of the department at that point. Poole had felt the LAPD stymied him, and that the department's boss Bernard Parks had something to cover up, so the case got passed to Katz (who, as an African-American, seemed also a politically expedient choice). In particular, Katz was stuck on the theory that Suge Knight was behind Biggie's murder. I told Katz, "Don't get stuck on just one theory—you should look into, and exhaust, *every* theory."

Admittedly, there were more than a few theories going around to get through. To my mind, though, there were in fact only *three* plausible theories about who was responsible for the killing of Biggie Smalls. One theory is that, because Biggie and Bad Boy didn't pay the full price for protection (or Tupac's hit), the Crips hired a hit man to kill Big, dressing him up in Fruit of Islam uniform to throw the police off the scent. Perhaps Suge Knight hired the guy. I also knew from talking to law-enforcement sources that Suge hated Biggie, and that Suge had enough resources and connections in the streets to put something like Big's gangland-style execution together. And while it's unlikely, maybe Big's killer actually was a rogue member of the Fruit of Islam? All of these theories deserved a follow-up.

Worst of all, this crime might've been preventable. I learned from my informants that before Biggie went to Los Angeles, there were constant, very real, and ominous threats directed toward the Bad Boy camp—somebody was going to get killed. And someone had to know about it in advance.

My personal feeling, deduced from everything I've learned in my law-enforcement career, is that the Crips were significantly involved in Biggie's homicide. What made me think so more than anything is that, after Biggie was killed in Los Angeles, there was a war between Crips and Bloods. Biggie's murder in such close proximity to gang territory sparked a deadly paranoia; gang rivals were shooting each other down like crazy.

The LAPD was caught off guard by the bloody aftermath of Biggie's death, as was made clear when I talked to my friend Ken Knox at the time. "Hey, Parker, this Biggie thing is getting huge," Knox told me. "They are killing people out here like crazy." Knox described numerous incidents involving cold-blooded murders and drive-bys. Biggie's murder had obviously made someone very mad.

For one, people on the street assumed that Suge Knight had something to do with the murder of Biggie Smalls. As Suge is a member of a Bloods-affiliated gang, and comes from a Bloods neighborhood, then he'd have hell to pay from the Crips. The post-Biggie gang holocaust went like this: a Crip shot two Bloods. The Bloods retaliated, killing two Crips. A Crip then kills another Blood in revenge; next, two Bloods kill another Crip. And so on. *Ad infinitum.* Following the idea that the Crips were involved, my theory on who's behind the Biggie murder looks something like this:

Biggie contacted a guy connected to the Crips gang asking for protection. A financial arrangement was then made between the Crips and Biggie for a decent amount of money: less than a million most likely, but a big fee regardless, totaling in the tens, maybe even *hundreds,* of thousands. But then Biggie reneged; he didn't give the Crips the second part of his payment. *That's* why I think he was killed.

Word was also the LAPD believed Big's shooter was an actual member of the Fruit of Islam. They wanted to explore any conspiracy involving members of the Nation of Islam involved in such a hit, and looked actively to support this idea. I thought that was a stretch, despite some circumstantial evidence. Biggie had supposedly gone into the House of Blues and gotten into a dispute, which a Fruit of Islam security guard had responded to in order to keep the peace. As well, Nation of Islam leader Louis Farrakhan and his son had also supposedly attended parties that weekend around the Soul Train Awards.

Personally, I didn't think much of these theories implicating the Nation of Islam. For one, I wasn't surprised that the Fruit of Islam would be at either a House of Blues rap show or a *VIBE* party. Fruit of Islam were in vogue as the politically correct security of choice for rappers, and *VIBE* magazine had already caught flak in the media about hiring party security from the radical Farrakhan. Farrakhan's contentious relationship with the American Jewish community even caused *VIBE*'s then top editor, Alan Light, who is Jewish, to be scandalously excoriated by certain Jewish groups for his association, however minimal, with the Nation of Islam. And I knew, as an African-American, that it wasn't surprising to see members of the Nation of Islam at gatherings of important black people— controversial or not, the Farrakhan and his Nation remain a part of the black community, whether the powers that be like it or not.

I believed exploring the Islam connection was key, however, to discovering the identity of Biggie's shooter. Eventually such a person of interest was identified as someone born with the name Harry Billups, but more commonly known as Amir Muhammad, came to the attention of investigators.

Amir Muhammad knew the corrupt LAPD cop David Mack. Mack was not only a Blood gang member with the street name D-Mack whom authorities discovered signed his prison correspondence "M.O.B." (for "Men of Bloods"), he was also in deep with Death Row Records. Adding to the conspiracy theories, according to Coker's *Unbelievable*, Muhammad was Mack's old college buddy. In fact, the first person to visit Mack in jail after he was busted for bank robbery was Muhammad, who curiously signed in with a phony address and Social Security number. Indeed, the statements of eyewitnesses just kept leading me to consider Muhammad.

In my opinion, after talking to Lil' Cease, the guy he described in the composite drawing made from his eyewitness account resembled the description of Amir Muhammad. Furthermore, a bodyguard named Eugene Deal, who had accompanied Biggie and Puffy to the party that night, reported that he had seen a Nation of Islam "guy" who seemed to be "checking them out." In Nick Broomfield's penetrating documentary *Biggie & Tupac*, when Broomfield shows Deal Muhammad's picture, Deal says "That's him. That's the guy who came up to me." I mean, when things come together like that, it's pretty clear to me that that's a guy you want to look into.

Deal also states in *Biggie & Tupac* that he has never seen a picture of Muhammad before, from the LAPD or anybody else. Muhammad wasn't even in the LAPD's six pack. And yet there were obviously those in the LAPD who were looking into any potential involvement by Muhammad in Biggie's murder: in Broomfield's film, Kevin Hackie, another former LAPD officer controversially close to Death Row, opines that Muhammad might be involved. Also, according to Randall Sullivan's December 2005 *Rolling Stone* story "The Unsolved Mysteries of the Notorious B.I.G.," "an inmate described by the L.A. County Sheriff's Department as an 'ultra-reliable informant,'" had reported hearing that the shooter in the Biggie Smalls case belonged to the Fruit of Islam and went by the name Amir or Ashmir.

Still, Amir Muhammad has never been arrested or charged with anything involving the homicide of Notorious B.I.G. At least one LAPD detective has told the press that Muhammad was no longer a suspect. Muhammad has repeatedly claimed innocence, stating he is a mere mortgage broker—and no criminal. And although he was originally named as an individual defendant in the wrongful death action brought by Biggie's mother, she later dismissed the claims against him. However, based upon the information and experiences I've just described, it's my opinion that Amir Muhammad deserves further attention. And even if Muhammad had any connection to the shooting, it remains unclear who, if anyone, was pulling his string and whether there is any link to Biggie's rumored troubles with the Crips.

To this day, Biggie's murder has never been solved, yet the legal pileup left in its wake continues. On July 6, 2005, a mistrial was declared by the federal judge overseeing a wrongful death suit filed by Biggie's mother, Mrs. Voletta Wallace, against the city of Los Angeles. The trial had been going on for over two weeks when an anonymous phone call indicated that the LAPD was willfully withholding evidence in the trial. In particular, a jailhouse informant, Kenny Boagni, supposedly indicated that LAPD officer—and Rampart scandal veteran—Rafael Perez was more involved with Death Row Records than had previously believed. According to this informant, Perez, an accomplice of David Mack's, was on security detail for Death Row on the night of Big's murder.

The suit initially had charged that Mack had arranged for Big's murder via the instruction of Death Row honcho Suge Knight—and the LAPD was behind a cover-up of whoever killed Big. Adding credence to Mrs. Wallace's legal stance is that, in the wake of these revelations, my old friend, LAPD detective Steven Katz, revealed in a deposition that he had "forgot" the log book that recorded his meetings with this informant in his desk drawer—a flimsy assertion the presiding judge, U.S. District Judge Florence Marie-Cooper, ridiculed from the stand.

I agreed with the judge that it didn't sound right that he "lost the file." That's not too cool—Steve's actions will not only damage his credibility, but his high-noon revelation could be a turning point in this multimillion-dollar lawsuit.

Furthermore, these last-minute turnabouts strongly suggest that the LAPD has something to hide. Bernard Parks, the LAPD's chief at the time of Biggie's homicide, has been accused by Russell Poole of engineering numerous cover-ups in the Biggie case. "For years, there have been rumblings that Parks's daughter Michelle, a former civilian clerk with the [LAPD], had been buddies with rogue cops Perez and Mack, who wound up in prison," claimed a July 3, 2005, story by Michelle Caruso published in New York's *Daily News*. Parks's daughter Michelle was also arrested in Las Vegas in 1998 for allegedly selling cocaine. The charges were later dismissed for lack of evidence. Whatever the real story is, it's clear that Bernard Parks and the LAPD have something to conceal when it comes to Biggie Smalls. I think Parks had bigger aspirations beyond being police commissioner, and he didn't want the scandal to get out and taint him. Los Angeles already had the O. J. Simpson case and the Rodney King riots smearing their reputation; this would only besmirch the LAPD further, adding fuel to the fire of the seemingly never-ending Rampart scandal.

In the end, Biggie's and Tupac's murders provided the beginning of hip-hop's blood marketing. The Notorious B.I.G.'s posthumous album, *Life After Death*, released on March 25, 1997, entered the charts at number one, and just didn't stop selling; it would go on to be given a rare "diamond" certification by the Recording Industry Association of America—"diamond" indicating sales of over ten million copies.

Bling, bling indeed: the industry discovered via Tupac's and Biggie's example that murdering rappers could turned them into big-ticket martyrs—post-mortem icons à la Elvis Presley, Jimi Hendrix, or Kurt Cobain. Sometimes rappers sold more records after they survived a shooting—or even if they didn't survive. Once dead, every utterance they recorded now was imbued with new value, as Tupac's endless volley of posthumous recordings have proven. Soon every rapper would be predicting his own death, would be boasting about how many bullets they've taken on the street, how many times a rival drug dealer sent them to the emergency room. A brush with death made for even better marketing than a prison stint—it was proof of the rapper's invincibility, a crucial part of the persona of any hip-hopper claiming any street cred.

For me, the more disturbing trend was that these murders would never be solved. It was a trend that would reverberate throughout what was becoming a hip-hop crime epidemic. Apparently, neither the cops nor the hip-hop community had learned anything from Biggie's and Tupac's deaths. If anything, niggas were more emboldened to bust their guns in the club than ever, regardless of who might catch a bullet. And law enforcement was even more confused than ever about how to deal with such developments.

I had my job cut out for me.

8.

THROW YA GUNS IN THE AIR, AND BUST 'EM LIKE YOU JUST DON'T CARE:
Puff Daddy, the Club New York Shooting— and the Birth of "Rap Intel"

> *Bust shots at your crew, another charge . . .*
> —Shyne, *"Bad Boyz"*

> *Y'all know it's all fucked up now, right? What the fuck I'ma do now?*
> —*Puff Daddy, "Victory"*

SEEING the aftermath of the Biggie and Tupac murders, you'd think that the NYPD would be united in trying to figure out what to do about rap-related crime. *Hell, no:* alas, by the late '90s attitudes toward hip-hop in the NYPD still remained divided. I was hearing about it all the time in Cold Case.

And it was coming from the top. Cold Case's lieutenant commander John Dove told my commanding officer Ray Ferarri that he thought this rap stuff was still just bullshit. Let me tell you, I was getting real sick of Dove and his square, by-the-book attitude. Six-foot-one with a buzz cut and very piercing blue eyes, Dove started as a cop in the Transit division before it got merged into the NYPD; he'd done a brief stint in Internal Affairs, but he wasn't famed for his homicide work. Dove was very regimented in how he wanted things done and that was a problem for me. Hip-hop crime didn't do things in a regimented way, so I needed flexibility—not grief. I was mad at Pollini for putting me with this guy. I even had a year more on the job than Dove. Most of all, I knew homicides.

Thankfully, surprisingly, NYPD top brass was starting to recognize what was happening with hip-hop crime and prioritize accordingly. Biggie and Tupac provided a wake-up call of sorts, and the NYPD top brass' new attitude was made loud and clear when Chief Anemone put out an official memo on the subject: it said every squad was instructed to notify me, Derrick Parker, on all rap-related investigations. There were so many more cases coming in because of rap violence, so the precincts were smartening up and taking preventive measures, like with an upcoming outdoor Fugees concert in Brooklyn, which had Brooklyn North's commander, Chief Esposito, on edge.

Esposito was worried about a potential riot, and with reason: at a previous Fugees concert in Harlem, a concertgoer shot a round in the air during a dispute, causing the crowd to scatter. With hundreds and sometimes thousands in attendance at such events, the significance in terms of public threat is massive. An innocent could catch a bullet—and if panic ensued, there could be a stampede to rival Puffy's City College tragedy.

Members of the public aren't the only ones in danger. By the late '90s, rappers were almost in as much danger themselves—or more: with their visibility and lavish "livin' large" lifestyles, they'd become hard targets to the stick-up kids and resentful have-nots back in the 'hood. I was seeing a trend popping off in the streets and the clubs: rappers as victims of robberies and shootings. In reaction, rappers were often taking the law into their own hands. That meant a lot more eye-for-an-eye retaliation in the streets, plus more busts for illegal gun possession among hip-hop crews.

Rappers had reason to be scared: this was the peak of the "bling-bling" era, the moment where ostentatious "jiggy" materialism had taken over hip-hop. In videos, rappers began rocking more ice than the North Pole; in rhymes, only the most expensive of everything, from Bentley cars to Cristal champagne, received shout-outs. Hip-hop was now the sound of success; as a result, rappers were being targeted in home invasions, getting jacked for their money, their cars, and their jewels. Wu-Tang wildman rapper Ol' Dirty Bastard took a bullet in a robbery at a relative's apartment in Brooklyn's Brevoort projects. Busta Rhymes was shot and robbed *twice* during this period. The home belonging to Foxy Brown's mother was violated in a home invasion focused on looting her famous daughter.

It's clear from this violent uptick that rappers were not safe anywhere; in the club or on tour, shootings and violent incidents began sparking up even more, often in public places with thousands of people around. In a dispute over bootlegging, Jay-Z stabbed Biggie's former right-hand man Lance "Un" Rivera at Studio 54's Kit Kat Klub in midtown Manhattan on December 1, 1999. Even as hip-hop left the 'hood to swim in the mainstream, crime kept following close behind, recognizing no borders or law.

More beefs kept popping up as well. It was clear from the murderous tenor of the day's rap rhymes that the hip-hop nation hadn't learned anything from the deaths of Biggie and Tupac. Back in the day, beefs between old-schoolers like Kool Moe Dee and LL Cool J existed primarily on wax, resulting in put-down dis rhymes of thrilling ingenuity. But by the late '90s, if anything, hip-hop was more bloodthirsty than ever. Rap beefs were no longer delineated along regional lines like "East vs. West." Even if you were from the same city, the same neighborhood, the same project house, a beef was possible, as the escalating row between female rappers Lil' Kim and Foxy Brown demonstrated.

On the surface, Kim and Foxy appeared to have a lot in common. Both hailed from rugged Brooklyn 'hoods, where they were protégées of famous male rappers—Kim began as part of Biggie's Junior M.A.F.I.A. crew, while Foxy was cultivated as a mic talent by Jay-Z. At one point, Kim and Foxy were friends and planned a collaborative album called *Thelma and Louise*. The notion of rap's two hottest female rappers working together was irresistible.

Unfortunately, the Foxy-Kim connection was too hot to handle: Brooklyn apparently wasn't big enough for the both of them. The root of their beef was never made explicit, but to outsiders it was about competition more than anything—i.e., who was the baddest bitch from the B.K. on the mic. Foxy and Kim's lyrical catfight seemed to erupt around the time both were nominated for Soul Train Best New Artist award in 1997. The insults started piling up in the media—for example, Foxy claimed Big had approached her first, not Kim, to be Junior M.A.F.I.A.'s female rapper; soon, however, the dissing moved to wax, where it grew more serious.

Kim got off the first sonic salvo with a venomous verse on a now-classic 1999 remix of Mobb Deep's "Quiet Storm," which slashes Foxy as an "embezzler" while savaging the rap skills of Kim's rival and "*u-n-o* competitor." Foxy Brown retaliated on a remix of a song called "Bang, Bang" by the thuggish Queens duo Capone-N-Noreaga. On "Bang, Bang," Foxy breaks Kim down hard, claiming to be the true ghetto gangstress between them. Foxy pulls no punches here, calling out her rival as a slut.

Throwing fuel on the fire, Foxy's "Bang, Bang" verse implied that Kim's whole reputation stemmed from her association with Big. "Let the nigga rest in peace," Foxy instructs, "and hop off his dick, bitch." And when Foxy recorded another dis track with a different mistress of Biggie's named Charli Baltimore, the heat was really on; this beef would ultimately result in one of New York's most infamous hip-hop-related crime incidents, a shooting that would tear hip-hop apart at the seams. Between Foxy and Kim, beef was definitely personal, not business.

With hip-hop beef, though, even business is personal, as I learned in 1999 when I received a call from One Police Plaza. On the line was Deputy Inspector James McCool, a friend of Anemone's who had been following my rap-related investigations. Ever since the Biggie funeral, McCool had even nicknamed me "Puff" after Puff Daddy; however, on this day he was calling about an incident involving the real Mr. Combs himself. "Yo, Puff," McCool said to me, "I have a case you can probably help me with. You gotta come to with me to Midtown North—there's been an incident involving Puff Daddy and some guy named Steve Stoute."

Stoute's name in the mix made me curious. Puff Daddy's name needed no introduction to the public by now, but Steve Stoute was a more behind-the-scenes character in the rap game. A longtime hip-hop player, Stoute started at the bottom of the ladder while working with groups like Kid 'N Play in the '80s before rising to become a major-label executive and the on again–off again manager of hardcore rap superstar Nas. I'd seen Stoute around the hip-hop scene for years; in fact, Biggie was on his way to a party hosted by Stoute when the rotund rapper was killed. I'm surprised to hear the name of a Big Willie like Stoute in this context. As he's a real businessman above all else, Stoute stayed above the fray when it came to violent bullshit.

In the car on the way to Midtown North, Deputy Inspector McCool debriefed me on the situation. Apparently that day, April 15, 1999, Puffy and some of his accomplices allegedly assaulted Stoute with a champagne bottle, giving him a real good beatdown.

By this time, I'd already spoken to my informants to get the low-down on what sparked Puffy's assault on Stoute. I learned everything that happened: according to my informants, Puff got heated over the editing of a Nas video for the song, "Hate Me Now" that he appeared in. The initial edit of the "Hate Me Now" clip featured shots of Puffy crucified on a cross. However, Puff eventually decided that the Jesus Christ pose might be too controversial even for him. To that end, he asked Nas' then-manager Stoute to edit the crucifixion scenes out.

Stoute refused Puff's request: he wanted to put the video, complete with offending cross shots and all, on MTV. It was a standoff, Big Willie vs. Big Willie, and Stoute lost when Puff called his bluff. Stoute's obstinate attitude resulted in an unannounced visit with an angry Puff Daddy, and the subsequent champagne beatdown. For once in hip-hop, the victim actually called the police, so Puffy was arrested and brought to the Midtown North precinct, where we connected with him. The Stoute case was my real introduction to Puffy, and I would get to know him better. Believe me, this would not be the last time we'd meet up in a precinct house.

At Midtown North, the lieutenant let me handle the investigation. The powers that be didn't want big media swarming, so we tried to keep things under wraps as best we could. I started by identifying the perps: I had already begun monitoring people with criminal records in the hip-hop industry, so identifying Puff and his security team wasn't hard—I already had photos of 'em. Puffy and I talked in an interview room in the Midtown North precinct; he was "lawyered up," so his counsel was present during questioning. I handled Puffy with kid gloves. I knew if the case was going to be prosecuted successfully I had do everything right.

This being hip-hop, however, suddenly I had a noncooperative complainant in the case's victim. Steve Stoute, who looked pretty badly beaten up to me, and his lawyer, Harvey Slovis, abruptly informed me they were no longer pressing charges. I don't know if Puffy got to them, nor do I know if a financial settlement was made; both sides claimed there wasn't, but I kind of doubt it. The reason I think Stoute called the police in the first place was if the incident wasn't reported to the authorities, there could be no basis for legal proceedings, and therefore a settlement. Regardless, Puffy managed to get exactly what he wanted, as usual: he stayed out of jail, and his crucifixion scene was edited out of the "Hate Me Now" video.

Personally, I found Puff's alleged assault on Steve Stoute shocking. Then again, maybe Puffy was understandably tense. For one, rap was changing. The ghetto-fabulous era led by Puffy's Bad Boy camp had peaked, and was starting to fall out of favor. In fact, in the Nas song "Hate Me Now," which served as the basis for the controversial crucifixion video, Puff addresses his growing legion of "haters" wanting to see him fall, who are blaming him for everything that's wrong with hip-hop. By the time of the Stoute incident in April 1999, it had been just over two years since Biggie's death; while Biggie's posthumous album *Life After Death* had proven a massive success, selling over ten million copies, finding an heir apparent for Bad Boy's big poppa wasn't proving so easy.

Puffy tried to position himself as that heir—and indeed, he did find success as a performer, evolving into a superstar icon in his own right. Puff's 1997 solo debut, *No Way Out* by Puff Daddy and the Family, gained multiplatinum sales thanks to its numerous massive hit singles like the Biggie tribute "I'll Be Missing You" (which interpolated The Police's "Every Breath You Take"), "It's All About The Benjamins," "Can't Nobody Hold Me Down," and "Been Around The World." But Biggie had left a void that Puff couldn't fill, as the Bad Boy mogul proved more a new-style pop idol than a credible hard-core rapper; as one of Puffy's trademark raps made clear, "Don't worry if I write rhymes—I write checks." In musical terms, Puff's credibility on the streets was waning without B.I.G.

Indeed, by the late '90s it seemed like Puffy's empire was crumbling around him. Bad Boy's other remaining flagship rapper, the more pop-oriented Ma$e, announced he was retiring from rap music and devoting himself to Christianity following his second album, *Double Up*, which fell quickly from the charts after its release on June 15, 1999. As well, the Lox, Bad Boy's most hard-core rappers tied to the streets, had started an embarrassing "Free the Lox" campaign to get off the label. Puffy needed to find another Biggie to make up for the defections from Bad Boy's roster; in a way, he was almost too successful in this mission when he signed Shyne.

By 1999, a rapper named Shyne (real name: Jamal Barrow) was getting hype in hip-hop circles for his rhyme skills, making him the unsigned flavor of the minute for record-company talent scouts, which resulted in a bidding war between the major labels for his services. Shyne proved an unlikely success story: he was a troubled young man of West Indian descent who had come out of the tough Brooklyn neighborhood of Flatbush. His mean-streets Brooklyn provenance and ethnic heritage weren't the only things he shared with Biggie: eerily, his vocal tone and rhyme style were almost identical to those of the late, great Christopher Wallace. It was eerier still when Sean "Puff Daddy" Combs won Shyne's bidding and signed him to Bad Boy. By sounding so similar to the deceased Notorious B.I.G., it was almost like Shyne was a more stand-in for the dearly departed than the real thing.

As well, Shyne and Puffy's partnership would be marked by blood as well. Like Biggie, Shyne would all-too-soon become a magnet for deadly mayhem, in a case that almost destroyed both his and Puff's careers. This case would also debut my role in the NYPD's newly formed Rap Intelligence Division, or as it's informally come to be known, the "hip-hop squad."

That the NYPD would even consider forming a special unit devoted to hip-hop crime was at earlier junctures almost unthinkable. But just as hip-hop was evolving, the NYPD was evolving, too. After the murders of Biggie and Tupac, the NYPD slowly came to understand that rap-related crime was something to pay attention to, and that they needed an expert on the beat—*me*.

One thing that affected the NYPD's attitude to hip-hop in the late

'90s were changes in leadership, namely Bill Bratton. Under New York mayor Rudy Giuliani, Bratton was doing a fine job as commish, lowering crime rates across the board. But Bratton took too much credit in the media; this rankled omnipotent, all-powerful, hype-craving Giuliani, culminating in a tense back-and-forth in the newspapers between the two. As a result, the mayor replaced Bratton with an NYPD outsider, Howard Safir. Safir, like Giuliani, acquired his law-enforcement background as a former federal agent with a spectacular prosecution record.

Other than his aversion to press grandstanding, Safir was similar to his predecessor in that he favored fully modernized law enforcement, and embraced technological innovations in computers and DNA research. If anything, Safir had even more zeal than Bratton for cracking down on crime, which got him in trouble with civil-rights groups, particularly in the black community. Three particularly infamous cases tarnished Safir's legacy: the savage beating, torture, and sodomizing of a Haitian immigrant named Abner Louima, which set new standards for police brutality; the shooting murder of an innocent West African man named Amadou Diallo by a group of NYPD officers, who mistakenly emptied forty-one rounds into him; and the killing of an innocent African-American security guard, Patrick Dorismond, by an undercover officer in a botched drug sting.

No doubt, Safir was as hard-charging and stealth as Giuliani. If Safir was to be faulted for anything, as the racial scandals on his watch made clear, it was that he was too involved, too intent on crushing crime at whatever cost—including that of civilian's lives; his shoot-first-and-ask-questions-later attitude wasn't exactly a civil-rights landmark. It comes as no surprise that the hip-hop squad was formed under Safir: as commish, he wanted to control everything, to have his finger on every pulse.

In 1996, when Safir assumed power, the new commish didn't rock the boat on what Anemone and Norris had started with the Cold Case Squad. In fact, at this time I received a lateral promotion within Cold Case, taking me out of the Brooklyn squad to work in the Special Projects unit with my mentor Pollini, which I was happy about. My projects were getting a little too "special," however. Since Anemone put out the interdepartmental memo that I was to made aware of all of the NYPD's hip-hop-related crime investigations, I was consistently getting pulled into them. My Cold Case superiors were upset with me because the NYPD chiefs kept yanking me off cases to assist with hip-hop-related investigations, and they couldn't do anything about it—they were outranked.

There was a lot going on in the hip-hop world that needed surveying, too: I was going to awards shows, concerts, in-store promotions, album-release parties, clubs. All the while, I got the sense I was being evaluated and observed by the higher-ups. This was made clear to me when I was called in to investigate a rap-related shooting in Queens.

I was off duty, coming home from a Halloween party dressed as Zorro when I got a call from my captain around 6:00 A.M. concerning a rap-related shooting at the Owl Club in Queens's 105th Precinct. I could tell from his voice that the captain wasn't happy: apparently nine people were involved in the shooting, with two sustaining serious injuries, the rest getting off with graze wounds. I was informed that Deputy Inspector McCool would be joining me as I responded to Queens's 105th precinct house.

I found that last bit of info particularly interesting: word circulating around the department suggested that McCool—with whom I'd had a personal relationship with since 1982, when we were both coming up as rookies—was getting ready to start a special gang-intelligence unit in the Intel division. From what I'd was heard, this unit would deal with what had become an epidemic: organized gangs like the Bloods, Crips, Latin Kings, and Netas—many brought in from other cities—had infested New York's ghettos. Throughout the boroughs, gang "colors" were running deep: their presence was followed by a spike in violent initiations, gang shoot-outs, and, of course, drugs. Nor were their activities limited to their own turf, either; these crews operated all over.

When McCool and I got to the scene of the Owl Club shooting in Queens, we were debriefed on what had happened. During an album-release party for an underground rapper, some guys came in and, following a dispute, started shooting. As soon as I walked in, I saw people I recognized from working the streets and hip-hop clubs. McCool was amazed at how I could walk into a room like this and people would actually know me. Furthermore, witnesses were actually willing to talk to me, while the other cops on the scene were getting nowhere.

The scene was a mess. I couldn't believe how the cops there were treating the witnesses: they'd been sitting there for hours, but weren't offered as much as even a cup of coffee. I told the lieutenant he should buy them pizzas, doughnuts, *something* to eat immediately. Once they had something in their stomachs and got relaxed, I started interviewing the witnesses. McCool asked to sit in on my interview with this one very scared girl; afterward, he told me he was amazed at how people confided in me. McCool left early that morning, while I stayed on the set until three in afternoon: we made our arrests in the case and moved on. That was it, or so I thought.

I found out later that that moment in Queens was a test. Not only was McCool indeed starting a gang unit in the NYPD's elite Intelligence division, he planned to include a specialized, clandestine "Rap Intel" squad within it—led by yours truly. McCool was savvy enough to connect the dots. It wasn't just that some rappers were established gang members themselves; it was that all gang members were into rap. Gangbangers wanted to hang out with rappers; with increasingly frequency, they were emulating rap stars, getting into their world by offering their services as "protection." If all else failed, they would just jack them for their loot.

That McCool wanted me to leave Cold Case and work in Gang Intel riled up my comrades and superiors. When Ray Ferrari, the commanding officer of Cold Case, got wind of McCool's plans, he blasted him for "stealing detectives" to start a new NYPD dynasty. Back at Cold Case's headquarters, meanwhile, Pollini tore into me about what he was hearing.

"I know what McCool's up to," Pollini yelled in my face. "You gotta remember you don't work for him, you work for *me*." Pollini made me feel two feet tall, but what could I do? I was caught in the crossfire of NYPD politics and power grabs.

Despite the interdepartmental friction on the subject, at this point a special unit devoted to hip-hop seemed inevitable. In the spring of '99, I found myself moderating a panel for a "Policing for the Millennium" conference being held at the Hilton Hotel. It was a conference on gangs for law enforcement all over the world—Japan, Australia, you name it. My panel explored how the crime picture was shifting—in particular, how the rap world related to gangs.

Chief Anemone was among those attending the conference. After my panel concluded, the chief approached me. "Parker, I'm transferring you to the Gang Intelligence Division," he told me. "McCool tells me you're getting a lot of flak, and I'm tired of it. Where I'm putting you, you'll work for me and everybody in the NYPD. You're not limited to any person—you can go everywhere and anywhere. It'll better serve the whole department."

I couldn't agree more, but then again, I didn't have a choice: Anemone made me an offer I couldn't refuse. So in May of 1999, I made my way to the new Gang Intel unit within the Intelligence Division. At first Intel was housed in a dilapidated old school building on Poplar Street in downtown Brooklyn that the department most likely got for cheap; after a short time, though, Intel moved to a new building by the Brooklyn Army Terminal on the waterfront near Staten Island. The new Intel digs showed NYPD's commitment to the division, with brand-new office equipment, new computers, new everything.

I was happy about my new assignment, as an Intel post is very prestigious—it's as high as you can get without becoming a Fed. All in all, Intel comprised three hundred assigned personnel, many of them veteran detectives. The mayor's office detail and Gracie Mansion security is housed in Intel, as is security for politicians and judges and all manner of public security—i.e., bomb threats, U.N. missions, and any kind of threat to national security or political hot-potato work. Intel works closely with the Feds, for example, whenever the president comes to New York. The NYPD's Organized Crime Unit is also housed in Intel.

In fact, me and my partner in Intel's hip-hop squad—Kevin Bryant, a short black guy with a background in undercover narcotics—

wound up sharing an office with NYPD Intel's mob guys. The mob guys were very interested in my rap investigations, always asking, "Can we go with you?" when I went into the field. That's because they were on the verge of becoming obsolete: throughout the NYPD, it was becoming known by insiders that rap was the new mob. The traditional Mafia was losing power, while the hip-hop industry was gaining it. And there was a lot of overlap between hip-hop and the mob: drugs, gangs, the music industry, radio promotion, clubs, general gangsterism—even bootlegging. Jay-Z's public stabbing of Lance "Un" Rivera over an alleged bootlegging was a classic mob-style retaliation and humiliation all in one. We had to keep up with all of it.

Once we were situated at Intel, Bryant and I started a central warehouse to keep and store data: an authoritative, in-house database on rappers and their affiliates with criminal records. The formation of my rap unit in Intel came at just the right moment, as one of the biggest cases of my life was about to fall in my lap.

I was home asleep one night when I received a series of intriguing calls starting around two, maybe three in the morning. First I got a call from one of my street informants close to the rap game. An incident has just happened, and once again, Sean "Puff Daddy" Combs's name is involved.

Hearing this, I was afraid that Puffy had been murdered—the latest rap casualty à la Biggie and Tupac. My informant assured me that wasn't it: Puff was alive, but he was in hot water. "Puffy's got a little problem, that's no joke," he told me, "but I think it's going to turn into a big deal. You watch." And then he hung up.

When my phone rang again just moments later, it was Steve DeLisi, the lieutenant on duty at Intel's "hot desk." DeLisi informed me I was to respond to a shooting at a midtown Manhattan nightclub called Club New York involving some big names. The lieutenant added that Sean "Puff Daddy" Combs had been arrested, along with his then-girlfriend Jennifer Lopez. Also taken into custody were members of Puff's entourage, including Jamal Barrow, aka Bad Boy's hot new street rapper "Shyne."

DeLisi broke down the basic story for me. On December 27, 1999, Puffy entered Club New York, located at Forty-third Street and

Eighth Avenue in midtown Manhattan's Hell's Kitchen, accompanied by a high-powered entourage: J.Lo, Shyne, and Puff's infamous bodyguard Anthony "Wolf" Jones. From the minute he walked through the door, Puff became the life of the party. When a particularly hot dance-floor jam started booming through the speakers, Puff exuberantly started tossing money into the crowd. All was well until a patron took offense at the gesture and threw money back at Puffy's face as a challenge. His attitude was like, "You're Puffy? *So what*. I'm a big man, too—you think I don't got money?"

Seeing this, Puff's crew sprang into action to defend their don. Shyne in particular was particularly heated, and a dispute ensued. Within moments, Shyne pulled out his gun. In the ensuing confusion, shots rang out, causing injury to three innocent bystanders (victim Natania Reuben took a bullet in the face). At the first sign of gunplay, Puffy, J.Lo, and Wolf ran out of the club into a waiting Lincoln Navigator SUV driven by chauffeur Wardel Fenderson. Shyne, meanwhile, was caught by uniformed cops standing in front of Club New York with his gun in his waistband.

Hearing this news, I hustled on the double to the Midtown North precinct, where Puffy, J.Lo, Shyne, Wolf, and Fenderson had been arrested and detained. When I reached the precinct house, it was chaos—a clusterfuck of uniformed cops, lawyers, and press reporters everywhere.

All the attorneys for Puffy's entourage were stuck behind the barricade in reception, which was not a good sign. In rap circles, there's always a rotating pool of high-powered attorneys, a colorful group of characters that handle all the high-profile cases; I knew them all. The group collected in front of me made for an intimidating cross section of top-shelf New York celebrity lawyers: Larry Ruggiero, Ed Hayes, Murray Richman (best known as "Don't Worry Murray" for his sure-shot powers of acquittal), and Puffy's initial choice of counsel, Harvey Slovis (who'd just flown in from the Bahamas, cutting his vacation short) were all there. And when the lawyers saw me come in, they started applauding.

"Finally someone who had brains is here," Ed Hayes grumbled. "Let's get this show on the road."

Hayes pulled me aside and told me that the police were not letting them see their clients—NYPD's big fuck-up *numero uno* in the case. "They've been depriving my clients of due process," he noted pointedly. "In particular, they're denying their Fourth and Fifth Amendment rights."

I couldn't disagree, so I rushed over immediately to the Midtown North duty chief who responded to the arrest. He was the highest-ranking officer on the precinct's night watch, the one in charge of coordinating any major incidents that might come through the door. This was about as major as it gets, and it was getting bigger by the minute: the chief told me that two guns had already been recovered—one from Shyne, the other from Puffy's vehicle (a third would be discovered later). The weapons compounded the Puffy posse's legal problems even further: once a firearm is recovered from a vehicle, everybody in the car goes in for gun possession. Now even *J.Lo* had a gun charge (although it was quickly dropped).

The duty chief, meanwhile, didn't know what to do with this motley crew. He admitted to me that he didn't know a damn thing about hip-hop; he'd never heard of Puffy, let alone Shyne. "Parker, you're the expert," the duty chief told me. "I'm the chief here, but you're in charge."

"Well, Chief," I responded, "the first thing you need to do is separate the defendants and allow them to speak to their attorneys. Right of counsel is attached: they can't speak to police at all and their attorneys are present—it's a violation of law. And these are not your regular bad guys, either. These are high-profile people, and you have to let them see their attorneys, because you don't want to get them in court saying you deprived them of their right to see their counsel. You're not going to get anything out of them anyway until then."

As I talked to the duty chief, I saw all the NYPD's big-boss cops come in, led by Anemone. They knew that the Club New York shooting was going to hit the press in a big way, so they were here to make sure everything was handled just right. Together, we did a debriefing, collectively deciding that as Club New York was located in Midtown South, we had to transfer the arrested parties to that precinct. What happened was, Puffy's car got stopped in Midtown North, but the shooting itself happened in Midtown South, so everything and everyone had to be moved back to the precinct of occurrence.

I went to check in on Puffy, who after the Steve Stoute incident called me by name. As soon as he heard my voice, he started bellowing, "Derrick, Derrick, Derrick—I gotta talk to you, man" as I approached his cell.

"Hey, Parker—what's going on?" he asked, obviously concerned. I told him we had to separate everybody and take them individually to the Midtown South precinct. Puff was worried about having to do a perp walk, but I told him I wouldn't let that happen. Outside, the press had already assembled into a feeding frenzy, but I assured Puff perp walks are just *not my style*.

A perp walk past the tabloid paparazzi serves no purpose except to embarrass people and let ignorant officers get their jollies humiliating someone more famous than them. It serves only to convict suspects in the media's eyes before they've seen their day in court, and I'm not into that; a perp walk is no way to build trust with the people under arrest, let alone a big name. If you want perps to cooperate in an investigation, especially if they're celebrities, skip the perp walk. To that end, I'd blocked the entrance to the precinct house so the media couldn't come in.

In fact, the growing media presence outside numbered over three hundred reporters and paparazzi. The media, however, was ultimately more interested in Puff's girlfriend J.Lo than him: they were standing on top of cars with cameras, frothing at the mouth for a glimpse of the infamous diva caught unawares by tragedy.

When I went over to see Jennifer Lopez, she indeed appeared traumatized. I was shocked at what I saw: the cops had her handcuffed roughly to the top of the cell cage. Still in her little club outfit, a long pink coat with fur on the collar, J.Lo was crying and upset—her agitation exacerbated by the fact that her arm has been locked upright in an uncomfortable position for at least an hour. That's no way to treat a lady, especially a V.I.P. like J.Lo. Talk about drama—the lady was understandably very upset. The cops that night were just overwhelmed by J.Lo's presence. As I uncuffed her, a uniform cop got in my face.

"What are you doing?" he snarled at me.

"She's not your problem anymore," I snapped back. "Go away."

I tried to be as considerate as I could've been with J.Lo: she could end up as a crucial witness in the case, and I didn't want her to grow alienated this early on. As I got her a glass of water, I told her I was going to treat her like a normal person, not a criminal, and to that end she wouldn't be handcuffed with her hands in the back. Instead, I assured her she'd be cuffed loosely in the front so that when her coat was on, the cuffs wouldn't be visible.

I sent my partner to Midtown South with Puffy, who pulled his hoodie tight around his head to remain as incognito as possible. Meanwhile, I rolled with J.Lo in an unmarked Crown Victoria; a detective from the squad was driving, while J.Lo and I sat in the backseat. She was very quiet but obviously distressed. And then J.Lo's mother called, which added to the tension. A very heated discussion between Mama Lopez and J.Lo ensued. From the Spanish that I'd picked up over the years, the conversation consisted largely of the mother telling J.Lo stuff like "I told you not to go out with that *moreno,* this *moreno* is trouble"—*moreno* being a Spanish slur for "dark-skinned black man."

When we arrived at Midtown South, Puffy and J.Lo were taken upstairs to the detective squad area: Puffy was placed in a detective squad cell, while J.Lo got a room all to herself. Meanwhile, Wolf, the chauffeur, and Shyne headed downstairs to the cells with the rest of the hoi polloi.

The Midtown South detectives were angered by the Bad Boy mogul's presence; they were grumbling about how Puff Daddy wasn't going to get V.I.P. treatment anymore. He'd been arrested numerous times before, so they weren't interested extending him any additional courtesy. Puff was starting to get a reputation around the NYPD: some cops just didn't like him—they considered him a criminal, a perp, a bad guy "just like the rest of 'em." Puff was nervous that night—he could tell his red-carpet treatment by the NYPD was running out.

My graduation from
the police academy.

(From the author's collection)

As an undercover detective I used to buy kilos of cocaine. This was my very first buy.

(From the author's collection)

That's me playing college ball for the St. John's basketball team.
(From the author's collection)

Tiny Lister and Tommy Hearns pose with me at Jack the Rapper.
(From the author's collection)

As the hip-hop cop I had interactions wi some of the biggest names in the industr This is me withthe famous DJ Red Alert.
(From the author's collect

That's me with Heavy D.
(From the author's collection)

Me and MC Lyte.
(From the author's collection)

Boxing champion Evander Holyfield slugs it out with me.

(From the author's collection)

In addition to my duties as an NYPD detective, I used to promote parties. This is me at one of those notorious events.
(From the author's collection)

My Hero KRS-One.

(From the author's collection)

Gettin' fresh with Will Smith.
(From the author's collection)

The original "Yo! MTV Raps" VJ Fab 5 Freddy.
(From the author's collection)

At Midtown South, detectives were interviewing the witnesses and Club New York's security guards like mad. Trying to piece together what happened, we were asking questions like, "Why were these people let in without being searched?" According to the club's security, it was all about fame, like, "This is a high-profile celebrity—I'm not going to search this guy." In other words, the club proved very lax when it came to security for the boldfaced names in attendance. That was a big problem.

Another problem came up almost immediately. Of the overwhelming majority of witnesses from the scene that I spoke to, all claimed they didn't see Puffy with a gun. The two or three real victims, however, were saying the opposite. Hearing all these conflicting stories, I started thinking, "*Hmmm*, maybe there *is* a problem here." I knew Puff, and while he gave off a little attitude sometimes, I'd never heard anyone say, "Hey, Puffy pulled a gun on me."

Making the rounds, I went first to J.Lo's room. "Ms. Lopez," I said, "I'm going to take the handcuffs off, and your attorneys are going to speak to you." At this point J.Lo was quiet no more—she was really breaking down. "I didn't do anything!" she cried out. "I don't know why I'm here!"

"Ms. Lopez, there was a shooting at a club and three people are shot," I responded. "That's why you're here. I'm not saying you did anything, but we're going to have to iron this whole thing out."

By dawn, the press has pounced on the Club New York shooting story in a big way. It was all over New York City's 1010 WINS news radio station and the New York One news channel, and reporters were calling the Midtown South precinct nonstop. The scene was so intense, additional security was placed outside the station to quell the crowds. Then the squad commander, a lieutenant named Martin, came in to coordinate everything. My job was solely to assist and advise detectives on investigations, so my time was done; Martin was taking over from there. The Club New York case was out of my hands, which concerned me. I knew those handling the investigation were not going to handle it well, as was reiterated when the district attorney arrived.

When the D.A. got to Midtown South, he made sure everybody knew he was there, and that he was in charge. This particular D.A.,

Matthew Bogdanos, had his own agenda. He came in exuding an of-
fensive, take-charge attitude from minute one. Bogdanos had very
specific orders that everyone was to follow—or else: no one was to
speak with the defendants in the case, and he wanted a chronological
breakdown of everything that had happened since Puffy and his
people were in police custody. Bogdanos, a former marine who
would later be chosen by George W. Bush to cope with the looting of
Baghdad's priceless ancient artifacts during the Iraq war, was playing his cards close to the chest because he saw a big prize in Puffy.

Bogdanos may have wanted to be bumped up to prosecutor of the
year, and he may have figured taking Puffy down was the fastest way
to make that happen. He was aware that if he was the D.A. that finally put the evil rap czar Puff Daddy in the slammer, it would
make New York legal history; such a victory could turn Bogdanos
into a celebrity, and prove valuable politically. Giuliani had transformed his successful prosecutions against the Mafia as a federal
prosecutor into political capital during his mayoral campaign, and
his example wasn't lost on Bogdanos. But this was a high-stakes
game he was playing. As rappers were the new mobsters in the public eye, a Puffy conviction could prove to be a nice stepping stone for
a savvy D.A. If Puffy triumphed, though, the aftermath could alternately prove career ending.

Unfortunately, this D.A. was not as savvy as he thought he was.
Before the Club New York case even landed in a courtroom, Bogdanos made his first crucial mistake. Bogdanos initially tried to
make a deal with J.Lo's lawyer, Larry Ruggiero, who was very smart:
he requested that Puff and J.Lo immediately be separated at the
precinct. Bogdanos told Ruggiero that he wanted J.Lo to testify
against Puffy, and made an offer: the D.A.'s office agreed to grant
Lopez immunity if she testified against her boyfriend Puff about
having a gun in the car.

Larry Ruggiero proved too smart, too slick, for Bogdanos, however. Ruggiero agreed to have Lopez testify, but made the D.A. give
up something in the bargain. Ruggiero wanted it made official that
Jennifer Lopez would not be charged in any way in regards to the
Club New York shooting. Furthermore, Bogdanos had to grant her

immunity *first,* without conditions; only then would she agree to co-operate with law enforcement and testify in the case.

Unbelievably, Bogdanos threw the dice and consented to Ruggiero's request; he thought J.Lo was going to cooperate, that she would "do the right thing." Ruggiero made him think that J.Lo was mad and resentful of Puffy for putting her in this bad situation, so Bogdanos released her; it was J.Lo's on-again, off-again manager, Benny Medina, who picked her up at the precinct. Of course, once J.Lo was cut free of charges, she decided not to testify. No grand jury testimony, nothing. The Club New York case score board now read thus:

Puffy: 1 point. Bogdanos: *zero.*

J.Lo was only part of the district attorney's problem in handling the Club New York case. Throughout the investigation, all the witnesses started to recant or to change their stories. It was unclear what was happening. There were a number of possible scenarios in play, all of them bad: the witnesses appeared either genuinely confused, or were being tampered with, or had other motives for changing up their stories.

For one, two of the shooting victims, Julius Jones and Natania Reuben, as well as Puff's driver, Wardel Fenderson, all filed civil suits of their own against fat cat Puff Daddy; of course, a conviction in his criminal case would undoubtedly help their civil suits. Reuben even claimed to place Puffy at the scene as the shooter, which I believe was bullshit. Bogdanos, however, became obsessed with prosecuting Puffy as the shooter; this obsession would, in fact, prove to be the D.A.'s Achilles' heel.

The Midtown South detectives on the Club New York case weren't going to help Bogdanos too much, either. They were good detectives, sure, but as usual, they didn't know anything about hip-hop, and had no interest in learning; I could only help them so much. Detective Artie Cadogan, the investigator assigned to the case, was immediately put off by my presence and started giving me and my partner a hard time. In Cadogan's dominion, we were considered interference. He and his partner Anthony Nardi were two real sourpusses: they didn't care for outside units coming in, and gladly got in my face to challenge my authority. They had all the squad tricks down, like after they interviewed someone, they wouldn't come out and tell me what the guy had said. I mean, come on—I knew all those tricks, too.

At the time, Cadogan, doubting my partner Kevin's skills and abilities, humiliated him by questioning all the police commands he'd worked at. When these guys found out Kevin's background was primarily narcotics, they laid into him as if he was a loser. "What gives you right to be here when you never worked in a detective squad?" Cadogan snarled.

I, however, had worked in detective squads for almost ten years by that point, and the toughest ones at that—way tougher than Midtown South! When Cadogan stepped to me about my abilities, I told him I'd probably responded to twice as many homicides as he'd investigated in the previous five years. When I mentioned I'd worked homicides in the 75th Precinct, in East New York, all questioning ceased. If you came from the 75th's squad, you were a god in the homicide world. "I can't question you," Cadogan responded humbly. "That's an 'A' house, for sure." In fact, I was sure could teach Cadogan a few things about homicide investigations, and told him so.

"You guys are just rookies," I said. "Sit back, and you might learn something."

Back in the D.A.'s office, meanwhile, additional challenges were piling up, making the Club New York case even more complicated and harder to prosecute. Some of the issues were internal. While Bogdanos was very neat and thorough—he had a bulletin board up in his office documenting the case's progress, and his paperwork was always very clean—he was anal to a fault. Word got out that his colleagues didn't want to work with him because he wanted to try the entire case by himself, without any help.

Additional challenges to the case kept accruing. The D.A.'s office wanted to amend Puffy's charges to include bribery and witnesses tampering. In particular, the chauffeur Fenderson was claiming Puffy and Wolf intimidated him; even more damaging, Fenderson claimed they tried to bribe him, with Puffy allegedly offering up an expensive platinum ring and $50,000 in exchange for the driver to change his testimony and not to cooperate with the D.A.

As developments in the Club New York saga continued to amass, Bogdanos became more and more insistent on tying up every loose end. In particular, he was obsessed with finding the guy who started everything by throwing money in Puffy's face. I told the D.A. I was going to identify that guy.

"Yeah, *right*," Bogdanos shot back. It was a typical Bogdanos mistake to underestimate me, as it took me about two weeks to track down the individual in question: Matthew "Scar" Allen.

The reason I was able to identify Scar was, again, my experience in the hip-hop universe. In particular, I'd spoken with a couple of girls in the club world that knew him, including one that dated him. Once I heard his name, I remembered who Scar was, too: a known felon from Brooklyn's 77th Precinct, where he grew up at 802 Washington Avenue.

Scar was facing domestic violence and weapons charges and had a prior conviction for gun possession. And Scar had contacts in the rap world. I was searching all over to find this guy when I discovered his name had come up in a home invasion involving Foxy Brown and her mother. When Foxy's mother responded to her doorbell ringing, two young black men at the door claimed they had been sent by Scar to return some clothes to Foxy's brother. This was their way of gaining her trust so she would let them into her home: they knew she would know Scar from the local neighborhood. That said, police had no reason to believe that Scar was actually involved in the invasion.

With a rap sheet like Scar had, it wasn't too hard to get a photo of him, which I passed to Bogdanos, who was shocked. "Wow, Parker," he said, "you do know what you're talking about!" But then, Bogdanos himself didn't like talking, especially when it came to this case. All of a sudden, I heard scuttlebutt that there were leaks. Someone close to the prosecution was apparently leaking information to Ben Brafman, Puffy's defense lawyer. This was made clear when a fax containing information from the D.A.'s office was sent to Brafman, and then traced to a line inside a Housing Authority police building.

The paranoia surrounding the case was getting unbearable. By

the gist of his conversations with me, I knew I couldn't trust Bogdanos; he even made a complaint to the Internal Affairs Bureau trying to link me to the leaks. He was looking for a scapegoat for the
leaks in case he failed—he could always blame it on the NYPD, and
I would be a perfect target for such talk. I called the lieutenant and
told him I no longer wanted to work with Bogdanos—he was on his
own now. I knew he was looking for a fail-safe, and I didn't want to
be vulnerable to that.

Additionally, Bogdanos was fixated on getting Puffy convicted as
the shooter, which I thought was ridiculous. I wanted no further association with this line of thinking—why would Puffy pull the trigger on anybody when he'd surrounded himself with armed thugs
like Wolf and Shyne? Puffy puts it out there, sure, but he's too
smart to be caught in a club busting caps. I told my bosses I would
monitor the investigation from afar, but as far as I was concerned, I
would no longer aid the Club New York case.

During this time, however, NYPD top brass was concerned about
what was happening at the trial, so I kept getting dragged in. I heard
from my good friend Mike Pacific, then a court sergeant in the Manhattan D.A.'s office. In particular, Pacific told me the big bosses
were concerned about community unrest and riots in the streets if
Puffy were to be convicted. After the magnitude of Biggie's funeral,
they were taking no chances with notorious rappers.

To this end, Pacific gave me a surveillance list of everyone who's
attended the trial. He wanted to know if I thought there was anybody on this list whom the NYPD should be concerned about. I told
him that in my opinion, if Puffy was convicted, then there would
probably be an outcry, but I didn't think it would explode into violence. Then again, I didn't think Puffy was going to get convicted after seeing Bogdanos in action.

Bogdanos, in fact, put me on the stand during the trial: I testified
in the hearing about the rap music industry and whatnot, but kept
my distance from him. It was a colorful trial. Even though Bogdanos
had what he claimed were telephone records indicating that Puffy
had spoken to some of the witnesses in the case, it was no use. The
jury found Puffy's counsel far more compelling. For one, Puff's le-

gal team had been joined by Johnnie Cochran, then a media sensation in his own right due to his successful defense lawyering in the
O. J. Simpson murder trial. And to this day, Ben Brafman remains a
very prominent attorney, and rightly so: he'll take every little piece
of paper you've ever written and refute anything you've ever said.
He's that good, and that was exactly his approach in Puffy's defense.

As such, Brafman and Cochran hammered home what they felt
were the trial's injustices and inconsistencies—like the fact that the
only witnesses testifying that Puffy had discharged a gun at the
scene were also suing him for big bucks in civil cases. Puffy's legal
team then put it into the jury's mind that these witnesses' testimony
was compromised, as they stood to profit from a criminal conviction.

As well, Puffy's legal team took a number of high-intensity risks
that paid off handsomely with the multicultural jury of five Cau-
casians and seven African-Americans. For one, they put Puffy on the
stand, which could've destroyed their case if it went the wrong way.
But for all his arrogance, Puffy proved himself a charismatic, sympathetic, and believable witness; he seemed more of a victim of the
shooting himself than the actual shooter.

With so much seemingly contradictory evidence and testimony,
the jury felt if the accusation did not fit, they had to acquit. For one,
Scar had given two differing, contradictory accounts of the incident.
As well, one of the guns Bogdanos displayed at the trial as a key ex-
hibit for the defense proved more confusing than conclusive: it was
actually registered to someone in Atlanta—but with the serial number filed off. In addition, "traps"—i.e., hiding places—had been
found in the Lincoln Navigator escape vehicle containing cocaine
residue.

Despite the case's growing complexities, Bogdanos stubbornly remained a one-man show. He was going at Puffy's superstar counsel
completely alone; he didn't even have an assistant D.A. working
with him. He needed another trial attorney up there, maybe a
woman—*someone* who the jury could identify with and perceive as
sympathetic.

Bogdanos climaxed his prosecution with a predictably dramatic flourish. In his closing arguments, he warned the jury that Combs must be punished—or they would be responsible for "adding names to the to the list of victims in the case." The D.A.'s moral threats proved all for naught, however. In the end, the judge and jury ended up acquitting Puffy of all charges on March 16, 2001, which I learned almost immediately as it happened.

I was downstairs outside the courthouse at that very moment, and it was easy to tell what had just happened inside. I knew Puffy had beaten the rap thanks to the proverbial ghetto communicator, the two-way pager—people inside the courthouse were two-waying messages to their friends on the outside saying "Puffy was acquitted!" the second the verdict was read. People in the streets started screaming, "Puffy's free!" It was actually liberating to watch—there were hundreds of people there celebrating. When Bogdanos came out, the crowd booed him, calling him every nasty name they could think of. Now that he was the villain, the failed D.A. was silent at last: he just jumped in his SUV and sped off.

Puffy's acquittal just added to his myth of invincibility, certifying his status as hip-hop's "Teflon Don." It was after beating the case that he changed his name for the first time, to P. Diddy, in the hopes of making a fresh start and leaving the traumatic past behind (in 2005, he would shorten it to just Diddy). His beating the case made me think about what they always used to say about cockroaches. Like those hard-to-kill critters, no matter what one thought of him, Puffy was a survivor above all else: he would probably still be styling around in a Versace suit after a nuclear-war apocalypse had wiped out everybody else.

More than anything, Puffy now seemed more powerful than ever. For Bogdanos, the exoneration of Puff Daddy demonstrated a massive failure on law enforcement's behalf: the not-guilty verdict in the Club New York case resulted in making the D.A. the laughingstock of the prosecutorial world, but it was his own fault. He just didn't want any help; no opinion that clashed with his version of the events was given voice. The D.A.'s office had gotten great evidence together, yet Bogdanos went about the entire prosecution solo (no wonder the Bush administration likes this guy so much).

The D.A.'s zealous attitude I believe affected jurors' views as well. Bogdanos was so fixated on getting Puffy that, even with the evidence the D.A. did have, no one was going to believe that Puffy, a well-known figure in the rap community, would pull a gun out where everyone would recognize him. No matter how much evidence Bogdanos presented, no one believed Puffy pulled the trigger. The D.A.'s relentless fixation on this flawed theory ultimately led to the demise of his prosecution.

Even though the big fish got away, there were still convictions in the Club New York case. While Combs's associate Wolf got off scot-free, Shyne wasn't so lucky: the fledgling rapper got convicted and sentenced to twenty-five years, of which he had to serve anywhere from eight to ten. Of course, this was no great judicial achievement: anybody could've gotten Shyne because eyewitnesses had no problem identifying him and, most importantly of all, *he had the gun that matched the ballistics of the shot bullet tucked in his waistband.*

As a result of the trial's verdict, however, Shyne grew very bitter toward Puffy. Shyne claimed he was made the Bad Boy mogul's sacrificial lamb, and that Puffy didn't do much for him in terms of legal help. The conviction did a lot for Shyne's rap career, though—it was the best marketing he'd received yet. Like Jesus turned water into wine, a prison sentence transformed Shyne into an instant Tupac-style martyr, a rebel persecuted by the system. Shyne's conviction provided him with a story, a narrative dimension that had been missing from his persona previously.

Now Shyne really was seen as a true soldier of the streets, and he fed those flames, calling himself a "spiritual prophet" in missives from his jail cell. In the process, Shyne paradoxically became a more valuable property in the wake of his imprisonment. In 2004, he signed a multimillion-dollar deal with the Def Jam label, even though he wasn't due to be released from prison anytime before 2009! The resulting album, *Godfather Buried Alive*—which included raps reportedly recorded over the jail telephone dissing Shyne's new enemies like 50 Cent—alas didn't perform on the charts. As well, Shyne was temporarily unable to profit from the Def Jam deal, as New York's "Son of Sam" law (named after the notorious serial killer) prevents felons from exploiting their crimes for cash.

Shyne wasn't as innocent as he portrayed himself to be—the Club New York shooting wasn't the first time he'd been wilding out with a gun. It has never come out to the public, but I was actually summoned to the scene of another Shyne shooting that occurred earlier in 1999, *before* the Club New York incident—a dispute with someone believed to be an associate of Biggie's crew, Junior M.A.F.I.A.

Junior M.A.F.I.A. were beefing with Shyne at the time, as they felt he was ripping off the late, great B.I.G.'s style. The group's feelings on Shyne were made clear in dismissive, challenging lyrics like these from Lil' Kim's "Notorious K.I.M.": "Everybody wanna shine off of B.I.G./Get it, Shyne try-na sound like him."

One night, Shyne started an altercation in front of Puff Daddy's recording studio, Daddy's House, on Forty-fourth Street between Eighth and Ninth avenues. Daddy's House had off-duty corrections officers in its security detail who tried to break up the fight, but then supposedly Shyne started shooting. When that happened, the corrections officers did the right thing.

They called *me*.

I knew these corrections officers—they were moonlighting from their duties at the city jail, Riker's Island; they felt comfortable with me, and were totally open about the situation. This is how they described the incidents that led to the first Shyne shooting:

Punches at first were thrown between Shyne's entourage and the Junior M.A.F.I.A. crew outside the studio. Everyone then regrouped to continue the dispute in a parking lot across from Daddy's House; that's when Shyne started shooting—and all parties dispersed. Thankfully, no one was hurt. The incident resulted in a little property damage—a car window got shot out—but that was it.

I arrived at the scene right behind the uniform cops. The corrections officers moonlighting as security guards didn't feel comfortable until I got there, though, and only wanted to speak with me; with me, they were cooperative and tried to help as best they could. Then the uniform duty captain at the scene asked the guard where he worked. He identified himself as a Riker's corrections officer. The guard was a straight shooter, but this duty captain decided to burn him anyway. The captain made a moral judgment: he figured, "What is this *cop* doing working for Puffy, who's an enemy of the police?" The duty captain wanted the corrections officers to notify their bosses that they were was employed by Puffy. I felt that wasn't necessary, but the duty captain wasn't going to just let this go.

The duty captain put a notification in to the inspector general's office, which is the equivalent of Internal Affairs for prison police. The I.G. then called in the corrections officer from the Shyne shooting because he didn't have his off-duty employment application properly filed. Then everything snowballed.

Once the Corrections Department learned they had officers working for rap acts like Puffy, I found myself fielding calls from Commissioner Michael Caruso of the I.G. office; Caruso also called my commanding officer at Intel, John Odermatt, wanting to know if other correction officers were working in the rap industry— regardless of whether they'd properly filed their moonlighting applications or not. In particular, he wanted me to supply a list of every NYPD and corrections officer moonlighting in the hip-hop world.

What made Caruso's request problematic to me was the fact that they weren't able to read the shades of gray between the lines. This wasn't the corruption-infested LAPD for one—this was the NYPD. I knew most of the officers that worked as bodyguards and security for rappers, and, while a bad apple would reveal itself from time to time, they were for the most part good men just trying to add to their paycheck. But more important, they were valuable as potential sources within the rap industry, or as even just another set of eyes coming from a more rational point of view, as the officers in the Shyne incident proved. Often they had useful information, and sometimes prevented crimes from happening just by their legitimate presence.

When the incident at Club New York went down, there was a corrections officer involved who I knew personally and helped me out with my investigations. His open cooperation could've gone another way if he'd felt persecuted by his peers in law enforcement; otherwise, he might've just kept what he knew to himself. Going after guys like him would just alienate key sources within law enforcement. Therefore, when the I.G. guy asked me for the list of NYPD and corrections officers working in the music industry, I turned him down with a flat "no."

The I.G. didn't stop there, though. They even contacted Billy Tartaglia, my section captain. The I.G. inspector told Tartaglia he wanted to know who Derrick Parker knew—especially any corrections officers who had helped in my prior investigations. When Tartaglia questioned me about this, I hit him with the truth.

"These are not informants," I said, "but *law-enforcement officers.* If I expose them for no reason other than that they've worked with rappers, then it would only hinder us in future investigations. It would certainly put me in an awkward position if I needed help from these guys in the future."

I knew a lot about law-enforcement guys running around with rap guys, and I didn't want to burn them. If I did, I'd be branded a rat and these guys would never talk to me again. I'd also noticed that, nine times out of ten, if an off-duty officer was present at a rap-related incident, he would tell you straight up if it was just some bullshit or something real you should be concerned with.

"I refuse to give them up," I concluded to Tartaglia, "because they did *nothing wrong.*" My proof involved a shooting up in Harlem, where the driver of Bad Boy producer Mario Winans was involved with a vehicle licensed to Puffy's Bad Boy Entertainment company. Winan's driver got into a family dispute where shots were fired by some unknown person, and he departed the scene in an SUV registered to Bad Boy. There was a corrections officer with the driver who didn't know what was going on, and inadvertently got caught up in the aftermath.

The detective squad of the 28th Precinct in Harlem had the case, and as I was to be informed of all rap-related incidents, they notified me immediately. I went uptown to Harlem, where the lieutenant briefed me on the situation. He didn't have much: no witnesses were talking to him, so there wasn't anything to go on.

Then I spoke to another corrections officer who also worked for

Puffy's security team: first I explained the situation, then brought the lieutenant into it. This corrections officer told me, "Derrick, the police are putting pressure on my guy and he didn't do anything. He doesn't have to talk, so they can wait until a corrections superior, or union delegate, comes down—or they can wait until it goes to court. They need to follow proper protocol."

I then switched the conversation to the lieutenant. "Are you looking to arrest the corrections officer for the assault?" I asked him. The lieutenant responded no, explaining that he was a fair man and understood what was going on. "I don't believe the corrections officer had anything to do with the dispute, but I have to find out the truth," the lieutenant told me. "I need his story and I don't want to wait until he goes into the system."

Because of the Bad Boy/Puffy connection, there would be pressure on the precinct coming from downtown top brass to handle the case's business immediately, making it bigger than it needed to be. I told the lieutenant I can probably get the corrections guy who was moonlighting as Bad Boy security to talk. I then made his corrections superiors assure me that if I can get him to talk and clear the matter up, we won't violate his rights. The corrections superior grudgingly agreed to the terms: "We'll deal with you, but we don't trust them." The corrections officer ended up telling me everything, which led to his case being severed. It was determined through an investigation that he wasn't involved in the dispute—and neither was Bad Boy. Thankfully, I'd averted another public-relations disaster involving Puffy and the NYPD.

Regardless of my reasoning, my refusal to cooperate against my fellow officers enraged the I.G. further, so they started going after corrections officers on their own. They were out to get a friend of mine who was working as the lead corrections officer moonlighting for Puffy's security detail: he was to be made an example of. The I.G. inspector told this guy that, even though all his official moonlighting paperwork was legit, he was forbidden to go to Puffy's office. If anything happened while he was working with Puffy, then I.G. didn't want the Corrections Department attached to the incident. The corrections officer agreed to the conditions, but when he went to Puffy's office to pick up his final check and personal effects, the I.G. was there watching. He was subsequently disciplined and left the force. (Once he left the department, this same officer started working for Irv Gotti, the embattled founder of Murder Inc. He was also instrumental in getting me hooked up to do security with Murder Inc. when I myself departed the NYPD in 2002.)

Not all NYPD guys working for rappers always did the right thing, however. One time around '97 or '98, Busta Rhymes got pulled over in car stop, and the officers on the scene discovered a gun in his limo. Also present were two NYPD guys moonlighting as security for Busta; they were from the 67th Precinct in East Flatbush, Brooklyn.

These officers from the 67th were moonlighting legitimately—all their paperwork was in order. The problem was, the lieutenant and commanding officer of the 67th squad, Vincent Didonato, was already touchy on the subject. He felt that having his people working for Busta Rhymes could open his precinct up to unnecessary exposure. Lieutenant Didonato didn't want to be embarrassed if they were present at an incident. Didonato had several problems with the situation: for one, he suspected that Busta smoked marijuana, say, and he didn't want anyone from the his precinct present not doing anything about it.

"Do you think I don't know Busta might be smoking weed and my guys could be with him and something could come back to embarrass me?" he asked me. Instead, guys from the 67th embarrassed him with a rap-related gun charge.

The two guys from the 67th were in the car the day when Busta got busted with his gun. These plainclothes cops made their mistake the minute they vouched for Busta. They said to the cops that stopped vehicle, "Hey, we're on the *job*"—i.e., "While you think this guy you think is a criminal, he's actually with an NYPD guy, so everything is cool. Please move on."

The cops at the scene knew Busta had a gun, however, and weren't going to let that fly. The captain present told Busta's cop pals to stay out of it, but they persisted: "Busta's a good guy, we all work for him," yadda yadda. The cops got pissed that other cops were trying to intervene for a rapper on a gun charge, so they went straight to

the 67th guys' inspector. The inspector next called their commanding officer, and they got in a lot of trouble.

With more and more officers working in security for rappers, and
more and more criminal incidents involving hip-hop, the pressure
from I.G. to reveal rap moonlighters never let up on me, but actually
increased: the drive to rout out corrections officers working for rappers turned into a full-on witch hunt. I.G. even threatened to start
putting pressure on the police commissioner's office to force me to
give them the names and information that I.G. wants.

I beat I.G. to the punch, however. I called my best friend LaTonya
Meeks: at the time, she was the executive assistant to Police Commissioner Bernard Kerik, who had replaced Safir in 2000. I told
about her my situation, and she communicated my feelings to
Kerik, who told the I.G. in no uncertain terms to *back off.*

Kerik squashed the whole thing, but in a sense his action came
too late. By now the paranoia about hip-hop crime begat by the Club
New York case had permeated throughout the entire NYPD. Detectives even thought *I* was going around trying to find cops working
for rappers; a detective in the 67th queried a friend of mine behind
my back to see if that was the case.

Within the department, the idea was that higher-ups were trying
to purge hip-hop of the NYPD element, and vice versa—even if it
was legal and on the books. I had hoped to mediate and to stem such
destructive behavior within the department, but it was getting
harder and harder to do so. There weren't many people the NYPD
on its own could reach out to at, say, record companies, or in the
seamier sides of the music industry connected to the streets. My job
was to reach out to people that were unreachable, and the NYPD
was just making my job harder.

Trust was deteriorating both within the NYPD and on the street.
Internal Affairs was more curious than ever about the seemingly
close relationships some officers had within the hip-hop world. A
new rule was instituted as a result of all this intrigue: if you worked
for the NYPD and you were caught working for rappers, you would
be disciplined.

By this time, the rap patrol was a real thing in the NYPD: there were officers out there just waiting for rappers to fuck up so they could bust them. It was definitely there. The problem was, how effective was this kind of effort? Were they a positive force? Or were they just making enemies? Either way, I was caught in the middle, and I refused to be destroyed by the paranoia.

Later, when I retired from the force in 2002 and started my own security company, P. Diddy was one of the first people to work with me. My company ended up working many of his Sean John fashion parties and exclusive affairs, which were always attended by numerous celebrities.

I was impressed with his growth as a person, and his natural intelligence. Diddy always asked a lot of questions: he wanted to limit any negative publicity, and was working to make sure he kept looking good in the public's eye. From what I could tell, he had learned from his mistakes and was largely committed to following the rules. If he was throwing a party, he wanted to make sure the police were notified, and that he had a good relationship with them.

At the same time, being around Puffy's Bad Boy crew as a civilian, I was privy to things I wasn't able to see as a cop. I must say that, after what I saw, I better understood both points of view when it came to hip-hop crews operating on a street level. I now comprehended that Diddy needed to have a certain element in his camp—dudes so respected on the street that nobody will fuck with them. With such O.G.s on his side, he could keep other camps out to get him at a distance. I now believe, and want both the public and law enforcement to know, that when that East Coast–West Coast dispute began to grow, it was essential for Puff have certain people with him for protection. Confronting that hard truth confirmed what I had always suspected during my time running the hip-hop squad: what a visible rap target like Puffy was facing on a daily basis was not a game.

This shit was bigger than the police.

Way bigger.

KILLER QUEENS:
Clocking Hip-Hop on "Giuliani Time"

I'm coming from Queens, motherfucker, carrying guns in couples
And wilding.
—*Mobb Deep, "Q.U.—Hectic"*

As the late '90s slid into the dawn of the millennium, things were starting to boom around the hip-hop squad. For one, the block was *hot* in my home borough of Queens, New York. Several criminal incidents involving rappers were popping off in Queens, which on one level wasn't so surprising. Queens was already a hotbed of both hard-core crime and hard-core rappers.

Queens has served as a legendary hip-hop haven since the genre's birth, spawning rap legends ranging from Marley Marl and the Juice Crew to A Tribe Called Quest, Nas, and 50 Cent. As well, this outer borough has also served as the longtime home to some of New York's most notoriously thugged-out housing projects like the Baisley and Queensbridge houses.

And at any time of night around the Baisley Houses, you're sure to see cars stopped in the middle of the street as guys with bandannas tied around their heads like Tupac lean into car windows to make "transactions." Back in the day, you might have seen the younger, not-yet-famous 50 Cent hanging on Guy Brewer Street, hustling not far from Carmichael's Diner. Most infamous, however, may be Queensbridge, which, located at Forty-first and Twelfth streets, lies in the shadow of the Queensboro Bridge. Queensbridge is home to rap icons like Nas and Mobb Deep—and a whole lotta drama.

Following the pattern of my entire career, I started seeing Queens
dudes that were once drug dealers developing affiliations with rap
artists, funding studio time or working in security or as a manager or
a road manager. All of this resulted in a spike of rap-related crime,
and I found myself responding to all kinds of bullshit. Shootings.
Murders. Robberies. On Queens streets, anything goes.

Indeed, all the grimy reality the baddest Queens rappers rap
about is based on something real—as their rap sheets make clear.
Even the hardest, most thugged-out niggas were targets once they
got a little paper. Around this time, Queensbridge-spawned gangsta-
rap group Mobb Deep, who make albums filled of self-titled "murda
music," found themselves victims of a violent robbery in their own
hometown 'hood when local thugs relieved them of their jewelry.
And while rapper Capone, of the group Capone-N-Noreaga, hailed
from the Queensbridge slums (his partner-in-crime Noreaga repped
the hardcore Lefrak projects, known as "Iraq" on the streets), he
found trouble at Queensbridge around this time, too: the ex-con and
his crew became involved in gunplay at a Queensbridge-area strip
club that ended in a shootout with police. I was off-duty at the time,
but I got a call from the first deputy police commissioner demanding I report to headquarters right away for a meeting with the
NYPD's top brass, including the commissioner himself, to discuss
the incident. Despite the fact that charges against Capone were
dropped in the strip-club incident, they requested the name of
every rapper who came out of Queensbridge. Out of that initiative,
I even created an all-borough chart indicating specifically which
housing projects rappers came out of. The NYPD was right to be
concerned: a new era of hip-hop crime had begun, more flagrant,
public, and brutal than ever before.

As well, this era found Queensbridge's most celebrated rapper,
the visionary lyricist Nas, entering into one of hip-hop's most infa-
mously venomous beefs of all time: a brutal spat on wax with Jay-Z.
Queens has been the home for some of rap's most notable beefs, like
the legendary late-'80s turf war between Queens rappers led by MC
Shan (who threw down with the Queensbridge anthem "The Bridge")
and Bronx bad boys like Boogie Down Productions' KRS-One (who

responded, and I would say won the flight, with the amazing "The Bridge Is Over," an all-time hip-hop classic). Queens-bred LL Cool J, meanwhile, scrapped mightily with old-school legend Kool Moe Dee in another classic beef from the hip-hop history books. But the verbal brawl between Jay-Z and Nas, arguably contemporary hip-hop's lyrical leaders, threatened to eclipse all beef that had come before.

At one time, Jay-Z and Nas respected one another greatly: on his 1997 track "Where I'm From," Jay-Z states that hip-hop's greatest M.C.s are "Biggie, Jay-Z, and Nas." The animosity appeared to have begun with Jay-Z associate and Roc-A-Fella rapper Memphis Bleek, who was heated over a derogatory Nas rhyme Bleek felt was directed at him. After Bleek blasted back at Nas on the 2000 single, "My Mind Right," the Queensbridge king retaliated against the *entire* Roc-A-Fella label roster on the underground mixtape dis track "Stillmatic Freestyle," saving the choicest barbs for Jay-Z himself. Here, Nas took extra care to savage the Roc's leader as "the rapping version of Sisqo."

Jay-Z retaliated in a big way against Nas, dissing him from the stage at New York radio station's Hot 97 annual Summer Jam event in 2001; Jay-Z's other foes (and Nas's Queensbridge homies) Mobb Deep got slammed even more potently than Nas at Summer Jam when Jay-Z projected on the stage's screen a giant picture of Mobb Deep's Prodigy as a youth wearing an embarrassingly form-fitting dancer's outfit. Hip-hop's leaders were now truly at war, and tensions brewed between their rival boroughs, Brooklyn and Queens.

In the wake of Jay-Z's fresh taunts, Nas got on rival station Power 105 and went buck wild with accusations: in an interview with radio personality Steph Lova, Nas claimed he was banned from Summer Jam because he wanted to hang a Jay-Z effigy as a stage prop. Furthermore, in the same radio interview Nas not only suggested that Hot 97 was in cahoots with Jay-Z against him, he implored rap fans to attack Hot 97's star D.J. Funkmaster Flex and steal his chain. Nas's airing his provocations over the airwaves may have led to a later physical altercation between Funkmaster Flex and Steph Lova, where Lova was allegedly battered and strangled by Flex. After pleading guilty to a lesser charge of harassment, Flex would end up receiving thirty-five hours of community service as a sentence.

As it evolved, the basis of the Jay-Z and Nas dispute seemed to alternate between the rappers' involvement with the same woman (Carmen Bryan, Nas's "baby momma") and who was New York's greatest on the mic now that Notorious B.I.G. was deceased. In response to Nas's jabs, Jay-Z responded with the song "Takeover" (released, coincidentally, on September 11, 2001). "Takeover" doesn't just question Nas's street authenticity—it claims Nas has made just one good album in his ten-year career. Here Jay-Z also gives Nas's Queensbridge pals Mobb Deep a further lyrical beatdown, even making fun of their "stolen jewels" in reference to their getting jacked in their very own Queensbridge 'hood.

Nas responded to Jay-Z's jibes with "Ether," possibly the most potent dis track ever. Taunting his opponent with homophobic slurs, Nas here answers his own question about who's the best in hip-hop, putting himself a long side Notorious B.I.G. and Tupac. "Ether" escalates the violence in the beef, too: Nas threatens to "put a burner to the side of [Jay-Z's] dome" if the Roc-A-Fella mogul didn't "kneel and kiss the fucking ring." "Super Ugly," Jay-Z's freestyle response upped the verbal violence ante even more—"I got more shooters in Queensbridge than you," Jay boasts. As well, "Super Ugly" made the two rap kings' beef even more personal with lines directed to Nas claiming that Jay-Z left condoms on [Nas's] baby seat.

During the Jay-Z/Nas fracas, the streets were burning up with speculation; the 'hood was taking bets as to whether the beef would move from mere song to real violence. Thankfully, Jay and Nas's fighting was kept on wax and never escalated into actual violence, but this pressure cooker could've boiled over at any minute. What scared me most about the Jay-Z/Nas beef was the fact that in Queens, beef can quickly turn to blood. That was made clear when rapper Freaky Tah of the local rap group Lost Boyz was killed over a 'hood dispute in his own native Queens habitat. The Lost Boyz were responsible for giving Puffy's uptown '90s jigginess an inspired roughneck Queens makeover on club anthems like "Lifestyles of the Rich and Shameless" and "Jeeps, Lex Coupes, Bimmas & Benz."

The Boyz's 1996 major-label debut album was called, naturally, *Legal Drug Money*.

Legal or not, the group's success ran out, however, when Freaky Tah, one of the Boyz's four-man M.C. crew, was killed on March 28, 1999. The perp, a ski-masked gunman, shot Tah in the head as the twenty-seven-year-old rapper was exiting a party at the Sheraton Hotel in Jamaica, Queens. The shooting occurred around 4:00 A.M. Just twenty minutes later, Tah was dead.

Incidentally, the Freaky Tah shooting ramped up the paranoia about hip-hop within the NYPD. In the Tah case, there was a cop present at the party the Lost Boyz rapper was leaving. It was an off-duty narcotics detective that actually was working the door—but he left with all the other witnesses instead of remaining and speaking with the law enforcement that responded to the scene. Following the Inspector General's paranoia about corrections officers moonlighting as rappers' security guards, this NYPD officer's misled actions at the scene of the Freaky Tah homicide only made nervous whispers around the department even more prevalent. Who, my NYPD peers wondered, was working for whom? Who could be trusted? My worlds were coming—no, *crashing*—closer together.

Around this time, I first became aware of the rapper known as 50 Cent, another victim of Queens beef bloodletting. Before he turned into a superstar, 50 sold drugs, got involved in altercations that alerted the NYPD's attention, and did some time behind bars. But as 50's fame grew, so did the murderous stakes surrounding him.

I was amused that 50 had borrowed his name from a true criminal, the legendarily fearless, archetypal stick-up kid who was himself killed over some Brooklyn bullshit. Unlike his namesake, 50 Cent wasn't from Brooklyn, or even Queensbridge like Nas and Mobb Deep. 50 represented Jamaica in Southside Queens, where he was raised a true child of the streets. 50 never knew his father, and in 1984, at the tender age of eight years old, he saw his drug-dealing mother murdered before his eyes. Regardless, just a few years later, he entered the family business and started slangin' crack rocks on street corners.

All the while, however, 50 nurtured rap dreams, and his skills on the mic eventually got the attention of another Queens hip-hop hero, Jam Master Jay of Run-DMC. Jay took 50 under his wing and nurtured his talent, eventually getting 50 a recording contract with the Sony/Columbia label. 50 Cent would make an auspicious recorded debut with the late 1999 single "How to Rob," or as it's better known in the streets, "How To Rob An Industry Nigga."

With his very first record, 50 was already starting beefs as a way to gain attention. In fact, "How to Rob" might be the *ultimate* beef record, as 50 takes on literally every notable rap artist of the day on it, describing how he would violently stick up a veritable who's-who of hip-hop: Busta Rhymes, Juvenile, Heavy D, Wu-Tang Clan, DMX, Jermaine Dupri, Missy Elliott, Master P, Will Smith, Big Pun, Jay-Z, Ol' Dirty Bastard, Foxy Brown, and Ma$e all get called out. Some get it worse than others: in his lyrics, 50 threatens to kidnap Lil' Kim (whose career he would help revive with their 2003 hit collaboration "Magic Stick"), and even claims he wants to "stick Bobby [Brown] for some of that Whitney money."

While "How to Rob" instantly made 50 notorious in the underground, it wasn't necessarily the best kind of attention. Upon the song's release, the hothead on the mic from Jamaica, Queens, found himself persona non grata in the rap game; many of his song's subjects didn't find "How to Rob" very funny. Heads grew heated, and rappers like Ghostface Killah and Jay-Z lashed back at 50 in song. On "It's Hot (Some Like It Hot)," Jay-Z blasts the newcomer in a brutal verse stating, "I'm about a dollar, what the fuck is 50 Cents?"

On "How to Rob," 50 Cent is begging for someone to call his bluff, pull his card—that's proven to be the defining motif of his entire career. Another motif in 50's lyrics is a continuing association with the criminal element; "he calls himself a crook with a deal" on another memorable rhyme from "How to Rob." Both motifs came together when someone *did* call 50's bluff soon after "How to Rob" appeared: on May 24, 2000, 50 was shot nine times in Jamaica, Queens, outside his grandmother's house.

I got the call and responded to the scene, but by the time I got there 50 was already on his way to the emergency room. On the scene, I met up with my friend Lt. Richard Bellucci of the Queens

Homicide Squad, who gave me the details: according to Bellucci, 50 was in a car when two other cars blocked him, at which point some guys jumped out and shot him numerous times. As well, apparently 50 was not cooperating with the police, cursing everybody out on the way to the hospital.

Lieutenant Bellucci, like any other good detective, wasn't gonna waste a lot of time trying to convince 50 to talk, especially if he didn't want to help himself. As a result, no one ever figured out who shot 50. However, Kenneth "Supreme" McGriff of the Supreme Team quickly surfaced as a prime suspect. 50 himself had similar suspicions about McGriff, and even said as much on songs like "Fuck You," where he speculates frankly about just which Queens gangsta pulled the trigger on him.

In addition to Supreme, "Fuck You" also calls out McGriff associates Freeze and Tah-Tah, who have their their own links to hip-hop. In particular, Tyran "Tah-Tah" Moore has a child with Sandra "Pepa" Denton from the groundbreaking female rap duo Salt-N-Pepa; eventually Tah-Tah was arrested following a standoff with police. In 50's 'hood, Supreme reigned as the local kingpin, with his cousin Gerald "Prince" Miller providing feared muscle. 50 even mythologizes 'Preme's and Prince's exploits on another song, "Ghetto Qu'ran (Forgive Me Part 1)."

Part of 'Preme's business activities apparently involved the music industry. McGriff was down with the Murder Inc. record label, home to rapper Ja Rule; he was a neighborhood hero to Inc. founder Irv "Gotti" Lorenzo and his brother and Inc. partner, Chris. The streets whispered that 'Preme, the notorious cocaine trafficker accused of two homicides, was the label's muscle, their "protection." McGriff was an O.G. so intimidating, so *down*, that no other crew would dare fuck with Murder Inc.

I knew 50 blamed Supreme and Murder Inc. for his 2000 shooting, especially after an assault involving him and the Gottis at a midtown Manhattan recording studio. Just three months earlier, 50 had been involved in an altercation between himself, Murder Inc. honcho brothers Irv and Chris Gotti, and Inc. rapper Black Child at the recording studio Hit Factory. The dispute ended with 50 being stabbed, sending him to the hospital for lung injuries. This incident was the moment when 50's activities became a focus of my concern.

The link between 50 and Supreme was titillating. That an organized crime figure like Supreme was possibly behind 50's shooting wasn't a far-fetched idea to me. The animosity between 50 and 'Preme was thicker than water: 50's mother had reportedly worked for Supreme at one time, and McGriff had been rumored to be one of her killers (a rumor that 50 has always rejected). As well, 50's shooting resembled a premeditated gangland execution more than anything else: with it, I could see a pattern of violence increasing, and becoming more organized.

At the time, 50's shooting had more resonance in the criminal world than in hip-hop, as far as the media or the NYPD was concerned; at the time, he was just an up-and-coming rapper in Queens, barely on the radar, with a rep on the streets from dealing drugs and provoking disputes. His 2000 shooting almost ended 50's hip-hop career: Sony dropped him soon after, fearing that he would prove to be too much trouble. They weren't wrong; even after he was dropped, 50's drama continued, with reverberations of his shooting echoing through the hip-hop world. I knew about beef between 50 and Ja Rule's Murder Inc. crew long before it hit the papers, well before 50 was famous.

50's issues with Supreme have always been fairly out in the open, but the root of the beef between 50, Rule, and Murder Inc. remains more murky. Ja Rule has claimed that this dispute stems from 50 feeling disrespected at a Murder Inc. video shoot; however, what I heard on the streets at the time—and what 50 has corroborated in numerous interviews—was that the beef began over a robbery. Allegedly an acquaintance of 50's stole some valuable jewelry from Ja Rule, and 50 refused to intercede.

Regardless of who put out the hit on 50, it was clear someone in Queens wanted him dead—all of which, of course, became a crucial part of 50's marketing when he signed a million-dollar deal with Eminem and Dr. Dre in 2002.

In fact, 50's first national hit "Wanksta" was a taunt directed at Ja Rule, in which 50 hilariously ridicules his rival's gangsta authenticity. In every interview, 50 mentioned surviving his would-be assassins' nine shots, his videos morbidly re-creating what was now ghetto mythology. He passed up no chance to mention his feud with Rule, either, creating a hip-hop Hatfield-and-McCoys saga bar none that proved irresistible tabloid fodder.

By having a dispute with the high-profile Murder Inc. and then coming out on top, 50 transformed himself into an underdog hero, an invincible ghetto soldier—rap's number-one thug. Like Puffy and 'Pac before him, 50's involvement with violent crime, even as the victim, buffed up his status among hip-hop fans. And it's been a continued, successful campaign: 50's latest album, 2005's *The Massacre*, came shrouded in all-new, highly organized and orchestrated beefs with fellow rappers Fat Joe, Jadakiss, and even the newest recruit to 50's G-Unit crew, L.A. rapper The Game, a discovery of Dr. Dre's whose smash debut album, 2004's *The Documentary*, was executive-produced by 50. That 50 would go after Jadakiss, who also records for 50's record company Interscope, and *his own G-Unit crew member* the Game, showed that 50's trash talk knew no boundaries. And it wasn't all just hype: an associate of the Game's was shot in a dispute related to this beef outside New York's Hot 97 radio station on March 3, 2005, while 50 was inside doing an interview.

(I would later have an odd, indirect association with 50 Cent. One day in the recent past, my friend Glen called me asking for a favor. Glen worked with 50 for some time as a member of his security detail; he'd learned that a relative of 50's was involved in a fight where he and another man ended up stabbing each other. Glen asked if I could find out about his condition and make sure that he was being treated fairly by the police, which I did. I spoke to the arresting officer, who advised me that 50's relative was in stable condition; as well, he assured me that he would be treated like a gentleman while en route to court. This was more of a personal favor, nothing more, with nothing expected in return. I doubt 50 even knows about it himself.)

Not everyone was as lucky as 50, however. During the end-of-the-'90s era I encountered a young Queens rapper named Eric Smith, who's better known to rap heads as E-Money Bags. E-Money Bags had roots in Brooklyn, but he found greater acceptance in the other borough; he would end up working mostly with Queens rappers like Nas, Nature, Mobb Deep's Prodigy, and Noreaga, who dropped a verse on E-Money Bags's track "Thugged Out." E-Money would be killed in Queens, however, his career on the mic extinguished in another gangland-style execution that the borough was becoming infamous for.

From the professionally orchestrated hit that ended his life to his own disputes with "Supreme" McGriff, E-Money Bags's story is very much like 50 Cent's, in fact—except for the fact that as of this writing 50 is the world's biggest-selling rapper and E-Money Bags is six feet under. Like 50, E-Money Bags found initial infamy by taking on hip-hop's sacred cows. E-Money's greatest moment of notoriety occurred when he got into an on-air spat with Jay-Z on Hot 97, claiming a rapper on Jay's Roc-A-Fella label had stolen his name. Jay-Z let it be known that he didn't appreciate this obscure renegade thug entering his spotlight. In addition to a big-mouthed fearlessness, E-Money Bags also shared with 50 Cent a career in crime, having served prison time for a double-homicide felony. But on July 16, 2001, his crime past (and present) caught up with E-Money Bags, cutting his career short.

On that day, E-Money was driving in on 111th Street in Queens Village when he was killed sitting in his Lincoln Navigator SUV. E-Money Bags's murder was a highly premeditated execution: it was put in motion by an organized crew who left ten slugs in him, a group rolling up just like the gang in the movie *Dead Presidents*. E-Money Bags took just one more bullet than 50 Cent, and it proved to be one too much: he didn't survive the ordeal. 50 himself was apparently aware of the paradoxical hand of fate that spared him yet took E-Money Bags from this earth: he gives the deceased rapper a poignant shout-out at the end of his underground anthem "Ghetto Qu'Ran."

Unlike 50, however, E-Money Bags's killers were eventually found. I had an interesting conversation with E-Money's girlfriend, a young woman named Tomika. She didn't say much to the Queens detectives who interrogated her; when I took her out to dinner one night, however, she told me that everybody believed Kenneth

"Supreme" McGriff was behind E's murder, but no one could prove it. Per usual, there were no witnesses.

Then in August 2000, authorities caught a break in the case when they raided a house in Baltimore, Maryland, which Supreme supposedly used for criminal activities. At Supreme's Baltimore stash house, Federal agents discovered, in addition to narcotics and tens of thousands of dollars in cash, a crudely shot videotape. This tape featured footage of McGriff, as well as extensive surveillance of E-Money Bags right up until his final moments.

Authorities contended that the E-Money Bags surveillance tape was shot by 'Preme associate Dennis "Divine" Crosby and his girlfriend Nicole Brown (Brown later admitted that the videotape was shot from her home). Documents included in the Feds' indictment indicate that a C.I. told authorities that Supreme had ordered the E-Money Bags hit, allegedly in retaliation to the narcotics-related homicide of McGriff's close Supreme Team affiliate Colbert Johnson (aka "Black Just") in December of 1999. I wasn't surprised to hear this. I had learned from my informants that E-Money Bags had been bragging in the streets about pulling the trigger in Colbert's murder. I also knew that Queens detectives were all over Supreme in connection with several murders (McGriff would later be charged with two additional homicides).

Meanwhile, I'm continually surprised at what the Feds have been learning about hip-hop crime, Queens-style. Government law enforcement even hoped, in 2005, to pin Irv and Chris Gotti of Murder Inc. to Supreme's homicidal schemes (both Gottis were ultimately acquitted of all charges). In specific, the Feds futilely claimed that Murder Inc.'s record-company executives had prior knowledge of McGriff's revenge plan against E-Money Bags. E-Money Bags wasn't the end of Queens' all-out hip-hop crime wave that was welcoming in my millennium, though. Soon I'd find Queensbridge rappers going at New York's own invincible king himself, Mayor Rudy Giuliani.

Giuliani himself had a new NYPD Commissioner, Bernard Kerik, who was nearly as gung ho as the mayor—if not more so—when it came to keeping crime down. Giuliani's previous commish,

Howard Safir, was a good leader but proved a scandal magnet. Not only did his administration endure some of the NYPD's most racially divisive moments in the Diallo, Louima, and Dorismond cases, but Safir also caught flak for accepting a flight to Los Angeles on Revlon C.E.O. and socialite Ronald Perelman's private plane to attend the Academy Awards; as well, his wife was known to use NYPD detectives on the clock as chauffeurs, which raised eyebrows, too. After all that hassle, Safir—never a fan of a hostile press—was looking to go into private industry to make more money with less public accountability.

When Safir decided to leave in 2000 after four turbulent years, however, the NYPD started buzzing about who was to be the new commish. It was a close race, with many cops making their bets based on rank. Rank in the police department kind of follows the star system in movie reviews. The police commissioner technically has five stars; the first deputy commissioner and chief of department have four. Once you're that high, commissioner is really the only remaining step up.

At the time, Joe Dunne was the four-star chief of the department, and many expected he was going to be next commish. Dunne and I had a good relationship from Brooklyn. I'd helped him as a liaison to smooth out problems between the NYPD and the local black community, whose controversial activists—like Bishop Anthony Monk (who once invited me to a sit-down dinner with Rev. Al Sharpton)—often showed me a grudging respect, despite my badge.

Dunne wouldn't get the NYPD's top spot, however. When Giuliani appointed Bernard Kerik as commish, it surprised many, including Dunne—but not me. My best friend LaTonya was Kerik's secretary and special assistant: she was very close to Kerik—she paid his bills, went shopping for him, and coordinated his schedule—so she was in a position to know what was going on on the down low. Well before his appointment was announced, LaTonya gave me insider info that Kerik was going to be the next police commissioner.

I didn't get involved in politics of the race, but I had nothing bad to say about either Dunne or Kerik. Dunne did have serious credentials in the department, but Kerik already had actual commissioner experience, and could claim numerous impressive achievements on his résumé. As head of corrections, he had turned around New York City's notorious Riker's Island prison; that was something real that Giuliani could use to "sell" Kerik politically.

While some grumbled that Kerik didn't know as much about the department as an NYPD insider like Dunne, Kerik was a former NYPD guy who came up through undercover narcotics. I liked Kerik personally: as corrections commissioner, I had to see him a lot in regards to a lot of my cases. He was known as a tough guy, a tough boss, but fair; I didn't hear much bad about him.

Whenever there's a new chief, certain people in the department who are close to the incoming candidate get excited. They assume they're going to be promoted and taken care of within the system— you know, "That's my man, Kerik's gonna hook me up"—but it wasn't like that as he took power. Kerik was more interested in transforming the department, shaping it in his own ruthless, crime-fighting image—well, his image and Giuliani's, to whom he was very close, and whose needs were never far away.

Kerik's reign ended being very good for me personally; we had a good rapport. Since I had a lot of hooks in the entertainment world, Kerik would ask me to get him tickets for operas, plays, and concerts, and I didn't mind doing it. I had a lot of contact with him; I'd go to his office and say hello when I was at One Police Plaza. He knew who I was, and I could always call him if there was a problem.

Kerik also appreciated my Intel work with the hip-hop squad, which he saw as being on the cutting edge of law enforcement. One day, LaTonya told me on the down low that I was going to be promoted to detective first-grade—the highest rank of detective one can achieve in the NYPD. "The Commissioner knows you've done a lot of favors for him, and he knows he owes you," LaTonya told me. "And he knows that you were on call with this rap industry stuff all the time." Unlike many others in the NYPD, Kerik was beginning to understand the usefulness of my work dealing with hip-hop crime. "By making it look like he understands the rap stuff, you're helping him to look like a superstar," LaTonya explained. "He looks like he's on top of it in an innovative way, and he appreciates that."

Morale was good under Kerik—he didn't rock the boat too hard, but during his leadership one was expected to do Giuliani's dirty work. After a while, you could say that part of the job affected my morale. What I learned during Giuliani's administration was that it would never be easy for me to reconcile my love of hip-hop and police work. There were things I did as Giuliani's hip-hop cop that I wasn't so proud of, that made me uncomfortable; still, I had no choice because it was my *job*. Giuliani was an enforcer, and Giuliani considered the NYPD his enforcers by extension. Of course, one of the biggest crimes that needed enforcing was, naturally, disagreeing with the mayor—or just saying bad things about him. It all came down when I get a call from my commanding officer.

"Parker," he says, "you gotta go out to Queens and deal with the Screwball case."

"*What* Screwball case?" I respond.

My C.O. filled me in: Screwball were an underground rap outfit from the Queensbridge Projects. The group had garnered some media buzz in late '99 with a song called "Who Shot Rudy?" In it, Screwball fantasizes about assassinating the mayor, claiming with Malcolm X–style revolutionary rhetoric that "the devil died, and nobody cried."

"Who Shot Rudy?" became a minor sensation, and a problem for the NYPD, landing on Kerik's desk just as he was taking office. In Intel each morning, we would circulate a press dossier of everything that might hold potential intelligence interest that day—news stories on the mob, on third-world political developments, on the latest hip-hop murder. Next thing I know, there's Screwball in the press dossier, with "Who Shot Rudy?" mentioned in a clipping from *Jet* magazine.

In no time, Screwball were baiting the mayor all over local New York City media, their flagrant behavior irking the boys in blue. As soon as they got wind of "Who Shot Rudy?" NYPD top brass wanted all the members of Screwball identified, with their real names and criminal histories; if they had anything outstanding on their record they were to be picked up immediately. My order came direct from the police commissioner—it wasn't sanctioned, it wasn't written down, but I knew where it was coming from: Rudy Giuliani apparently did not think Screwball's song was funny.

I did some research into Screwball, which didn't prove difficult. I talked a reporter friend about how to get more info on them. He suggested I call Screwball's record company Tommy Boy and tell them I was a writer for a magazine, and that I needed a press release and all other pertinent biographical materials for a big Screwball story. Tommy Boy gladly faxed over to me everything I requested. After going over the material, I gave the NYPD Warrants division all of Screwball's background, everything from their names to the members' arrest histories. Some members of Screwball had been in the system a bit on some drug-selling charges, maybe a larceny. It was all pretty minor stuff, but they had some outstandings, which made them vulnerable.

Sure enough, the next day, the Queens warrant squad went out to pick up the member of Screwball who performed under the stage name "Hostyle": he had a bench warrant for failing to appear in court over a minor drug charge. At 7:00 A.M. I saw Hostyle being walked into the precinct. As I took him up to the "cage" to process him, he was acting pretty damn salty.

"Yo, man—the only reason you're picking me up is because of my song about Giuliani," he snarled.

"You shouldn't be making records about the mayor," I shot back. "That's not too smart, especially if you have outstanding warrants for your arrest. It's 'Giuliani Time' on the streets right now—you know what that means."

In the end, Hostyle was very apologetic and asked me to tell the mayor he was sorry if his rap offended his honor. Hearing that, I just laughed: I mean, c'mon—tell the mayor you're *sorry* for writing a song about killing him? Not too "gangsta" now, are you? Still, the whole Screwball experience put a bad taste in my mouth.

I was conflicted. Was it totally cool that the mayor was using the police department to settle scores? No. Was it an abuse of power? *Maybe* . . . But the guy *did* have a warrant out for his arrest. If Hostyle hadn't committed a crime in the first place, NYPD couldn't have gone after him. Still, I didn't join the force in the first place to do the mayor's dirty work.

Then again, I didn't always have a choice. My spell clocking "Giuliani Time" wasn't over. Another of Rudy's enemies with hip-hop connections soon came up on my docket. Soon after the Screwball situation died down, an investigation came up concerning Khalid Muhammad. Muhammad was a radical black-community activist who was originally associated with the Nation of Islam but broke away from Farrakhan and his ilk; Muhammad's racially divisive hate spewing was too extreme even for *them*. Police didn't like him, either, on account of his vitriolic protests against racism in the NYPD, especially involving police brutality and racial profiling. But more than anything, Muhammad was a sworn enemy of Giuliani's, and he was making big problems for the mayor in minority communities.

The directive to investigate Muhammad came down from Mayor Giuliani's office. In particular, the administration was worried about community unrest involving an outdoor rap concert and rally against police brutality up in Harlem that Muhammad was planning; the event was to feature politically outspoken activist rappers Dead Prez, among others. It was clear to me why Giuliani had fears: Muhammad indeed could be a very volatile figure. He said people should rise up and attack the cops, which turned out to be the rally's theme.

Muhammad sure knew what buttons to push when it came to Giuliani's goat—so the mayor called Intel in on him. Intel's plan called for complete surveillance of Muhammad throughout the entire rally, a covert operation for which they needed the participation of undercover African-Americans. In other words, *me*.

To get briefed, my partner and I went up to Harlem's Apollo Theater on 125th Street, where the planning was clandestinely taking place. Once there, I was shocked by the scope of the Muhammad investigation: detectives were keeping tabs on the activist from the time he got up in the morning to when he went to bed at night.

My partner and I, meanwhile, were to pose as civilians attending the rally in order to keep a close eye on Muhammad. I was dressed as inconspicuously as possible: plain T-shirt and dark pants, but with an automatic pistol tucked in my waistband. I was also wearing a fanny pack equipped with a camera—just like Chris Rock's informant character Pookie in *New Jack City*. The whole scene made me recall Richie Bushrod's stories from his experience during the COINTELPRO era, when he was doing surveillance on Afeni Shakur and the Black Panthers.

We stayed in Harlem the whole day, and it was good thing I was undercover: police were the crowd's number-one target that day. To Muhammad, the NYPD was the butt for all the black community's issues, and not without reason. African-Americans felt stung by the racially explosive Diallo, Louima, and Dorismond scandals. As well, they felt persecuted by the hard-charging Giuliani administration's desire to rub out crime at whatever cost. Young African-American males took the crackdown as a personal attack; inner-city youth felt Giuliani considered all of them criminals first 'til proven innocent. "Giuliani Time" *was* one of New York's most racially divisive moments; I hadn't felt such tensions since the late '70s to early '80s era.

To that end, at one point during the rally Muhammad began inciting the crowd to beat the police with their own nightsticks. The potential for a full-on riot hung heavy in the air—cops almost came to blows with protesters chanting that classic hip-hop mantra, "Fuck the police!" And when the crowd started throwing rocks, bottles, and bricks at the cops, NYPD retaliated with riot gear. It was just getting ugly when I heard my lieutenant yell "Get out of there!" over my radio wire. The lieutenant thought it was too unsafe to continue useful surveillance from within the crowd, and he was probably right.

After the rally ended, however, our work still wasn't done: we had to keep following Muhammad. As he drove away at the end of the event, me and other NYPD officers followed his vehicle in five unmarked cars; two cars were to stay with him at all times.

This was the most ridiculous surveillance I've ever done in my life—a cat-and-mouse game played out on the streets of uptown Manhattan between two obstinate forces. Muhammad knew we were following him, so he kept pulling over abruptly to see how we would respond. The more attention we gave him, the more he would use it against the NYPD: "The police are following me—see, I'm not paranoid!"

Muhammad was being tailed by law enforcement, no doubt about it. The police presence made him seem more powerful than he was: the excessive law-enforcement attention legitimized him and his views, and he used it to his political advantage. Muhammad and Giuliani were playing a high-stakes game of chess, and to us police on the frontlines, we were the pawns.

Still, it was cool to go up to Harlem that day. I've always loved Harlem—the stores, the people filling the busy streets, the overwhelming heritage of African-American culture permeating the atmosphere. Harlem always feels nostalgic for me; my grandfather was a performer at the legendary Apollo in Harlem's heyday, after all. At first when I was asked to participate in the Muhammad investigation, I didn't have a personal stake in it; there was a job to do, and I knew I'd make a lot of overtime cash. As I was there, however, the reality of what was happening around me started to nag at me: here I am, in the capital of African-American culture, chasing around other African-Americans.

The cruel irony wasn't lost on me. The Muhammad investigation ultimately didn't amount to much, a trend I discovered was becoming all too common when it came to rap-related investigations. I was beginning to question the NYPD's real commitment to constructively and effectively fighting crime within the hip-hop community. Was going after people like Screwball and Khalid Muhammad an abuse of power that threatened those citizens' civil rights as COINTELPRO had, or were those men truly public dangers? Did the NYPD really want justice—or did it just want to serve its own increasingly politicized needs?

At the same time such doubt was seeding in my mind, things were heating up on the streets—more and more cases were going Federal, but too many of them ended up going nowhere, putting potential criminals back on the street. In the middle of this confusion, I found myself returning back to the bloodiest borough, Brooklyn, for the most shocking and complex case my hip-hop squad would take on yet.

And would lose . . .

10

BACK TO BROOKLYN:
Losing the "Commission"—
The Ones That Got Away

In the Commission, you ask for permission to hit 'em.
—Notorious B.I.G. verse from "Victory" by Puff Daddy

B Y 2001, it was open season on rappers. It was possibly the worst epidemic of hip-hop crime yet, and this time, the rot was coming from the *inside*. Indeed, no rapper was safe on the streets, as I learned when I commenced on what would eventually be known as the Commission Case. It was labeled "Commission" because of some crucial lingo dropped in the jailhouse confession that got the case rolling. The case involved an organized band of individuals allegedly performing robberies on rappers, which frequently escalated to violence. This crew was known alternately as G-Squad, or BGS (for Brevoort G-Squad); however, this grimy group of Brooklyn thugs was best known on the streets and to law enforcement simply as the Commission, a name taken from the crew's slang—as in "I'm going to go out and commission shit," as if each robbery was a commissioned job. What was interesting about the case was that not only did it include big names from the rap game, it also concerned *future* hip-hop idols who hadn't yet graduated from the school of hard knocks into fame.

The boys in the Commission crew—many of them just high-school age—were an all-star team of junior criminals culled from Brooklyn's most dangerous housing projects. At first, the Commission acted mostly as boosters, stealing from big-name stores and then reselling the loot on Brooklyn's inner-city blocks. Working

213

across New York City, Gotham's Westchester suburbs, and neigh-
boring New Jersey, the Commission lifted brand-name clothes and
other merchandise from big chain stores like Macy's, Blooming-
dale's, The Wiz, Coconuts, and Coach. Wherever there was fly shit,
the Commission was there with sticky fingers. The Commission really got the authorities' attention, however, when some of them
graduated to gunplay, shamelessly robbing and shooting people in
their neighborhood.

The Commission was headed up by a guy we'll call Da Kommander. Barely into his twenties at the time, Da Kommander would
hang out at housing project basketball tournaments, where he'd recruit and meet potential Commission members, who spanned the di-
aspora of Crooklyn's crime-riddled housing projects: these children
of the streets hailed variously from the Pink Houses in East New
York, the Red Hook Projects, Seflow in Brownsville, Fort Greene's
Ingersoll Houses, Tompkins, Summer, and the infamous Brevoort
in Bed-Stuy, which was Da Kommander's home base. The future rap
superstar Fabolous, who was known back then as Fabolous Sport,
also came up in the Brevoort projects; interestingly, several of the
Commission members reported knowing Fab back in the day.

Da Kommander and his boys liked to hang around black Brooklyn's vital main drag, Fulton Street. Fulton's multitude of clothing
stores, hip-hop record shops, and fast-food restaurants meant a constant stream of potential customers for the Commission's stolen
gear. But that was just the beginning—like many increasingly successful business ventures, the Commission was looking to expand.
Eventually, the Commission had hooked up with a corrupt security
guard who worked with big-name rappers; it was he who would help
them plan bigger, more spectacular jobs. That's when I came in.

The Commission investigation officially began on April 16, 1999.
The case came into being when I got a call from the 81st Precinct ad-
vising me that they were holding a suspect named Thomas Ryan
(aka Booney) at Riker's Island in the alleged murder of a cab driver.
What they thought would interest me, however, was that Booney was
giving up inside information on a crime ring specializing in robberies and assaults on rappers.

Jimmy Kuzinski, an investigator in the 81st's detective squad, called me and said they'd arrested some kid who was thought to be involved in a livery cab homicide: Booney and another boy had allegedly murdered a gypsy cab driver in Brooklyn. Booney eventually was acquitted of all charges in the case, but getting picked up at all was Booney's biggest mistake. Once you get arrested for murder, you go into what cops call the "blue room." In the blue room, detectives know how to get answers out of people; there, this kid admitted he and an organized gang were setting up big-time rappers to get robbed. Booney thought that giving up this information might help his chances in the case with the cab driver. He went on to detail the names, associates, and illegal activities of a group known as the Commission.

After I got Kuzinski's call, I quickly hustled myself over to the 81st Precinct, where Booney was being held in custody. I interviewed him there, where he unveiled with little prodding the Commission's elaborate schemes to rob hip-hop luminaries. It took all my resolve to keep my jaw from dropping when Booney started giving up the details.

According to Booney, the Commission's operations expanded beyond small-time larceny when Da Kommander met a guy who'd worked as a bodyguard for rappers, someone we'll call Bigg Micki. Bigg Micki served as an experienced, Fagin-type role model to young Brooklyn criminals, mentoring his Commission charges in the wealth-enhancing world of organized crime.

I learned that this guy knew a lot about the rap music industry and had a lot of contacts. In particular, Bigg Micki exploited his connections to other security guards who worked for rappers, whom he would pay off to apprise him of their bosses' daily agendas. As a result, Bigg Micki knew where rappers would be hour by hour, which ones were carrying big sums of cash, who had jewelry, what the rappers' security situation was, what clubs they were scheduled to appear at—he could even find out if a rapper was wearing a bulletproof vest on a particular night. Bigg Micki would accordingly direct Da Kommander and the Commission to potential cash-rich victims.

Booney's confession included numerous useful details about the Commission, including the group's ties to the Bloods gang and how some members would sell guns out of the trunks of their cars. But what blew my mind most were Booney's intimate details of some very prominent crimes involving hip-hop's elite of the day.

Three cases described by Booney stuck out to me. According to his confession, the Commission had been responsible for a shooting and robbery of Ol' Dirty Bastard. As well, Booney claimed the crew had been behind two robbery-assaults directed at Busta Rhymes and a home invasion targeting Foxy Brown.

There was another wrinkle to the Commission case that made things even more interesting. Bigg Micki had connections to law enforcement himself. This made the case *way* more complicated. I now had to be very careful about who I spoke to regarding Bigg Micki and the Commission, as there could be leaks to him among my own people inside the NYPD.

In addition to bringing on two more detectives from Intel, the Commission case soon became a joint NYPD-F.B.I. investigation. It had all the earmarks to go federal: because the gang's alleged robberies possibly involved large amounts of money and expensive merchandise, that meant there were potential interstate-commerce violations to pursue. The Commission's alleged crimes also crossed state lines: as some rappers purchased their looted jewelry outside of New York or filed taxes in other states, then national commerce laws came into effect. Because there was a corporate, organized hierarchy to the Commission, complete with leaders and various lieutenants, now you had a "Racketeering Influenced Corrupt Organization" situation, otherwise known as a RICO case. Mix a little homicide in with the Commission's robberies, drug activity, and firearm sales, and you have all the ingredients to cook these fuckers *good*.

Having the Feds get in on the case meant we had more, and better, resources—better vehicles, manpower, money, you name it. The NYPD doesn't have as big a budget for investigations as the Feds do, so when a case gets too big they turn it federal: the F.B.I. only wants to enter in when the stakes are highest and the defendants would likely be doing more time. And this case was getting bigger by the minute: the Commission's criminal activities spanned numerous jurisdictions, which would have involved too many individual district attorneys fighting for their piece of the investigation. Going federal, then, provided the ideal umbrella under which to pursue all the Commission's various acts of lawbreaking.

When the F.B.I. takes on an investigation, they have to open the case in their office and assign it both a case number with the U.S. attorney's office as well as a corresponding agent. My F.B.I. counterpart on the Commission investigation was a black F.B.I. agent named Kendall Hobson. Hobson was the case's main paperwork guy, filling out the endless forms required by the Feds' paperwork protocol. One of my captains would tease Hobson because he spoke proper English.

"Is he a *real* brother?" the captain would ask me.

"Yes—an educated one, with a master's degree," I'd respond. (Hobson later joined a number of other F.B.I. agents of color in filing a lawsuit against the F.B.I. for racial discrimination that made headlines in 2003.)

With the F.B.I. on board, the Commission investigation got kicked up a notch. Our big break in the case occurred when NYPD locked up a kid named Rome (born Jerome Hartman) for holding up a mailman at gunpoint in Bed-Stuy, a crime for which he ultimately did time. Robbing a postal-service employee is a federal offense but is not unusual for Brooklyn: sticking up mailmen was child's play in the 81st Precinct. Once he was locked up in police custody, it wasn't hard to Rome get confessing to all kinds of stuff. All these guys talk—get them in a room and they say everything. It's so easy to play them off each other—they're afraid their "friends" are giving them up in the other room, so they start racing to rat them out first. In all, I completed numerous interviews with Commission members—Rome, D-Mac, Booney, Ra-Ra, and several others—and the facts lined up neatly. In separate interrogations, the individual Commissions members all ended up telling me the same story from all angles.

Rome started by telling me about how he'd become involved with with the G-Squad gang, which I documented in "DD-5s," the official

NYPD case reports. "Every day we went to [a Commission member's] grandmother's crib and smoked weed," Rome explained. "On Marcy Avenue, we'd meet up with thugs there." For Commission member Booney, his entry into the gang took place when "[Da Kommander] asked me if I wanted to be down." According to Booney, the Commission seemed like a sure thing. "Bodyguards for some rappers were down [so] we knew when and where to rob them," he explained.

Rome laid out the gang's MO in ominous detail. "We took stuff and then sold it in [the] projects," he confessed. "We'd sell stolen shirts on Fulton Street to buy sneakers to match our clothes. Every Friday, we'd rob people in the projects, sticking up dice games, [or we'd] rob people at train stations. We'd pull chains on trains [then hit] the Moschino store."

Brand names meant a lot to the Commission's customers: according to an interrogation with another Commission associate, Gregory Blackman, the group went "to [Greenwich] Village to steal Moschino sweaters worth [three hundred dollars] apiece. After, we went to downtown Brooklyn to sell the sweaters to jewelry stores and Arab store owners." The boys eventually escalated to bigger and bigger crimes, however. "We never shot anyone at first," Rome added, "but in 1994 we started shooting people. If someone had a beef with us, we set it off."

My ears perked up when Rome admitted in his interrogation that he knew of a homicide involving the Commission. What Rome and his partners in crime described to me was like a scene from violent 'hood flicks like *Menace II Society, Juice*, or *Dead Presidents*—or maybe a contemporary ghetto remake of *The Outsiders*: when it came to violence, these kids were living the movie. In excruciating detail, their confessions led me step-by-step through the murder of a kid from the Commission named Antwan Jackson, who was known on the street as Indian Boy. "Indian Boy was a bad dude—he'd always stick up dice games," Ra-Ra told me during questioning.

One day, Indian Boy went with the group to steal shirts from department stores. When they returned to Brooklyn to sell the shirts on Fulton Street, Indian Boy started bullying the other guys around. He was the oldest boy in the gang, and bigger, so he felt entitled to take shirts from the other boys and sell them himself, keeping the cash. Rome took offense to Indian Boy's manhandling, sparking a dispute that resulted in Indian Boy punching him.

According to the DD-5s on which I recorded the interrogations, when the crew returned to the Brevoort projects, Da Kommander bragged to everyone how Rome got beat up. The talk got so heated about Indian Boy's antics that someone eventually busted out an AK-47 machine gun. "Rome was a little unsure because the AK was so big; he wanted a handgun," Gregory Blackman explained.

The group congregated at a spot on Brooklyn's Bainbridge Street to discuss how to take down Indian Boy. According to Blackman, a member of the gang was chosen to be the bait. "Go tell Indian Boy to walk with you," Rome instructed the gang member in question.

The murderous plan worked too perfectly. As Indian Boy and the gang member walked down the street, Rome, wearing a black Champion hoodie, hopped a gate and came up behind them. Rome then shot Indian Boy with the AK-47—at least four shots, maybe more, followed by some rounds in the air to clear the street of witnesses.

In a second, it was done: Indian Boy was dead. "I believe I shot him seven times," Rome explained in his confession. "I hit him, then fired four more shots, then shot three in the air. I left and went to Marcy Avenue and told [another gang member] that Indian Boy was dead."

The Commission had to get rid of the weapon pronto. Like a macabre game of hot potato, gang members passed the murder weapon from one to another until it reached Da Kommander. And where were the boys' parents during all this? Well, the boyfriend of Da Kommander's mother yelled at him when he discovered the gun, but then wiped it clean of fingerprints and left it on Brevoort's roof, where police would later find it. "We all leave and go to [a] house on Jefferson," said Blackman. "Rome kept saying, 'I really killed that nigga! He played me: I didn't want to look like a pussy! I did what I had to do!' " The next day, no one in the crew spoke about what happened. But the streets were talking for them.

Indian Boy's murder, however, was just the icing on the Commission's cake. Suddenly, many of my unsolved cases involving high-profile hip-hop stars began solving themselves as new Commission connections were revealed in the group's interrogations, including the shooting and robbery involving Ol' Dirty Bastard. According to D-Mac's confession, he and Da Kommander robbed Wu-Tang's madman rhymer, with D-Mac serving as the accidental triggerman. This was corrobated by interviews with other Commission members. "[Da Kommander] told me that he saw ODB go through the projects in a [an Infiniti QX4 SUV]," Booney explained. "ODB has family in the projects, and when he went to his family's apartment, [Da Kommander] and [D-Mac] went to get guns from [Da Kommander's] house."

Once fully strapped, the pair discovered that gaining access to ODB was easier than expected: according to Booney, when Da Kommander knocked on the apartment door, "someone answered and they bum-rushed in. ODB was asleep on the couch. They smacked him to wake him up; he said he wasn't giving up [his] chain so they shot him twice. They took his rings, money and his keys to the [SUV], and sold his jewelry."

Soon after, I attempted to contact Ol' Dirty Bastard (real name: Russell Jones) to corroborate the Commission's confessions. Through ODB's lawyer, Robert Shapiro (who was also a part of O. J. Simpson's victorious defense counsel), it was arranged that I would speak to ODB on November 3, 1999, at the Target Program Rehab Center, a rehab program run by the L.A. county sheriff's office where he was sent on court order.

In my interview with him, ODB was very open and appeared sober, even though he kept drifting in and out of lucidity. Despite his outfit of drab institutional coveralls, ODB's manic charisma shone through whenever he opened his mouth to flash his full mouthful of gold fronts. Accompanying me was an F.B.I agent, Christine Howard, from Kendall Hobson's violent gang squad; ODB kept telling Christine she was the most beautiful F.B.I. agent he'd ever seen.

We didn't get a lot out of ODB, but he was pleasant enough to deal with. ODB was most helpful in corroborating the events of the robbery and going over details: he stated to me that he was at his cousin's apartment on Ralph Avenue when the robbery took place. ODB was lying in bed asleep when he awoke to a black male with a ski mask slapping him and pointing a gun at his face; he assumed it was just some street guys who got the drop on him, which was pretty much the case.

As ODB and his assailant struggled with the gun, the rapper noticed another man standing behind him, also wearing a ski mask; he described the first of his assailants as six feet one inch, dark-skinned with a thin build, and wearing a blue short-sleeved shirt, while the other was shorter, around five feet nine inches, with a medium build and brown skin.

The first assailant, who I would learn was Da Kommander, demanded ODB's link chain necklace and the other jewelry he was wearing. The rapper finally complied and gave up his $10,000 chain, but D-Mac shot him anyway: ODB recalled taking a bullet in the arm and a slug ripping through his back. When the assault was over and his robbers long gone, ODB drove himself to St. John's Hospital, where he received treatment for his injuries.

D-Mac later confessed to his involvement in Ol' Dirty Bastard's shooting and robbery after he was arrested by Housing Gang Unit: he was picked up on an open warrant for a robbery in the 5th Precinct. I found D-Mac's account chilling and cold-blooded.

"I robbed that man—we needed the money," D-Mac explained. "It was me and [Da Kommander]. We were hanging out smoking blunts and I saw ODB come into the building and go into this apartment on the first floor. Some crack lady went to get him beers: I asked her what she was doing with all those [forties] and she said it was for ODB! We went back to [Da Kommander's] house and got ski masks; one of the masks were red and the other was black. We went to the apartment and saw someone, a female, come out; she left the door open, so we went in.

"I had a loaded black 9mm [on me]," D-Mac continued. "Inside, ODB was asleep. [Da Kommander] slapped him and said 'Get up!' ODB jumped up and tried to grab the gun, and the gun went off. We were about to leave and ODB said, 'Here, take it! Take the jewelry—

just don't kill me.' I thought it would be too hot to take because po-po would be around because of the shooting. But we took the gold chain and the ring and hid behind the building on a roof." The next day, Da Kommander and D-Mac went to a pawnshop on Pitkin Avenue and sold Ol' Dirty Bastard's jewelry for five hundred dollars, splitting the money.

The Commission boys also 'fessed up to Foxy Brown's home invasion case, which had stumped the NYPD. The incident took place on July 8, 1998. A supposed friend of Foxy's family allegedly drove the two suspected perps in the case, Da Kommander and an associate, to Foxy's house to show them where she lived. "When they got to the house, [Foxy's mother, Judith Marchand] came to the door," Ra-Ra explained in an interview. "They kept asking for Foxy, but she said she wasn't home. When they got in the house they put Foxy's mother in the closet."

I wanted to get Mrs. Marchand's version of the story, and she agreed to cooperate with the police. Therefore, on September 21, 1999, at 7:30 P.M., I visited Foxy's home with my partner, Detective Kevin Bryant, and an F.B.I. agent named S. A. Hopson. Mrs. Marchand answered the door dressed casually in slacks; also present was Mrs. Marchand's sister, Margo Berthout.

As far as hip-hop moms go, Mrs. Marchand is the greatest: she's a dignified, respectful person and refreshingly honest. She told us she wished her children would act better, adding that she's not always going to take the side of her children when they're wrong. And she didn't hold back on details about the home invasion incident, either. Mrs. Marchand's take on the events went something like this:

On the day of the incident, Marchand's daughter, Inga Marchand (better known as the rapper Foxy Brown), was dropped off at the house by her bodyguard, Joe, at 6:00 A.M., with her mother greeting her at the door. Having spent a long night in the studio, Foxy immediately went upstairs to her brother Gavin's room to sleep.

"I went back to sleep myself and woke back up about eight A.M., or maybe eight thirty," Judith Marchand recalled. "[Then a boy from the neighborhood] came looking for my son Gavin. I told him Gavin was not at home, and then went back to saying my prayers when I noticed that the dogs had messed in the hallway near the front door. I was at cleaning up after the dogs when my friend Alicia Evans called.

"As I looked up, I noticed this boy [ringing] the doorbell," Mrs. Marchand continued. "I went closer to the door with the phone to my ear. He said to me his cousin Scar told him to return this bag of clothes to my son Gavin." "Cousin Scar" had a familiar ring. Here, Mrs. Marchand was referring to Matthew "Scar" Allen, the thug who set off Puff Daddy's Club New York incident—yet another "six degrees of separation" moment between hip-hop criminals. It was strictly a coincidence, however: the perp somehow knew that Mrs. Marchand would recognize Scar, who had no connection to the Commission, as someone she'd know from the neighborhood, and used Scar's name to gain her trust. "I asked him to pass the clothes through the gate," Mrs. Marchand went on. "When that didn't work, I opened the gate door to reach for the bag, and he pushed it open."

Mrs. Marchand described the intruder as about six feet tall, skinny, with a dark complexion, wearing a blue cap and a long-sleeved crewneck T-shirt. And he wasn't alone. "As this male was pushing his way into my house, that's when I noticed this shorter black male: he was stocky with a wide nose, wearing a baseball cap— and he had a long black gun. I started yelling into the phone for Alicia to call the police, but then the taller male yanked the phone out of the wall with the cord attached and threw it in the corner.

"The shorter male asked me twice, 'Where's Foxy?'" Mrs. Marchand continued. "I told him that I didn't know where she was. He said 'Don't lie, because I'll shoot you right now.' I kept saying 'She's not here,' but I knew I couldn't let him get to my son Gavin's room—Foxy, Gavin, and her sister Shitara were on the top floor. I told him that Foxy was at the studio and that I had been asleep. He asked me where Foxy would sleep and I said upstairs. At this point, the taller male held one of my hands behind my back and the other over my mouth, while the shorter male took off his baseball cap and was trying to put on a black mask. He asked me where the bathroom was and I pointed down the hallway. The taller male then pushed me into the bathroom."

Kneeling down in the bathroom, Judith Marchand was terrified by what she heard outside. "The shorter one was about to go upstairs because his foot was at the first step," she recalled. But moments later, when Marchand opened the bathroom door, she saw that the hallway was dark, her assailants long gone. "I ran out of my house screaming, yelling at my neighbor, Mrs. Toppin, to call the police," she explained. "I said, 'They're in the house with guns!'" Then I ran to the store, and when the police came, both guys were gone."

The Commission's Busta Rhymes robberies proved to be the gang's coup de grace, however. Commission members admitted during questioning that the gang, in cahoots with Bigg Micki, had been behind robbing Busta. All in all, the jewelry the Commission took off Busta Rhymes was worth one hundred thousand dollars. As a thief, Da Kommander was so brazen he would even wear Busta's blue "laser" emerald earrings that were stolen in the robbery.

I would later interview Busta Rhymes himself about his robbery. I met with Busta at the Def Jam offices on Eighth Avenue in Hell's Kitchen, on the building's twenty-seventh floor. Busta was great: even though he had just been jacked for his valuables, he was still wearing a whole lot of bling—and anxious to help me figure out who set him up. At this meeting, the rap star was very honest and forthright: he would tell me of an additional armed robbery involving him as the victim. He stated he remembered being robbed *twice*— once at the parking garage and once at a barbershop.

At the garage, Busta remembered he was with the uncle of his child's mother, a guy named Tony Edgerton, aka E.T., who would also customize cars for the rap star. "I was there for the purpose of using [Edgerton's] garage to store my cars," Busta explained.

"The next day," Busta continued, "I was with E.T. again, dropped off at his garage. I'm listening to some music in the car when I see this kid wearing a baseball cap—he's five feet seven or five feet eight, with a slight beard, rough cut, dark-skinned. He asked me to let him by so he could get his car. As I let him pass, he puts a gun in my rib cage. I was stunned; he thought I was laughing at him, so he put the gun in my face and cocked it. He said, 'I'm not going to rob you of your jewels—I'm going to shoot you.' As I attempted to take off [my jewelry], he slapped me because it took too long. He then left with my car keys."

Busta then detailed for me another armed-robbery attempt on him, which took place at a barbershop on Church Avenue in Brooklyn on September 8, 1999. "I went to the barbershop after E. T. dropped me off at my mother's house," Busta recalled. "No one knew where I was going—I didn't tell anyone. It was just before the MTV Awards, and I wanted my hair cut before the show. While I'm at the barbershop, this Jamaican guy comes in like he's skipping. Then he tells everyone to go up against the wall; I saw this woman having a seizure or possibly a heart attack."

Rhymes described this man as dark-skinned with yellow pupils, around five feet eleven inches, weighing between 160 and 170 pounds; according to the rapper, he was wearing a baseball cap; jeans; a red, white, and blue shirt; and sneakers with no socks. He was followed by a second individual, a light-skinned male.

"I'll never forget his face," Rhymes told me. "He had his gun on me and didn't go anywhere else in the barbershop. The Jamaican guy gave him orders and took my property. I had a fifty-thousand-dollar bracelet on and a seventy-thousand-dollar necklace, and my car keys. No one else in the barbershop was robbed but me; if that's not a setup, I don't know what is."

The violent robberies of Ol' Dirty Bastard, Foxy Brown, and Busta Rhymes just set the tone; with greater visibility, rappers were now more vulnerable than ever, as a spate of robberies rocked the hip-hop world. The Commission's activities against rappers really weren't about beef but all about stickups, pure and simple: these guys were just robbing dudes for their loot.

It's the Brooklyn stickup kid tradition—no matter how famous, no matter how powerful, no matter how big on the streets, no matter: anyone is vulnerable, but no one more than someone that has something the stickup kid wants. And a Brooklyn stickup kid always wants it all, which is his fatal fault: he can't stop when he's got enough, because he never has enough. And in a way, robbery was a way to equalize between the haves and these have-nots. "Rappers are like regular people—they can get robbed, too," Booney from the Commission said in one interrogation.

As such, the Commission and stickup kids like them made it their business to put rappers in their place. Booney recalled going to a party celebrating hip-hop celeb Jermaine Dupri's award of a platinum album with Da Kommander and two associates. There, Booney remembered, they robbed a guy of his fur coat, money, and watch. That was a pretty good haul, but according to Booney, Jermaine Dupri was the real target. Indeed, big ballers made for prime targets all across New York City.

At the time, I spoke with a sergeant in the Midtown South detective squad about an incident involving Alexander Jay Martin, a partner in the hip-hop clothing line FUBU endorsed by LL Cool J. Martin was robbed on Forty-third Street while walking to a party with his bodyguard: his diamond chain pendant, Rolex watch, and diamond bracelet were all taken, totaling in all almost one hundred thousand dollars' worth of jewelry stolen. Around the same time, a guy affiliated with the Commission robbed the rapper Memphis Bleek, a protégé of Jay-Z, in one of the housing developments between Marcus Garvey and Lewis Avenues. Memphis Bleek was there with his boys when the Commission dude surprised them with a pair of 9mm handguns. "They took his platinum chain—it had circle links and diamonds in it," Booney said later. "[They] gave me two thousand dollars after [they] pawned the chain in Manhattan. I think they got sixteen thousand dollars [for it]."

Meanwhile, the Commission remained as active as ever. In 2001, a citywide scandal erupted over a shootout outside New York's hip-hop radio station Hot 97 involving Lil' Kim's entourage and rap duo Capone-N-Noreaga's crew—an incident that culminated in Kim's being sent to jail for perjury in 2005. However, I learned that wasn't the first shooting at Hot 97. The first one didn't make the papers, but the Commission was behind it.

The first Hot 97 shooting actually took place around 2000 and involved DJ Clue. Busta Rhymes first hipped me to this incident—it was him that got Clue to open up to me about it, as he felt it might have some bearing in his investigation. Busta wasn't too far off.

In my interview with him about this shooting, Clue told me that he was in front of the Hot 97 building at 395 Hudson Street when he was shot at by some dudes he didn't know. Clue had just finished doing his radio show: as he was loading up his car with his records, he saw three guys—one with a hood over his head—on the same side of the street he was.

"It looked like these guys were laying in wait," Clue told me. "When I walked across the street, they walked across the street. As I turned around to walk back, I saw one of the guys flash a gun." At this, Clue jumped into his car immediately, not a moment too soon. The shooter started firing at him, thankfully missing any human targets but damaging Clue's vehicle before he sped away.

After the smoke cleared, Clue came out to pick up the shell casings. I asked him why he would return so soon to the scene of the crime. "I wanted to see what they were working with—what caliber of firearms they were using," he told me. Clue ended up finding a .380 shell. In the streets, if guys are shooting a .380, then they are really shooting to kill. After the incident, DJ Clue asked Hot 97 management for the security tape; he told me they refused his request. In the end, staying true to the streets' code of silence, Clue never ended up filing a police report. Still, from my Commission investigations, I managed to figure out who was behind Clue's shooting: I learned from my interrogations that DJ Clue's car got shot up by Commission-affiliated thugs.

This was almost too much to bear. Now the Commission case was going in so many different directions. It was hard to keep track of all the gang's activities—there was almost too much going on with them, and it was putting strain on the investigation. The dam nearly burst when we learned that after collaborating with Bigg Micki to rob stars like Busta Rhymes, the Commission would then sell the loot from the robberies in New York City's diamond district.

In particular, we learned that the Commission fenced their spoils to a jeweler we'll call Mr. Vitae (not his real name), who would then melt down the stolen jewelry. This was particularly shocking news: Mr. Vitae's gaudy, diamond-encrusted creations are popular with big-name rappers, celebrity athletes, R&B superstars, actors, and whomever else can afford such bling.

All of sudden, the bigger picture in the Commission investigation focused on Mr. Vitae. With this new information tying him to the

gang, Vitae became the key principal, the real target, in the case.
This development didn't surprise me—the Feds always want the
biggest fish they can hook. Sure, some street thug got murdered, but
who really cared? Law enforcement's attitude was basically, this is a
kid from the projects—his murder is no big deal. After all, Indian
Boy was a part of the gang: he lived by violence, so the fact that he
died by it was no big deal. In the eyes of my superiors, Mr. Vitae's
involvement in the case was a much bigger problem. After all, it's
one thing to sell jewelry to gangstas; it's another thing to potentially
be a gangsta *yourself.*

As the investigation progressed, I learned surprising key facts
about Mr. Vitae's operation from the F.B.I. Not only was he caught
in an F.B.I. sting accepting stolen merchandise, Vitae was also involved with organized crime and trafficking activities. Mr. Vitae was
also the central figure in an investigation of a murder of another
jeweler in New Jersey, who had documents with Vitae's name on
them when he died. According to the investigation, Vitae loaned an
associate money to open a pawnshop; when he failed to pay, Vitae
put out a "wet contract" on him. A wet contract lets organized crime
figures know that someone is willing to pay to murder a specified
target; a "wet boy," therefore, is a hit man who kills for cash.

To pursue the Mr. Vitae leads, which meant expanding the Commission case even more into RICO territory, I called my friend Hector Carter. Back then, Carter was a detective in the Bergen County,
New Jersey, prosecutor's office (he's now a sergeant). I met Carter
during the preparations for Biggie's funeral and while doing surveillance at the annual Summer Jam rap concerts. Carter said he had an
informant that knew Mr. Vitae; supposedly, this informant could
arrange to fence stolen jewelry with him. This registered informant
turned out to be bad news, however. He was using the Bergen
County prosecutor's office for revenge on his rivals: he'd sell drugs
to people he knew, then call the police and turn them in. When this
informant went down we were stuck about how to bust Mr. Vitae and
make it stick, which wasn't proving easy.

Mr. Vitae had already been arrested as part of a sting operation by
the Feds in which he knowingly purchased and handled stolen mer-

chandise; however, the case was dismissed because at the last minute the informer who was the prosecution's star witness didn't want to testify. We knew Mr. Vitae was dirty, but we needed *more.* Then I found another C.I. who suited our needs perfectly. This guy was good—he knew Mr. Vitae, and he knew he'd buy stolen property.

Vitae's sting went like this. We took jewelry worth in excess of fifty thousand dollars to Mr. Vitae under the pretense it was stolen on two occasions. The sting was a success: Mr. Vitae bought all the supposedly hot bling off us, no questions asked.

As soon as we sold Mr. Vitae stolen property, the Morris County, New Jersey, prosecutor's office became very interested in our case against him. They told us he was involved, but never charged, in yet another murder of a jeweler *in addition* to the earlier New Jersey case; they couldn't prove it, however. According to Morris's investigation, Vitae allegedly murdered this rival jeweler in a hotel room over a dispute. If we were going to arrest Mr. Vitae, Morris wanted in on the investigation.

Me, I didn't want too many more people involved. The Vitae case was getting big—too big. The NYPD hierarchy was concerned about Mr. Vitae, and he definitely eclipsed the Commission case: his involvement meant serious racketeering charges involving big-time organized crime, a much larger deal than the activities of a bunch of Brooklyn street thugs. We had to notify the police commissioner, as there were already two major RICO investigations going on in the rap community: one was the Commission case, and the other involved the Staten Island, New York–based rap supergroup the Wu-Tang Clan. Wu-Tang Clan were being investigated for murder, racketeering, and money laundering by Staten Island detectives, who were also collaborating with the Feds.

Detectives in Staten Island had developed information that led them to suspect Wu-Tang's involvement in criminal activity. There were several murders being looked into in the Wu-Tang investigation, as well as alleged racketeering and money laundering activity involving legitimate banks, record companies, and clothing stores, in addition to firearms and narcotics trafficking. Wu-Tang's empire had even become the subject of a special dossier prepared for the

120th Precinct detective squad to aid in the investigation of a homicide of a man named Robert "Pooh" Johnson; authorities suspected a Wu-Tang connection in Johnson's murder, which occurred on New Year's Eve in 1997. (Ultimately no charges or indictments were served to any Wu-Tang associate in regard to Johnson's death.)

The Wu-Tang intelligence identified the group's suspected ties to the Five Percent Nation street gang (not to be confused with the Islamic Five Percent religious sect) and to other gangs like the Bloods. It was extensive, doggedly detailed research, listing all the outstanding warrants out on Wu-Tang members and affiliated individuals, along with all their social security, state ID, and license numbers, in addition to all known addresses, aliases, arrest records, and financial transactions.

This aspect of the Wu-Tang investigation connected the group to record companies and other businesses in the state of Ohio, where members of the group had family connections. The dossier indicated Wu-Tang's ties to businesses and record companies in Ohio. The dossier also provided graphs of Wu-related businesses and officers, including all the cash transactions and Citibank account numbers of Wu-Tang Management and Wu-Tang Productions: the graphs listed who cashed what checks, providing missing links and key details of Wu-Tang's finances.

With all these big cases on the docket, law-enforcement resources were becoming overtaxed. Therefore, the powers that be decided to reprioritize. Regarding Mr. Vitae, the U.S. attorney's office decided to drop the case against him. In the U.S. attorney's eyes, pulling Vitae in on stolen property wasn't big enough—they wanted him on murder, and if there wasn't enough to make that charge stick, it was time to let the case die.

As for the Commission case, we did more interviews that took us in a number of different directions, but the F.B.I. ultimately wasn't providing enough money for the investigation. The U.S. attorney's office wanted to get at least five-to-ten-year minimum sentences on drug charges and firearm possession. The narcotics element ended up dooming the Commission case. Across the line, I asked NYPD

Narcotics to come in, but they didn't want to put their best operatives on the case.

"Derrick, you want to take all my good guys," the narcotics chief
explained to me. "If I do that, I won't make my numbers." Instead,
Narcotics gave me people with not enough experience in these types
of investigations, which involved long-term buys. The cumulative
result of these actions left the Commission case dormant. It
could've been a good case, but it didn't go anywhere. Even with the
detailed confessions of murder and other crimes from the Commission members, I didn't have resources to put the case to bed.

I was getting increasingly frustrated—I suspected that it would
be more and more difficult to go after criminals in hip-hop. Law enforcement just wasn't equipped culturally or resourcewise to go after these types of gangstas. It wasn't like they didn't care; they just
didn't know how to turn that interest into something constructive.

Fabolous would make something constructive of his career, however: he would go on to become a platinum superstar thanks to hits
like "Breathe." And for the most part Fab has stayed out of trouble
and stayed serious about his career; other than a couple of gun possession arrests, which he ultimately beat, he hasn't proved to be a
real problem. For the most part, Fab has avoided the beefs and much
of the criminal bullshit that often comes with a rapper of his stature
from his neighborhood. The Commission's bad karma would come
back, however, to haunt those in its orbit. According to a statement
from Ra-Ra, on "Brevoort Day," some "little guys from Howard Avenue" came to rob Fabolous of his chain. Things quickly descended
to violence. In the ensuing confusion, some Crip gang members
milling in the street fair's crowd became involved and started shooting, hitting mostly innocent people in the dispute.

Since the Commission case was put to bed, I've even seen some of
the guys from the Commission become bodyguards for rappers and
fixtures in their entourages. They're shocked when I see them out in
the clubs, say, and recognize them from back in the day. I never forget a face, and there are a lot of ghosts out there from previous eras
of my life. Tough guys today are always shocked when I recognize

them and am able to describe intimate details about their lives—
their priors, the year they violated probation, what crew they ran
with back in the day. These are the ones that got away, just as the
Commission did, but I'm still always watching. Someone has to. And
it was just that desire to know all that led to the creation of the
NYPD hip-hop squad's notorious Binder that would prove so scandalous when its existence was finally revealed in 2004.

11.

WHERE'S THE BEEF?:
The Lil' Kim Shooting—
And the Birth of the "Binder"

Never snitch, never send a nigga to jail.
—Lil' Kim, "Notorious K.I.M."

SOME things are just considered sacred—even in "don't give a fuck" hip-hop. Then again, all sacred cows seem to get slaughtered sometime, don't they?

For years, the New York radio station Hot 97 was considered sacred ground for rappers—a bullshit-free zone. There was an unspoken rule in the rap industry: there would not be any beefs or violence at Hot 97 or you'd be banned from not just the building, but the airwaves. Hot 97 remains the biggest hip-hop station in New York City, serving as a crucial promotional outlet for any rapper wanting real success: it's the home to rap's biggest hitmaking D.J. Funkmaster Flex, along with legendary hip-hop personalities and mix-tape spinners like Kay Slay, Angie Martinez, DJ Clue, Miss Jones, Fatman Scoop and more. In the hip-hop world, Hot 97's star-studded roster wields national, and sometimes international, influence. The message? If you want a career in hip-hop, you play by Hot 97's rules.

On February 25, 2001, those rules were broken. This particular Sunday afternoon would see one of the most brutal public shootouts between rival rap crews in rap history play out right on Hot 97's doorstep.

That day was a particularly hot one at Hot 97, despite the wintry weather. DJ Clue, one of the station's flagship mixmasters, was re-

233

ally living it up on air during his show, even more than usual. A number of hip-hop luminaries had popped by the studio to honor the release of the second installment of Clue's popular mixtape CD series, *The Professional*, on Jay-Z's Roc-A-Fella label.

For Clue's show, performers and celebrities were going in and out in a constant stream. Around 3:00 P.M., Lil' Kim and her entourage were leaving the Hot 97 building when they encountered another posse called Murder Unit, the crew built around Queens's thugged-out ex-convict duo Capone-N-Noreaga, who were on their way in. It was an auspicious meeting, indeed.

A beef between Lil' Kim and her rap rival Foxy Brown had been brewing on wax for some two years; the dispute had heated up in recent months, however, after Foxy dropped a raw verse dissing Kim on a remix of a Capone-N-Noreaga track called "Bang, Bang." By allowing Foxy to use their song as a vehicle to dis Kim, it appeared that Capone-N-Noreaga were co-signing on that sentiment; as a result, the group became *de facto* enemies of Lil' Kim and Junior M.A.F.I.A. And when Kim's crew saw Murder Unit, which that day included Capone among their ranks, it was the spark that exploded a beef into a full-on street war.

As the crews faced each other, words were exchanged; before long, the dispute devolved into gunplay. All in all, *twenty-two* rounds were fired on a busy public street; one bullet managed to find its way into the back of Capone-N-Noreaga associate Efrain Ocasio, who miraculously survived the injury.

In the *Rashomon*-like descriptions of the event from the eyewitnesses, it was unclear who pulled the trigger first in the Hot 97 shooting. Although they claimed self-defense, two members of Kim's entourage, bodyguard Suif "Gutta" Jackson and Kim's manager (and sometime boyfriend) Damion "D-Roc" Butler, eventually pled guilty to weapons charges in connection with the incident. In court hearings, Jackson, who wielded a Mac-11 automatic machine gun in the fracas, claimed he acted as he did because "I was being fired on."

These were heavy dudes—and no strangers to guns. For one, Damion "D-Roc" Butler was both a convicted felon and a "made man" in the Junior M.A.F.I.A.'s inner circle due to his closeness with the group's deceased founder, Biggie Smalls. In Cheo Hodari Coker's book *Unbelievable: The Life, Death, and Afterlife of the Notorious B.I. G.*, the author claims that Butler, in classic mobster fashion, took the rap for a 1993 gun charge Biggie was actually guilty of, resulting in a four-year prison bid. That wouldn't be D-Roc's last stint in the slammer; in addition to sentences for other crimes, Butler would also do time for his part in the Hot 97 incident. The 2001 Hot 97 shooting would continue to have reverberations for years. In 2005, after a dramatic, highly publicized series of court trials, Lil' Kim would be sentenced to a year in prison for perjury in regards to her testimony to the grand jury deliberating the case.

The Hot 97 incident sent shockwaves through New York City—even more so than any other rap-related crime within its borders had before. For one, as politically incorrect as it sounds, the crime didn't happen in an outer-borough ghetto 'hood like, say, the Bronx, but an exclusive historical nabe. Hot 97 is located on the edge of the Hudson River in the famed Greenwich Village neighborhood, a tree-lined, quaint (and expensive) area of downtown New York City with a rich cultural heritage favored by fashion models and a significant gay population. Furthermore, like the scene from Brian De Palma's film *The Untouchables*, a mother pushing a baby carriage was nearly caught in the crossfire, resulting in community outrage.

The Hot 97 shooting didn't just enrage the community—it galvanized the NYPD's top brass into action. When I found out about the incident, however, I wasn't even in New York. I was in Las Vegas, moonlighting as security for Dwayne Johnson, the movie star and professional wrestler better known as "The Rock." Sure enough, I got a call on my cell phone from Intel telling me the NYPD's Chief of Detectives is looking for me. When I finally got the chief on the horn, he was not happy.

"Parker, where are you?," the chief barked at me.

"Chief, I'm out of town," I said. "I'm in Vegas. I'll be back in a day or two."

"Derrick, I need you to come back *now!* I'll have somebody pick you up at the airport," the chief shot back before hanging up. It was clear I didn't have a choice in the matter—this was serious: the chief wanted me to meet with the NYPD top brass at One Police Plaza as soon as possible. The Hot 97 crime mobilized New York's law-enforcement bigwigs in a way no hip-hop-related crime had yet. They were spooked, and wanted immediate results, as I discovered upon my return to Gotham.

Even before I get to New York, though, I started working the phone. I wanted to be fully briefed by my peoples on the streets; I needed to know exactly what happened and who was involved before I walked into a shark's den swimming with NYPD bosses. My informants and street soldiers always had better stuff than whatever I'd hear in any NYPD meeting anyway. Sure enough, the 'hood was buzzing with information.

The following day, I was picked up at the airport by my lieutenant, John Byrne, who took me straight to One Police Plaza. John was always a tough cop, but this particular day he was a little nervous. Nobody ever wanted to play with the big boys at One Police Plaza: such meetings usually mean big trouble (and a lot of work). New York cops call One Police Plaza "puzzle palace": you always get stuck with some pain-in-the-ass thing—an enigma, a puzzle—every time you walk through its doors.

John's anxiety wasn't unfounded. As we pulled into One Police Plaza, a car comes screeching up next to us. Inside is Bernard Kerik, the commish himself. Seeing us, Kerik leans out the window and screams my name.

"Derrick, I want those fuckers!" Kerik yelled. "And I want those fuckers *now!* Do you know what they did?"

"Yes, sir," I replied.

"I don't care how long it takes—I want these guys arrested!" At that, Kerik's driver hit the gas and zoomed off. Kerik was *pissed.* Lieutenant Byrne, meanwhile, was shaken by the exchange.

"I don't want to know the brass like this," John groaned as we exited the car.

Once inside, I went upstairs to the thirteenth floor to see the chief of detectives, William Alee, in his office. Bill Alee had worked his way up the ranks to earn three stars, and he was proud to be a detective. I knew Alee from Brooklyn as a captain and deputy inspector in the Detective Bureau. (Alee would also figure later as well in my investigation of the Jam Master Jay case.)

In addition to Alee, I was joined by Inspector Phil Pulaski, a one-star chief of detectives, as well as a third-grade detective named Vivian Potter. Potter was there representing the 6th Precinct: as the Hot 97 shooting took place in the 6th, Potter had been assigned to the case as the area investigator. Alee explained to us that Kerik was personally involved in this case's outcome: the commissioner was very upset not just at the large amount of rounds fired in the incident, but especially at the fact that a woman and baby were sent running to get to safety.

I wasn't so optimistic about the case's outcome. For one, Potter knew nothing about the rap industry. For the meeting, Potter and Pulaski had put together a little booklet on the case: it ludicrously suggested that the Hot 97 shooting was a result of a massive rap war between the East and West Coasts—total bullshit. Visibly skeptical, Alee next asked me for my take. Given the green light, I laid waste to Potter and Pulaski's analysis.

"Chief, there's no 'rap war' going on," I explained. "This beef is over lyrics." I explained how Lil' Kim and Foxy were rivals and had been dissing each other in their songs for some time now: the shooting incident resulted from that dispute, nothing more.

Alee didn't suffer fools, he made *them* suffer—and hearing this, he tossed the booklet back at Chief Pulaski. "I'm not giving this crap to the police commissioner!" Alee shouted. "Get out of here— I want to talk to Parker alone."

I was relieved when Potter and Pulaski left the room. "I hope you didn't believe their story, Chief," I exhaled.

"Of course not, Derrick, but I want you to make your own book," Alee explained. "I want you to put together a comprehensive book on rappers—not just the rappers in the Hot 97 shooting, but *all* rappers and their criminal histories."

I was shocked at the implications of what the chief was saying. Before, I frequently had trouble even getting the NYPD's attention when it came to hip-hop cases; now I was afraid they're ready to push too far in the opposite direction. To my mind, Alee was asking for trouble with this book business, and I told him so.

"I'm not cool with that," I said. "If I made such a book, it could be misinterpreted if it got in the wrong hands. If you were to circulate a book like this, it could lead to internal corruption and major civil-rights violations. People could start going after guys just because they have criminal histories."

What Alee was suggesting seemed problematic on a legal level: in this book, he wanted all rappers documented, regardless of their priors. After the COINTELPRO scandals of the '60s and '70s, where covert units were going after black activists, what became known as the "Hanschu" laws were established to protect minority and political groups from unnecessary surveillance and persecution. Hanschu stated you couldn't wiretap or perform a search and seizure on just anybody—you had to document probable cause; otherwise, you could be accused of illegal harassment and racial profiling. What the chief was suggesting could violate numerous civil-rights statutes and create disastrous publicity for the NYPD, especially after the racially divisive Diallo and Louima scandals. I explained all this to Alee, but what the commish wanted, the commish got.

"Do it anyway," Alee said.

"You know how long this is going to take?" I pleaded.

"I don't care," Alee snapped. "Just *do it.*"

I don't know why I was surprised—this was life under "Giuliani Time." Still, I held my ground, and eventually Alee met me halfway. After discussing the many issues involved in creating such a resource, it was decided that this project should be vetted first through the NYPD's legal-counsel office. Sure enough, the department lawyers said that such a book would be in violation of the law—*unless* the individuals included in it had known histories of criminal violations already accessible to the public. If everyone in this book or database already had criminal convictions, then there was a legitimate reason for its existence, absolving the NYPD of any potentially illegal misuse.

After being given a legal green light, I was on my way to creating the NYPD's first Rap Intelligence Book, or as it would become more commonly known as, the "Binder." Working nonstop with an analyst named Richie Lavacca from Intel, it took me about a week to compile the initial draft of NYPD's first full dossier on hip-hop crime. In what would swell to nearly a thousand pages, I detailed everything from rappers' criminal histories, gang membership, and crew affiliations to what nightclubs they hung out in, what other rappers they associated with—even the studios they recorded in.

When I finally gave the hip-hop Binder to Chief Alee, we further discussed its use and dissemination within law enforcement. Alee wanted the Binder to be fairly accessible, available openly to, say, borough commanders on a need-to-know basis. "Like a mug-shot book," he explained, "but on a higher level."

I wasn't too happy with this. The Organized Crime division in Intel had most of their records sealed, and I thought the Binder should be treated the same way—equally as confidential as any of the NYPD's Mafia intelligence research. When Alee overruled me, I knew the Binder would come back to haunt the NYPD. My Binder got distributed throughout the department, and I moved on to other things.

WELCOME TO MIAMI: BRINGING THE HEAT TO HIP-HOP'S NEW CAPITAL CITY

As 2001's Memorial Day weekend approached, I learned that law-enforcement authorities in Miami, Florida, had been reaching out for my help in regards to hip-hop crime. I got a phone call from Chief Dale in One Police Plaza's Patrols Office: Dale told me there were two Miami police officers requesting assistance in regards to major hip-hop events planned around the Memorial Day weekend in their city. Apparently, Miami PD had heard through the cop grapevine that the NYPD has a lock on rap—as well as rumors about New York's Intel unit devoted to hip-hop investigations.

Miami wasn't alone: both the media—and rappers themselves—had begun suspecting the NYPD had a special unit devoted to hip-hop intelligence gathering. A *New York Post* story by Larry Celona dated April 29, 2001, featured the headline CITY COPS LAUNCH NEW "RAP PATROL." Remarkably, the *Post* got a lot of things right. "The NYPD has a new hip-hop patrol that's been keeping tabs on rappers at their hangouts ever since a wild shootout on a Manhattan street corner two months ago [referring to the Hot 97 shooting]."

The *Post* article even reflected the rumored notoriety of the Binder's existence: "The Intelligence Division is compiling a book called 'Crime Trends in the Music Industry,' which so far includes information on more than forty rappers, including their names, nicknames, and photos. The book also lists the type of vehicle each star drives, what record label each belongs to, and what clubs they favor."

Reporter Celona proved remarkably fair and balanced in regards to the possibile existence of a "rap patrol." On the one hand, he noted the controversial potential of the NYPD creating such a squad. "There's a limit for what the police could use this information for," Celona quotes New York Civil Liberties Union's then-interim director Donna Lieberman as saying. "You can only stop people based on individualized suspicion, otherwise it would be rapper profiling." At the same time, the article quoted an unnamed NYPD detective who suggested the positive aspects of a rap patrol, comparing it to "how we look at other groups like the the Mafia and gangs like the Bloods or Latin Kings. Believe it or not," the detective continued, "it's also for the protection of the rappers, because a lot of times they are victims . . ."

Celona's article even featured an official statement from Police Commissioner Bernard Kerik himself. The commissioner proved characteristically crafty and ambiguous about the existence of a hip-hop squad within the NYPD. "We are not profiling rappers," Kerik was quoted as saying. "We go after criminals, people with guns, people who commit crimes. Some rappers are involved in criminal activity, and we will be looking at them."

At the time, the *Post* article disturbed me. To me, it proved that if the Binder did get into the media's hands, there'd be hell to pay for both me and the NYPD. That's also why I was a little nervous about helping out Miami.

Then again, Miami needed the help. Even though Miami had become the "rap Riviera" by this time, cops there didn't know about hip-hop. Rappers loved to party in Miami. They loved to record in Miami. Most of all, what hip-hoppers loved most about the city is that what happens in Miami stays in Miami for the most part. It's like Vegas by the beach: a naturally shameless oasis of hedonism, where the women are the most beautiful on earth, the weather's great, and, if you're a rap star, you can be sure to find a large number of South Beach hot spots bumping your latest hit. You'd think, then, that the city's law enforcement would be a little more up on things hip-hop—that they might be, say, innovative. In reality, Miami needed all the help it could muster.

Memorial Day in Miami had proven to be a good barometer of the city's racial tension—and hip-hop added fuel to an already cooking fire. During the previous Memorial Day, Miami was overwhelmed, wiped out, and torn up by the thousands of mostly African-American partygoers that descended on the city. The rappers destroyed South Beach, wilding out like the personas they depicted in their songs: it was yet another hip-hop life-imitating-art moment down in Miami.

The impresario at the eye of Miami's hip-hop hurricane is one Luther "Luke" Campbell. Campbell was better known as Luke Skyywalker, the head of '80s "Miami bass" raunchy rap group 2 Live Crew, until *Star Wars* creator George Lucas sued Campbell to change his stage moniker. A big Miami booster, Campbell has over the years become a true entrepreneur wired into the city of Miami, from his successful ventures into raunchy adult entertainment (2 Live Crew's biggest hit was the strip-club perennial "Me So Horny") to other business accomplishments. And on Memorial Day, Campbell throws an annual citywide party that can grow to include four hundred thousand rowdy revelers, all coming to see rap's hottest hitmakers in special concerts and club appearances.

The citywide party had gotten so rowdy in recent years, it had resulted in numerous incidents involving shootings, stabbings, robberies, property destruction, and public lewdness. On Memorial Day in Miami, it was not surprising to see throngs of people doing everything from barbequing on patios to wiping their asses on curtains. In 2001, however, Miami's Memorial Day *mishegas* featured a new wrinkle: that weekend, the city was also scheduled to host the 2001 edition of the infamous Source Awards. Not only have there been numerous incidents of violence at the Source Awards over the years, the event had a marked history in Miami specifically. In fact, the 1995 show, which took place in the city, was the beginning of a series of violent incidents that would taint the Source Awards' legacy.

In 2001, Miami police were afraid that, if something happened at the Source Awards, it could tarnish the city's image. As the event is such an industry magnet, and has grown in stature with every year, it assures that nearly ever rapper of note will be in attendance regardless of their beefs with other M.C.s. This is business, sure, but at the Source Awards even biz has a habit of turning violently personal. Reviewing this info, I started to comprehend why Memorial Day has got Miami so shook. They really needed the help.

Two of Miami Beach PD's finest, Major Charles Press and Detective Mark DeFusco, traveled to New York to consult with me on preparations for keeping the peace in the wake of the Source Awards. In particular, Press and DeFusco asked me to not only advise them, but to speak to their department roll calls and fully train their cops about crime trends in the rap industry. Press and DeFusco's attitude was refreshing, and surprisingly innovative, but then Miami law enforcement was going through an evolution itself, moving into a new era. For one, the Miami Beach department had an incoming new boss named Don DeLucca, a former assistant chief who was soon to take over from the four-star chief Richard Barreto, who was moving into retirement.

When I arrived in Miami accompanied by Lt. John Byrne, we were treated like visiting royalty. Miami Beach PD lived up to their city's reputation for hospitality, putting me and John into beautiful rooms at the Loews in South Beach and taking us on helicopter tours of the city. We were not the only cops visiting the city from other cities and states. Working with the mayor and city manager, Miami PD set up a Memorial Day strategy where other police departments were brought in to assist. We got to know the other officers on the scene when the department threw a beach barbeque for all the outside cops coming in to help.

For me, the trip wasn't really about fun and games, though. Soon after I touched down, I was rushed to meet with incoming Chief DeLucca for a briefing. From DeLucca, I learned how his department has been forced into a tricky dance. Local cops don't want to ruffle the feathers of rappers and tourists, or upset Miami's sizable minority communities; still, they need to know what's going on with violence, and what to do to prevent and contain it.

Tourism is the city's main industry, so law enforcement more than anything wanted to make it a safe week. To that end, I met for the first time with Eric B., the legendary rap D.J. and producer of "Eric B. & Rakim" fame. Eric was there acting as a liaison between the Source Awards and law enforcement. Despite the Source Awards' reputation, he was sincere about keeping the peace and making sure the event went off safely, and we became good friends; Eric's friendship will eventually play a key role in my solving of the Jam Master Jay case.

In Miami, *The Source* was playing its cards right, for the most part. For culturally correct event security, the Source Awards had hired Fruit of Islam guards. The F.O.I. (as Fruit of Islam are often referred to) maintain a calming presence: pledged to nonviolence against their fellow black man, F.O.I. are unarmed but righteously ominous in their incongruous trademark bow ties and screw faces. Regardless of what you think of Farrakhan, F.O.I. do a pretty good job of keeping the peace.

My instruction on how to deal with hip-hop crime hadn't totally sunk in with every Miami cop, however, as was made clear when a local officer got into a shouting match with a Source Awards attendee over a traffic dispute. I was in a car with Major Press when we got the call to respond to the scene. There we were met by Eric B., who was on hand to mediate and observe from the Source Awards' perspective. Once there, Major Press pulled the cop involved aside for some harsh words.

"Didn't we have a meeting about this?" Press laid into the surly cop. "Be nonoffensive unless something *really* happens. Got it?"

Indeed, the feeling in the air that year was that the Source Awards could jump off at any time. All the big names—and bubbling-unders, too—were there. Snoop. Cam'ron. Dr. Dre. Foxy Brown. Rumors ricocheted through the grapevine that Suge Knight was coming out, but I didn't believe them as Suge was on parole at the time and didn't need any more headaches. The only person to really cause any problems that year was, in fact, *Source* magazine co-owner Ray "Benzino" Scott.

We got a call that notorious problem child Benzino has been stopped for racing recklessly down Harding Avenue in a Ferrari doing ninety miles an hour, with a suspended license no less. The situation escalated into a physical altercation after 'Zino got aggressive with the officers who responded to the scene.

It got worse. Benzino next got on the phone with then Miami Beach chief Barreto, threatening to pull the race card on a national level. 'Zino was ready to drop the boom on Miami. If the city didn't drop the charges, he claimed, not only would he bad-mouth Miami law enforcement as racist and scream police brutality, he'd get Jesse Jackson and the National Association for the Advancement of Colored People on the case to boot. I was right there during that call, and I could see that Miami cops weren't about to be pushed around by a thug. "I'm not going to be extorted," the chief said as he hung up with Benzino.

Benzino went on to file a complaint with Internal Affairs against Robert Silvagni, the Miami Beach officer with whom he'd scrapped; as well, threats of a national boycott and protest marches emanated from *Source* co-owner David Mays. The situation, however, climaxed with Benzino pleading no contest to some charges, resulting in a year of probation and a moderate fine; as well, he mysteriously withdrew his I.A. complaint against Silvagni.

Other than the Benzino incident, the Memorial Day festivities and the actual Source Awards finished up relatively well. Other than a few minor disputes, it proved to be a safe, fun weekend thanks to the fact that the large police presence was well trained and well informed about the hip-hop industry presence. Working with Miami law enforcement, I experienced the positive results that can come about when police deal with hip-hop in a constructive and fair way.

Ironically, Miami would prove to be the weak link in keeping the Binder and my Rap Intelligence Unit covert and out of the media. *The Miami Herald* revealed both, as well as my training visit for the Source Awards, in a series of 2004 investigative exposés. I would be long retired from the NYPD, however, by the time the press had outed the actual existence of the department's organized, intelligence-gathering hip-hop squad to the public.

NO WAY OUT: EXITING RAP INTEL—AND THE NYPD

Back in the day, when I first started investigating the links between hip-hop and crime, no one in the NYPD was interested. Late 2001–2002, however, represented a new era for the NYPD: the department's cowboys now perceived the rap beat as a fast track to superstar careers in law enforcement. Following the media blitz of Biggie's murder and Puff Daddy's Club New York trial, combined with the buzz around the Hot 97 shooting, hip-hop had become *the* hot assignment.

To the NYPD's ambitious sons and daughters, solving a high-profile rap-related crime was seen as a glamorous way to move up the ranks quickly. Just a couple years earlier, the hip-hop beat was a slog that required selfless devotion: it was okay for anyone in the department to call me at three in the morning when they had a rap-related problem; I was on call twenty-four hours a day. Now I wasn't alone, however. Other cops were gunning for my spot, and would do anything to push me aside.

However badly the department's new jacks wanted to run NYPD's hip-hop investigations, they didn't always have the knowledge, passion, or love for the music required to get the job done. For the most part, my peers didn't get the nuances and gray areas hardwired into hip-hop crime investigations. To them, all rappers are all one-dimensional—dumb criminals that just happen to be famous.

Case in point: my nemesis Vivian Potter, the detective from the 6th Precinct whom I bickered with in front of Chief of Detectives Alee over the Hot 97 incident. It looked to me like Potter thought the Hot 97 shooting was the biggest case in the world and she might be made "detective of the month" if she cracked it. More than anything, Potter wanted an upgrade in rank; I can't blame her. But Potter's actions demonstrated that when it came to rap-related crime, she had a lot to learn.

Specifically, Potter started hard-charging the hip-hop community, not realizing that this was the exact opposite approach to getting results and solving cases. I learned from my industry contacts that Potter had been approaching security personnel at clubs and demanding lists of all the rappers inside. Hearing that, I was like, "*Huh?*"

One night, I caught Potter in action on the hip-hop beat. During my rounds, I showed up at the downtown club NV, and there she was, standing across the street doing surveillance with another detective, who's wearing a cheap suit; they were about as undercover as Pamela Anderson in the Tommy Lee porn video. When Potter spotted me, she was taken aback, like I caught her with her hand in the cookie jar.

"What are you doing here?" she snipped as I walked up.

"I could say same thing about you," I responded.

I left Potter alone, but this experience was pretty typical. I noticed she was sticking her fingers into every hip-hop case the NYPD had on the docket, desperately trying to tie all of them to the Hot 97 case.

On her watch, however, nothing happened with the Hot 97 investigation. Eventually, it was taken away from her by three other ambitious hip-hop cop wannabes: a sergeant, Hector Badici, and two NYPD detectives, John Bottone and John Keeley. Badici, Bottone, and Keeley pushed Potter aside. In their hands, they took the investigation to the Federal level and succeeded: shooters Suif "Gutta" Jackson and Damion "D-Roc" Butler received prison terms for their involvement. Badici, Bottone, and Keeley's triumph with the Hot 97 case emboldened them. Soon they were to go after my spot as the NYPD's top hip-hop cop.

I discovered that my role in the department was no longer safe in the aftermath of a particularly eventful trip to Atlantic City, New

Jersey. One day I got a call from an Atlantic City detective named Ray Davis. According to Davis, Atlantic City's gang unit had heard about me and wanted me to come down and help with gathering intelligence during a Hot 97 event featuring Busta Rhymes and Puff Daddy. Davis had received word from informants that a lot of gang members, drug dealers, and big ballers were going to be there, and he wanted any backup NYPD could provide.

This Atlantic City investigator wasn't the only one who wanted my guidance on hip-hop crime, however. I then received a call from Hector Badici, who'd heard through the grapevine about me going to Atlantic City. He and his pals Bottone and Keeley hoped to join me. In particular, Badici wanted to speak with Jimmy Cruz, then an executive at Def Jam Records, in regarding one of his investigations (today Cruz is part of 50 Cent's heavy-hitting management team). I told Badici I had no problem with him and his crew tagging along.

The Atlantic City Hot 97 concert proceeded without incident—or so it seemed at first. I introduced Ray Davis to Puffy and Busta Rhymes, and everybody got what they need. I brought my brother Ralph along with me, too; I figured Ralph might enjoy the event— Ralph works in the computer division for New York's Board of Education, and he doesn't get to go out to this kind of event too often. Mild-mannered Ralph, however, would become the billy club that my competitors in the NYPD would use to try to beat me out of the department.

Soon after I returned to New York, I was surprised to find myself in the whirlwind of scandal. The Internal Affairs Bureau contacted me soon after to explain that I was now the subject of an investigation into potential misconduct. Badici, had made allegations to the I.A.B. that my brother Ralph was falsely claiming he was an NYPD cop during the Atlantic City Hot 97 event. As well, there was an allegation from Matthew Bogdanos that I might have been involved with leaks during the Club New York trial.

At first, I was shocked to learn that people were out to get me. But then again, I was also confident, because I knew I had done nothing wrong. Bogdanos's leak allegation stemmed from the fact that Puff Daddy's lawyer, Ben Brafman, received a fax copy of a restricted

NYPD DD-5 report relevant to the case. However, the evidence about just who Brafman got the fax from points away from me: the fax had been traced to a fax machine within the housing bureau, to which I don't have access. As for the allegations that my brother Ralph falsely represented himself as law enforcement, that was just dead wrong. Ralph was as straight of an arrow as they come—cleaner than clean; he would never do that, and I was confident that eyewitnesses would back up my version of the events. The campaign against me worked all too well, however, even before I was given the chance to present my case.

Apparently the NYPD considered me guilty until proven innocent. Intel was concerned now that Internal Affairs was investigating me, so they transferred me to the 70th Precinct. I was pissed at how this was being handled—furious that my Intel superiors believed Hector Badici over *me*, their loyal soldier.

Badici had the ear of some influential people in the NYPD like John Cutter, the one-star Deputy Chief of the Intel criminal section. Suddenly, my peers were openly questioning my true allegiances, asking, "How close to these rappers is this guy *really?*" I also found out Internal Affairs was sniffing around in Atlantic City, asking cops there if my brother Ralph identified himself as a law-enforcement officer. As the investigation against me progressed, however, I believed that I.A.B. wasn't that interested in getting the full story.

For me, enough was enough; I refused to be persecuted when I'd done nothing wrong—especially after selflessly devoting two decades of my life to fighting crime. Therefore, once I transferred to the 70th squad, I decided I was going to retire from the NYPD as soon as possible. By this time it was November 2001, and I'd be eligible to retire in January 2002.

I worked in the 70th Precinct for about six weeks: mostly during my time there, I taught the detective squad everything I knew about how to close cases. The 70th's lieutenant was nice: he asked me to stay on, but I didn't feel like I could achieve much more there. For one, I felt alone in the department, caught out there; I still held some measure of power, but it wasn't the same as before. That was because most of my big-time backers had exited out of One Police Plaza themselves: Anemone had transferred to the Manhattan Transit Authority, while Norris went to work in Maryland.

Amidst the heavy shelling, though, I still had my boosters, and as word of my retirement circulated around the NYPD, they all came out of the woodwork to talk me out of my decision. Ferrari called, telling me I could come back to Cold Case if I wanted to. And when my union delegate from the Detective Endowment Association got wind of what happened, he let me know just how pissed he was about my situation.

"This is *bullshit*," the delegate exclaimed. "Everybody heard about this, and we all think it's bullshit."

Lieutenant Alfred King in the 60th Precinct let me know that he wanted me for Brooklyn South's homicide division. When we met to discuss his recruitment efforts, he very kindly told me how he felt I was a "great asset" to the NYPD. As we talked, King opened up about a traumatic event in his NYPD career that related to my current situation.

"Derrick, don't be upset and retire angry," King advised. "They tried to get me once, too—on a D.W.I. charge. I got through that, so you can get through this."

No one could do much to convince me to stay, however. In the end, a few more years of swimming with sharks and not being able to get done what I needed to get done just didn't hold that much appeal for me. People all around me were trying to get ahead, and I was becoming a target. At this point in my career, I was ranked a first-grade detective; I couldn't get much higher in the NYPD unless I went the management route.

As well, the department was going through big changes because of radical changes in society: 9/11 had just happened, after which much of the NYPD's resources were going toward a new villain far worse than any rapper—terrorism. This new emphasis on homeland security changed police work overnight. After 9/11 we did so much overtime, I was doing double and triple tours of duty. By the time I was to face Internal Affairs, I was exhausted.

I was almost retired. Technically, I was on terminal leave when In-

ternal Affairs called me in for my hearing. I was surprised to learn
that I was meeting with "Group One" of the Internal Affairs Bureau. Group One was the elite of the elite: it only investigated captains and above; it was almost a compliment to be asked in by them.
My case was assigned as a "GO-15": that meant I had the right to
have an attorney present at any departmental hearing. Actually, I
wasn't that nervous about my hearing—I was actually relieved; finally, *I* would be getting some answers. I had some questions for the
I.A.B. myself—if I had to go under the knife, I wasn't going to let
them off the hook, either.

As I sat down with my attorney by my side, a tape recorder was
placed in front of me. They hit "record," and I commenced the
meeting with a question.

"Why is Group One investigating *me*?" I queried the panel of
I.A. bigwigs facing me.

"Because you have a lot of power in the department," they told
me, "and a high-profile position."

Flattery didn't get them very far, though. The leader of the
Group One contingent, Katherine Donovan, well . . . to say we
didn't see eye to eye is a major understatement. Our conflict became
clear when she asked me if I knew the difference between police officers and special police officers—someone who might hold a gun
permit, say, or wear a shield like, say, a security patrolman. Of
course I knew the difference, I told her. Then Donovan got down to
brass tacks.

"Did your brother go to Atlantic City with you on the night in
question when you were assisting Atlantic City PD?" Donovan
asked.

"Yes," I responded.

"Did your brother ever say he was a police officer?"

"No. Never."

"Did your brother claim he was a gaming official?"

Donovan's last question caught me off guard a bit, but in a good
way. Now I knew someone was trying to get me. For my answer, I
spoke my words very carefully into the tape recorder, all the while
looking Donovan right in the eye.

"Of course not. *My . . . brother . . . doesn't . . . even . . . know . . . what . . . the . . . gaming . . . commission . . . is.*"

Group One still had a card up their sleeve, however—or so they thought. Next, Donovan questioned me about the Puffy trial. "Is it true you asked for a witness list from the Manhattan D.A.'s office?" she asked. Group One was playing their hand a little too confidently: it was clear from her smug demeanor that Donovan considered this her coup de grace. But I had an ace up my sleeve—the truth, which I knew they couldn't handle. With this parry, Donovan painted I.A.B. into a corner, because I had nothing to hide here.

"Yes, I did ask for a witness list in the Club New York trial," I responded.

"You did?" she asked, surprised at my immediate candor.

"Yes, Police Commissioner Bernard Kerik personally asked me to retrieve a witness list for him in regards to the Club New York trial," I said calmly.

Hearing Kerik's name, Donovan suddenly panicked. Her hand quickly moved to push the recorder's "stop" button, but I halted her.

"I'd like this to be on the record, Lieutenant," I said, bending down to speak directly into the recorder's microphone. "Police Commissioner Bernard Kerik ordered, through regular channels, that my chief should tell my captain to tell my lieutenant to tell my sergeant that I was to get a witness list from the D.A.'s office. Kerik was concerned about potential community unrest during the Puffy trial."

Suddenly Group One wanted to play nice. "Well, it was really a *loose* allegation, Derrick," they mumbled through forced smiles. "No harm, no foul."

"Just like this Atlantic City accusation?" I snapped back. "You know and I know this whole thing is about jealousy." I then handed my I.A. interrogators a typed report outlining how they failed to interview key eyewitnesses in my Atlantic City ethics investigation— especially *black* witnesses. From their actions, it appeared that I was the victim of a one-sided investigation. I figure I.A.B. could make up their own minds after I showed them the truth from my perspective. The sergeant flipped through my report nervously as I continued *my* interrogation of *them*.

"Why wasn't my partner Rosie Divine, who's black, inter-viewed?" I asked to a stone-faced response. "Why wasn't Ray Davis, who's black, questioned? And what about Hector Carter, who's also black? Why weren't these African-Americans approached for their side of the story, especially as they are *eyewitnesses* to the incident in question?"

The only thing Group One's sergeant could say to me was to rec-ommend *I just let it all go* . . . "Derrick, let's forget about all of this," he pleaded, his voice transforming from accusatory to com-forting. "You're only going to get a 'warned and admonished,' and it's going to get kicked back to Command level anyway. We know this is about jealousy."

"Why do you think this allegation came up now, anyway?" I queried right back.

"Well, your brother's presence in Atlantic City could've been misinterpreted," he said.

"What? That's a bunch of bull," I shot back. "You don't have to be a smart investigator to see what's going on here. For the record, I think you guys did a poor investigation."

By this point, as far as Group One was concerned, the hearing was over. The sergeant tried to shift the remaining moments to small talk, but I.A.B.'s pointed inquiry bubbled just underneath his words.

"So, what are your plans now that you're going to retire?" the I.A.B. reps asked ham-fistedly to conclude our heated little chat.

"Why do you want to know what my plans are?" I was in no mood to cooperate at this point. It was clear from their questions that the NYPD's paranoia about hip-hop remained at peak levels, and I no longer wanted anything to do with it.

"Well, are you going to work for the rap industry?" they asked, looking at me with three eyes.

"None of your business," I concluded, drawing the useless inter-rogation to a close.

In truth, I didn't know what I was going to do. I walked out that day largely exonerated by Internal Affairs, but I was still pissed. I.A.B.'s investigation into my affairs resulted in a "warned and admonished: conduct prejudicial to good order" ruling. When I heard that, I said, "What the hell does that mean?" My attorney explained that that this was just a weak catch-all that Internal Affairs had to issue in order to justify the closing of my case. In the end, I.A.B. told my squad commander to take whatever disciplinary action he thought fit, which wasn't much.

In fact, it was clear my lieutenant was only going to give me the lightest slap on the wrist: he told me I had to take a day or two from my vacation days, and that was it. I couldn't have cared less. At that point, they couldn't do anything more to me. My accusers weren't so lucky—karma's a bitch, it turned out. From what I was hearing through the grapevine, they weren't exactly rolling out the welcome mat for these guys around the department. No big deal—I was outta there. I would let those fools destroy themselves on their own time. They were no longer my problem.

Yeah, I could've remained in the NYPD for sure. I was getting job offers from chiefs spanning all the boroughs: they offered me weekends off, a car, anything if I would just stay on in the force and transfer to their precinct. I told them all, "No thanks." After being frustrated at every turn, then getting hammered by my fellow NYPD peers, there was a real bad taste in my mouth that refused to go away.

Still, I found it hard to stay away from the beat, as hip-hop crime continued unabated. Every day seemed to feature another hysterical *New York Post* headline implicating a rapper in some new crime or controversy. But Jam Master Jay's shooting upped the stakes a thousandfold. Even though I was retired, I felt drawn back in by hip-hop crime's tractor beam, almost against my will. But even after I retired, when I tried to work with the NYPD again to help solve Jay's homicide, I found that bad taste in my mouth was only getting more bitter by the minute.

12.

EXCEPTIONAL CLEARANCE:
Solving the Unsolved Homicide
of Jam Master Jay

Can't leave rap alone, the game needs me.
—Jay-Z, "Izzo (H.O.V.A.)"

Just when I thought I was out, they pull me back in.
—Al Pacino as Michael Corleone in The Godfather III

ERIC B. is a man of few words. When he speaks, it's usually about something important. And when he called me on November 1, 2002, what he had on his mind was no joke: the murder of Jam Master Jay. Eric was primarily concerned about two things. He was afraid that the police were mismanaging the case to the point that it would never be solved. As well, Eric worried about the witnesses in the case—both their rough handling by the police and the fact that they might be targeted next by Jay's killer. He was especially interested in the welfare of Lydia High, the case's key eyewitness.

"Lydia and the other witnesses, they're very afraid," Eric told me on the phone that day. "They don't know why someone wanted to kill Jay, and, as witnesses, if that someone may now want to kill them. And cops on the scene put Lydia in handcuffs the night of the murder, yelling at her and berating her just hours after her friend was killed in her presence. The cops thought she might've had something to do with it. Can you believe that?"

It wasn't hard to see why Eric was so committed to finding justice in the Jam Master Jay murder. Eric and Jam Master Jay had a lot in common : they were both rap icons, innovative D.J.s from two of the biggest groups from rap's golden age. Surprisingly, Eric and I discovered we had a lot in common, once we saw past our superficial differences: he was a rap star and I was "po-po," but in the end we found we were fighting a lot of the same battles.

At first, Eric B. and myself seemed like polar opposites. Eric is no stranger to the streets: with his group Eric B. & Rakim, he had helped create the ultimate stick-up kid anthem in their classic 1987 hit "Paid in Full," and their rhymes shouted out notorious underworld characters like Killer Ben, too. But when Eric and I met at the Source Awards in Miami a year earlier, I think we surprised each other. As the Source Awards' liaison to law enforcement, Eric showed me that there was a faction within the rap community that wanted to do the right thing and stop the violence, stop the craziness, and just let everyone be successful. At the same time, I believe I showed Eric that all cops weren't just racists who wanted to shut hip-hop down for good—that I was, in fact, a supporter of the culture and fought to save its soul behind closed doors at One Police Plaza. As a cop, I put myself on the line for hip-hop every day, doing everything I could do change perceptions within the NYPD, and I wanted Eric to know that.

As we got to know each other better, I would frankly educate Eric from the police side: I let him know, good and bad, about how law enforcement dealt with hip-hop crime. In the same way, he explained to me in greater detail about what was going down on the music side. Eric knew everybody in the rap game, and was concerned about its public image and ongoing health: he wanted to see hip-hop, a house he helped build, continue to flourish.

Deep down inside, Eric, too, was perturbed by all the violence, to him, the situation around Jay's killing served as a clarion call to end the bullshit once and for all. That's why he came to me: he didn't have anyone else that knew both the ins and outs of the rap game and the NYPD like I did. And since the Source Awards, a real trust had grown between us: he knew I would do the right thing. That's why he asked me to monitor the police's investigation and provide security for Lydia—there was no one else to go to. Lydia especially wanted to pay her last respects to her mentor, but didn't want to go to Jay's funeral alone.

"Lydia doesn't have any money for security," Eric continued.

"She can't afford it, and she's afraid to attend the service without serious protection."

I was glad to oblige—security had, in fact, replaced police work as my career when I left the force. In fact, the night I first heard about the Jam Master Jay murder, I was working security at a club. In 2002, when I retired from the force, a funny thing happened: I began experiencing the hip-hop world from the *other* side. I was a walking contradiction—no longer "po-po," but with "po-po" skills, a legit gun license, and a lot of knowledge and experience within the music business. All this translated nicely into the private sector. I was now working security for people who used to be the target of my surveillance in the hip-hop squad. As if things couldn't get any stranger, I was living life within the hip-hop industry's inner sanctum now more than ever.

Putting the skills and knowledge I gained in the hip-hop squad to continued use, I started up a company that provides security for nightclubs. I formed this company with a partner, Glen Beck, whom I met doing Intel surveillance. Glen's a former U.S. Marine; I was introduced to him by another marine, the district attorney in the Club New York trial, Matt Bogdanos, who knew Glen from his active days in the armed forces. Ironically, Glen was the doorman at Club New York when the Puffy/Shyne incident went down. Glen ended up testifying in the Puffy trial—but, tellingly, *against* Bogdanos. Glen has also worked security for artists like 50 Cent and G-Unit.

Our security company has worked with nearly every big Manhattan nightspot—Cheetah, Lot 61, Show, NV, Exit, Capitale, Boulevard, Etoile, Club 151; wherever the hot spot of the moment is for New York's elite hip-hop party crowd, we're there. In my new role, I was seeing the Puffys, the Jay Rules, the Jay-Zs, the Cam'rons all from a new, exclusive angle. In a way, I had my ear even closer to the street than I did when I was still a cop, which helped immensely when I jumped back into the Jam Master Jay investigation.

It'd been just a little over nine months since I retired from the NYPD. I felt myself wanting to spring back into action, like muscle memory. All my old moves came back as I tried to learn what really happened to Jay. The rumors surrounding Jam Master Jay's homicide started flying over the two-way pager "ghetto communicators" in the ensuing days after his death. And amidst the daze of whispered conspiracies on inner-city street corners, I was struggling to get the right story. One early rumor making the rounds was that Jay was murdered in Washington, D.C. I made a phone call to D.C. law enforcement, only to discover that the homicide didn't happen there. From my informants and industry contacts, what I came to first learn about the homicide is this:

Jam Master Jay's murder occurred at approximately 7:30 P.M. on October 30, 2002, at his recording studio located on 90-10 Merrick Avenue in Jamaica, Queens. Jay was there supervising a recording session for an up-and-coming group named Rusty Waters. The session was interrupted when a tall, masked African-American gunman dressed all in black entered the room where Jay is located, followed by an accomplice. The gunman then discharged a .40 gauge pistol into Jay's head, killing him.

Jay wasn't the only victim in the crime: a twenty-five-year-old hang-out buddy of Jay's, Uriel Rincon, took a bullet in the leg, but survived. The other witnesses on the scene included Lydia High, a pretty young black woman who worked as Jam Master Jay's business-affairs assistant and studio receptionist, and Lydia's older brother, Randy Allen. Of the eyewitnesses, I learned that Allen was closest to Jay. Randy Allen had grown up around Jay in the neighborhood; eventually, he became the Run-DMC D.J.'s business partner in developing new artists and making deals. Randy was partnered with Jay, for example, in developing 50 Cent early in the rapper's career, well before he became a superstar.

I'm shocked by other details that come my way concerning the Jam Master Jay case—like how police put Lydia High in handcuffs on the night of Jam Master Jay's murder. They didn't know how to deal with her at the scene, she was so upset. I was considering two possibilities: either Lydia knew who Jay's murderers are, or she was involved. Little did I know I was about to find out which was right.

Eric B.'s call was the linchpin that truly brought me into the Jam Master Jay case. I was intrigued: I knew being by Lydia's side during these crucial moments would bring me deeper into it—but I didn't know how deep. No, Jay's violent death would take me back to my home neighborhood of Hollis, Queens, as details in the case began to reveal themselves. My closeness to Queens helps put me on the right track to Jay's killers from the beginning.

Accompanying Lydia to Jam Master Jay's funeral, I saw all these guys from Hollis I knew growing up: Mookie, Ernest, kids I went to St. Pascal's with, guys I played basketball with in O'Connell Park, they were all there, dressed in black leather hats and white Adidas. That's how they sent Jay off—by dressing like him.

Then I personally witnessed the NYPD coming down hard on Lydia. I couldn't believe it when NYPD detective Bernie Porter and his partner followed me as I drove Lydia and her girlfriend Missy from Jam Master Jay's funeral. Even more shocking was when these Queens detectives going all out to pressure Lydia to talk. At that moment, it became clear that things were about to take a turn for the truly strange and complicated.

In particular, it remained obvious to me that if Queens law enforcement continued handling the witnesses in such a rough, hard-charging way, then the Jam Master Jay case would go nowhere. I understood on some level why these "Queens marines" acted so aggressively: sometimes the rough approach works to get info out of a suspect, especially on dumbshit criminals. But with Jay's murder, the cops weren't dealing with criminals: just because they were black didn't mean they weren't sophisticated. Jay was a superstar, not a common street thug, and treating the witnesses like thugs was absolutely the wrong way to solve his homicide.

And this case needed—no, *demanded*—to be solved, for the good of both law enforcement and hip-hop. Otherwise, it was going to grind toward a dead end just like Biggie's and Tupac's did. I knew my mission had to bridge the gap between two hostile tribes: Jam Master Jay's rap world and the NYPD. If I wasn't able to do that, his killer would never be brought to justice. And Lydia High was the link to make that happen: after all, she was the one that actually saw Jay's killer, face to face.

Moments after they came after Lydia following Jay's funeral, I received apologies from the two Queens detectives involved, Bernie

Porter Jr. and his hard-charging partner, as Lydia and her friend waited in my car. Turns out they were desperate to find more leads in the investigation. Porter felt Lydia was the crucial eyewitness necessary to cracking the case, and he was anxious for her to come to the 103rd's precinct house to talk.

"You can't force her to go to the precinct," I reminded them. "I'll ask Lydia and her friend if they want to go. But if they don't, they're not coming."

"Okay, fine," Porter grumbled back. "But give it a shot."

I returned to the car to speak with Lydia. I told her maybe it was better to get it over with: she was going to have to do it sooner or later, and if she did it sooner, then the police were more likely to leave her alone. I assured her that I'd call an attorney and make sure legal counsel was present at all times. Lydia agreed to cooperate, so I informed Bernie and his partner that we'd follow them to the precinct.

On the way to the 103rd I called Malcolm Smith, the state senator from Queens. When he heard how the police had handled Lydia, Smith became furious.

"I'm sending my attorney to the precinct," Smith informed me. "Don't say a word."

When we finally arrived at the 103rd precinct house, we all walked upstairs to the third floor. There they put Lydia and her girlfriend into a detective squad room together. Bernie was up there with his partner and another detective, waiting for Lydia's counsel to arrive. Lydia gave me explicit instructions for the Queens detectives as to how she wanted her interview handled: "When my attorney gets here, I'll talk. Until then, I have nothing to say."

While Lydia's lawyer was en route, Lt. Richard Bellucci showed up. Bellucci was the commanding officer of Queens's homicide division; I knew him from the investigation into Freaky Tah's murder years before. Also present was Lt. Al Murphy, the commanding officer of the 103rd Precinct, and the man in charge of the district's detectives. Seeing Bellucci and Murphy, I pulled them aside and asked if we could get everybody into a room to discuss just what the hell was going on with the Jam Master Jay case. Once we were behind closed doors, man, I really stuck it to the Queens marines.

"I can't believe you're trying to frighten the witnesses into talking about this case," I yelled at Porter. "What the fuck are you doing, Bernie? Do you know what kind of damage you've already done?" Turning to Lieutenant Bellucci, I told him, "I can't believe how you guys in Queens handle homicide investigations."

Bellucci gave me some insight into what was making heads hot around the 103rd, though. He explained that the NYPD needed Lydia's help in solving Jay's murder because this is a big case. Bellucci was afraid they might not crack it without her. He was right to be worried.

"I understand your concerns, but this is not the way do homicide," I fired back at him. "I've explained to Lydia the importance of her cooperation, but after how you've treated her, why waste my time—or hers? If NYPD is going to treat her like that, I don't blame her if she doesn't want to cooperate with you."

I was shocked at how this case is being handled. At the same time, these Queens cops are looking at me with three eyes; they're probably thinking, "Derrick, he was one of *us*—now look at him. He's working for the other side."

"Look, we could use your help," Bellucci pleaded. "If you could help us *at all*, I'd greatly appreciate it."

"Rich, you must listen to me: *this is not a conventional homicide*," I hissed through increasingly gritted teeth. "It involves a victim of stature who has money and influence in the community. Jam Master Jay wasn't just loved by locals, but by millions around the world."

I hoped I'd made my point, but I couldn't be sure. By this time, Lydia's attorney, Joan Flowers, had arrived, so we moved everyone into the interview room; I asked to be present during the interrogation, and Lydia and her counsel agreed. Once we were all seated, Porter asked Lydia to look at the NYPD's photo arrays: "We have some photographs we'd like to show you, to see if you can identify anyone from the scene of the crime." Joan Flowers made sure to protect her client. "You're not going to pressure Lydia into making an identification," she warned the detectives in the room.

Lydia was very calm as she inspected the arrays. Regardless, she

couldn't identify anybody from the photos. When she finished looking through them, Lydia's attorney informed the precinct they were
not to go near her client again. Before we left, I told Richie Bellucci
that I'd be in touch.

To me, the Jam Master Jay homicide didn't seem like too hard a
case to crack: you just needed witnesses to testify. Time went by,
maybe a week or two, but I never took my ear away from the street.
When the time seemed right, I began approaching the eyewitnesses
in the case again.

People in the street suspected Randy Allen had something to do
with Jay's murder. Threats were made against him, and he started
wearing a bulletproof vest. To me, however, Randy was never a credible suspect, as there was no evidence linking him whatsoever to the
homicide; I even got him to cooperate somewhat, but it wasn't easy
to get him to believe in me. Uriel Rincon was cool, meanwhile, but
strange and ultimately not cooperative enough for my tastes; I still
believe to this day that he could have done more to help the investigation.

To figure out more of Lydia's story, I spoke to Missy, her girlfriend who accompanied her to the funeral. She implied that Lydia
knew more than she was saying, but that she was afraid. Missy was
concerned about her friend: she knew the entire situation was eating
away at Lydia. Missy trusted me, especially as Eric B. had vouched
for me, and urged me to keep working on Lydia.

Bellucci kept calling me, meanwhile, trying to see if I could get
Lydia to talk. I let him know that I will work on this, but I needed
time. I let several weeks go by, so that everything died down as it
should. Still, when I approached Lydia again, she made it clear she
didn't believe the police could, or would, protect her.

"It's bigger than the police think," she explained. I knew this,
too, from my own poking around. I also knew Uriel Rincon and
Randy Allen may have had something more to say, also. However,
Lydia was the key eyewitness: she was the one who let the bad guys
in, who unwittingly buzzed the door open for Jam Master Jay's murderers.

Slowly I developed greater rapport with Lydia; in the process, I let her know that the only way I could effectively help her was to have her tell the truth. Eventually, she opened up to me with her side of what happened to Jam Master Jay that fateful October night, just one day shy of Halloween. Before he was killed; Lydia claimed, Jay was playing video games in the studio's chill-out area. Lydia had noticed Jay had been carrying a gun recently, which was unusual for him. But in the days before his murder, Jay's had received a number of threatening phone calls, and he was taking no chances. In fact, as he played games on the PlayStation, Jay kept the gun nearby, on the edge of the sofa, just in case.

Jay's burner wouldn't keep him from being slain, alas. For one, the shooters had little problem entering into the office building where Jay's studio is located, which typically suggests they are acquaintances of the victim. According to Lydia, when someone rang the studio's buzzer, their image would appear on the security camera—so Lydia had to know them if she let them in.

When the two gunmen entered Jay's studio, the first one pulled his gun on Lydia, ordering her to get down on the ground. They were moving so fast, by the time Jay was able to react and grab his gun, it was too late. When the shooter burst into the studio's chill room, Jay only had time to say "Oh, shit!" before he took a fatal bullet in his head. Another shot ricocheted, hitting Uriel Rincon in the ankle. Once the invaders were sure Jay was dead, they left.

I knew Lydia was having a hard time just living after such a haunting, traumatic ordeal; keeping the truth inside was eating away at her. Lydia knew who killed Jam Master Jay, but for two months she remained silent, causing her to have nightmares about the murder every night. It took me a long time to work on her and to gain her trust.

Next, I had to work on the NYPD, though. First, I approached my remaining supporters there. My Cold Case mentor Pollini was still on the job, so I asked him to get me an audience with Chief Alee. I felt I needed to debrief Alee about what I've learned about the Jam Master Jay homicide from *my* perspective. Alee agreed; soon after, I met with Pollini and the chief in Alee's thirteenth-floor office at One Police Plaza.

"Chief Alee, please listen to me," I implored. "I know the best way to handle the Jam Master Jay investigation, because the 103rd squad blew it."

Alee wasn't having it, however—and I could tell he questioned my loyalty to the NYPD now that I was retired. "Derrick, I can't get you involved in this case because there's been leaks to press," he said.

"Well, I'm not on the job anymore," I reminded him. "I'm retired, remember? There are no leaks coming from me."

"I can't trust anybody," Alee continued. "Look, the record industry is seductive like a woman—everyone wants to be in her, but not everyone can. Leave it alone."

Hearing this made me furious. "Chief, you have me all wrong," I shot back. "I'm not in this to be 'seduced.' I don't care about any of that shit. I'm in this to *solve murders*. Let me help you solve this murder so you don't end up looking like the LAPD did after the Biggie case."

"Maybe you should mind your business," Alee snapped.

"Maybe I should."

Shit, Alee was probably right. Now I was sure the NYPD wasn't going to get witnesses with the overzealous methods they seemed to prefer. Alee didn't want to hear what I knew, or so I thought.

"Look," Alee said calmly, trying to defuse the tension in the air, "why don't you just tell me what it is you know, and I'll handle it."

Yeah, right—in hell: that's what I'm thinking when I heard Alee try to play me like a sucker. After all my years on the force, you'd think they'd know me better, but no. I thanked Alee for taking the time, then got up to leave. After we walked out, I asked Pollini what he got out of that meeting. His response didn't surprise me.

"Derrick, if I was you, I wouldn't get involved in this anymore," Pollini said. "Alee's not going to listen. He's too regimented in his thoughts." I couldn't agree more. I didn't have time for this shit.

The Jam Master Jay case didn't go away, though—or maybe I wouldn't let it go. The media certainly didn't, as new conspiracies kept echoing through the tabloids. One name that came up as a potential connection was Curtis Scoon, another longtime friend of

Jay's from Queens. It was alleged that he, Jay, and another guy might've been involved in a dispute over unpaid monies in a drug deal. When Scoon got wind that his name was floating out there as a person of interest in the investigation, he immediately "lawyered up." For counsel, Scoon retained Marvin Kornberg, a very prominent attorney from Queens who really knows the ins and outs of New York's judicial system. I had testified for Kornberg, for the defense, in a gang trial months before Jay's murder happened.

That Curtis Scoon might've had something had to do with Jay's murder eventually got leaked to the media. An article by Sean Gardiner that appeared in the October 29, 2003, *New York Newsday* noted allegations that Scoon and Jay had made a $30,000 cocaine deal that went bad, and that Scoon demanded Jay make up for the loss. Scoon himself did an interview in *Playboy*'s December 2003 issue claiming not only had he not seen Jay for over four years, but that Jay's debt to Scoon wasn't a drug debt and that the late D.J. "did not owe me a dollar by the time of his death." However, in the same interview Scoon claimed it was common knowledge on the street that Jam Master Jay was involved in drug dealing "but nobody wants to talk about it because they don't want to tarnish his image."

The *Newsday* article, meanwhile, mentioned a man named Ronald "Tinard" Washington as a possible suspect. Here Washington backed up Scoon's claims about Jay's involvement in illegal narcotics, and a debt that might've led to his murder. Washington told *Newsday* "that he and Mizell [Jam Master Jay] met a drug dealer named 'Uncle' at a swank Washington, D.C., hotel last summer and Mizell negotiated a deal to receive $120,000 of cocaine on credit. The drugs were driven to dealers in Baltimore but those dealers then disappeared, never repaying Mizell the money." Washington added that Jay was scheduled to "meet Uncle's associates . . . the day after his slaying."

Washington was himself a potential suspect in Jay's murder. He had his own theories about who killed Jay, however, pinning the crime on two men named Darren Jordan (aka "Big D") and his son Karl ("Little D"); in the *Newsday* piece, Washington claimed he saw Darren and Karl Jordan running out of Jay's studio following gunshots on the day of his murder. Those weren't the only conspiracy theories floating around. One alleged that Supreme Team czar Kenneth "Supreme" McGriff may have been involved in a romantic relationship with Jay's wife (a claim that her friends have denied). Others suggested that Randy Allen was trying to profit from a life insurance policy taken out on Jay that would net $500,000 in the event of Jay's death, but the police eventually discounted that theory. A story on on sohh.com intimated Jay had purchased ten kilos from a Milwaukee, Wisconsin, trafficker, and was given protection by Washington to do so. I learned from my sources inside the NYPD that another weapon, a .357 magnum, had also been recovered from the scene; furthermore, it had been discharged, which suggested that someone had shot at Jay's killers as they left the scene.

Another story going around was that Jay had given his killer a hug before he was shot—implying that Jay knew his murderer personally. While Lydia might've been able to ID the shooter, she didn't know who might've wanted Jay dead. I myself wanted to find out the truth about all of these theories. Word got out in the street, meanwhile, that the police were going to question Scoon about a drug debt that Jay might've owed him. According to street-corner scuttlebutt, Jay wasn't doing very well financially from music, and he was involved in drug sales to make a little extra money to help with what some said was a half-million in debts. Supposedly, he wasn't handling drugs per se himself, but acting as more of a middleman.

The rumor one of my street informants related to me backed up the reports in the media: Jay may have introduced someone to a third party for a deal estimated to be worth anywhere between $50,000 and more than $100,000. When that third party maybe didn't pay, say, or made off with the drugs, Jay was likely held accountable because he'd made the introduction. Either way, Jay's murder was clearly payback of some kind.

By August 2004, I had made my own views about all these theories. Frustrating as it was, I was still trying to steer NYPD in the right direction. I didn't know why, but a blind hope remained within me that proper law enforcement would bring Jay's killer to justice.

To that end, I contacted Richie Bellucci once again, telling him that I had to talk to him as soon as possible. It was urgent, at least in my mind: I'd processed all the new info on Jay's homicide from my inside perspective, and I wanted him to hear me out. We agreed to meet at a diner near College Point in Flushing, Queens, the next day.

At the diner, I sat with Bellucci for two hours, explaining to him everything I knew about Jam Master Jay's homicide. Not only did I tell him my theory on how Jay got killed, I let slip that I thought he was killed by guys close to him; that was why Lydia and other witnesses weren't cooperating. Bellucci perked up when he heard my belief that Jay's supposed *friends* may have been the very same individuals responsible for his murder.

After absorbing all this, Bellucci wanted me to meet a Queens district attorney named Gregory Lasak. Lasak's the D.A. in charge of Jay's homicide: he always felt that Lydia knew more then she let on, and that she wasn't telling the truth. But if I was going to give something to Bellucci, he had to give something back to me.

"I'm gonna try to get the witnesses to cooperate and do the right thing," I stated, "But you can't approach it like conventional homicide. It took me a long time—months—to get Lydia to cooperate."

At first I had hope. I thought that maybe this time the NYPD would finally get a little innovative in this investigation. Early signs looked good. When I met with Lasak, he assured me that he'd assign one of his top D.A.s to the case. Furthermore, Lasak said that if I was able to convince Lydia to come forward, he could provide protection for her.

On Lydia's behalf, I had a few specific demands for Lasak. First, she needed full witness protection: if she was threatened in any way, the police had to take care of the situation for real and make sure nothing happens to her. Next, the D.A.'s office had to help her relocate to someplace where she felt safe. Lastly, Lydia needed financial support to get back on her feet: the D.A. would have to help get her a job. This kind of action on the D.A.'s part is common in, say, cases involving witnesses testifying against the mob. Unfortunately, it's not as common in cases involving hip-hop crime, even when there's a clear and present danger to the witness. It was a struggle to get the

D.A. to agree to even what he did—and there was always a chance he might go back on his word.

After I explained to her what the Queens D.A.'s office was promising, Lydia reluctantly agreed to cooperate with the investigation: she promised to tell them everything she knew if her safety was assured. Lydia, for her part, never believed that the NYPD would come through on their promises, however. Unfortunately, she was right.

That Lasak's deal with Lydia was going to go down the tubes became clear when the D.A. was to put all of its assurances of protection in writing so that her lawyer could review it. I called in my friend, the attorney Steve Brounstein, to assist Lydia in this matter. Brounstein set up a meeting with Lasak and asked when these things were to be taken care of. The D.A., however, claimed he needed to know what he was getting out of Lydia first; they wanted to hear what she was going to say. Still, Lasak agreed to put certain things in motion anyway, as a gesture of the D.A.'s good faith.

In the following weeks, the D.A. appeared to make good on some of his promises to Lydia. Lasak's office connected her with relocation staff, supposedly to help her move. When Lydia saw the D.A. might actually come through for her, she agreed to make a full identification of Jay's killer. The D.A., however, felt that Lydia was holding out—that she knew who the other perp was, but wasn't saying. Endlessly, Lydia kept repeating that she could positively identify only one perp—but not the actual triggerman in the murder. That's where the trouble began.

The person Lydia identified to the D.A. was Ronald "Tinard" Washington. Tinard, as he was best known, grew up with Jay in the Hollis, Queens, neighborhood they shared. Instead of becoming a rapper, however, Washington became a tough guy, and his name was always linked to a number of local robberies. According to Lydia, Washington threatened her and told her put her head down, but he wasn't the one who pulled the trigger on Jay.

As to the second alleged perpetrator, the main suspect for Jay's shooter, Lydia wasn't able to positively ID him. I suspected, however, that he was Carl Jordan, or "Little D." Carl Jordan is the son of

Darren Jordan, who's known around the hood as "Big D." Big D was a friend of Jay's from 'round the way: he was involved years ago in the music industry as a road manager, and was an associate of of the early Def Jam empire. Little D's involvement gained more credibility with me after I learned Lydia had received a call from Big D that she said scared her. "Hello? Oh, Lydia, is that you?" Big D reportedly said on the phone. "Sorry, I dialed the wrong number—I was trying to call somebody else."

I was hoping Lasak would pursue the possibility that Little D might have been involved. The thing was, without arresting Washington or any other credible suspects, we would never figure out the why, or especially the *who*, that was really behind Jay's shooting. This was the big factor. Did Jay's killers work alone—or were they taking orders from someone else? Jay's death was definitely a hit of some kind, but from what level of criminal? How organized were these crooks? Even if we had been sure who pulled the trigger, we still wouldn't know if they acted on someone else's behalf.

The media had a field day speculating that 50 Cent was somehow involved in Jam Master Jay's murder. The main evidence for this theory revolved solely around the mere fact that Jay *knew* 50—that the rap veteran had been a friend of 50's and was instrumental in setting up 50's first record deal. I found the idea of 50's involvement in the Jam Master Jay homicide ludicrous—total tabloid hype. 50 Cent had nothing to do with Jay's murder.

Finally, I caught a break in my investigation. I found out that Little D was wanted in another shooting: he'd allegedly shot this guy in the leg over some dispute, and I got the victim in that incident to come forward. The victim agreed to do an I.D.: this meant that Little D could be brought in to do a lineup, but he wouldn't know that it had anything to do with the Jam Master Jay case. I convinced Lydia to come to Little D's lineup so we could make a final attempt at identification.

Unfortunately, NYPD botched up everything. For one, the 103rd squad had problems finding fillers for the lineup. I was enraged.

"Out of all the people the world, and all the black people in Queens, how could they not get fillers?" I wondered aloud to anyone who would listen. This was sheer incompetence on the NYPD's part, and it frustrated Lydia; after couple hours of waiting, she wanted to go home. I was incensed at how the 103rd detective squad was handling this latest misstep. "This is bullshit," I told Bellucci.

Despite the NYPD's blunders, I wasn't yet giving up hope. Speaking to Lasak, I suggested that we try another approach. I explained to the D.A. that Lydia had identified Washington through photos, and we could work that angle more. Furthermore, I knew Washington's lawyer, Dana Grossblatt, a public defender whose acquaintance I made from prosecuting cases in my old Brooklyn murder days. If I got a friend like Dana involved, and if Washington was actually involved, I was sure she'd take a deal because her client wouldn't be prosecuted as the shooter in the case.

"You should offer Washington a plea deal to give up the shooter," I advised Lasak. The only problem with this plan was that it relies on a co-conspirator's cooperation—Washington's testimony wouldn't be enough to convict. However, it would advance the investigation significantly; a cooperative Washington could give up who else was involved, which would lead to more leads, more witnesses, and maybe even other co-conspirators.

Lasak kept balking, however. In our conversation, the D.A. continually reiterated that he felt Lydia wasn't telling the whole truth. I could tell he was going to renege on the deal he made with Lydia, so I let him know my exact feelings on the matter. "You're doing exactly what Lydia said you were gonna do—going back on the relocation, the job, money, protection, everything," I said. "You're blowing it." I felt so bad, I ended up giving Lydia five hundred dollars out of my pocket.

My little D theory hit a wall at the D.A.'s office. They just never did what they needed to do to find out whether Little D might be a plausible suspect. Meanwhile, Big D told the *Daily News* that his son had been questioned about Jay's murder but that he wasn't the killer.

After talking to Lasak, I told Lieutenant Bellucci I wasn't involved anymore. I was done trying to help the NYPD with the Jam Master Jay case: I put in over one hundred gratis hours in the investigation, got the primary eyewitness to come forward—and this is what happened? That was the thanks I get?

What happened with the Jam Master Jay case, which is still open and unsolved, remains indicative of other unsolved high-profile murders of hip-hop icons like Biggie and Tupac. All of these cases share some element of the same problem—law enforcement's repeated bungling. In the end, the Queens D.A.'s office had to share some of the blame, too.

My entire experience involving the Jam Master Jay investigation clarified exactly why the authorities can't get witnesses to come forward in rap-related investigations: if this was how the police were going to treat them, then why should they put themselves on the line? I couldn't blame them, to be honest. The NYPD just isn't culturally equipped to solve this case—that's my opinion that remains today after I watched the investigation unravel from the inside.

Yes, Jam Master Jay's case is still pending, but I'd be shocked if there were many new significant leads. If the investigation drags out too much longer, I'm guessing Jay's homicide would make a good candidate as an "E" case: "Exceptional Clearance."

Meanwhile, Lydia's since relocated; *everyone's* relocated. Me, I had to let it rest. I didn't get involved in the Jam Master Jay case to get paid, but to solve a murder; if they wouldn't let me do that, then I was no longer of any use. I'm the master of the game, because I invented the game, but sometimes a player just has to walk away from the sport.

No harm, no foul, right?

Yeah, *right . . .*

EPILOGUE

MURDER INC. WAS THE CASE:
The Federal Takedown of Hip-Hop Crime

If the "nine" don't kill 'em, then the truth will.
—Tru-Life, "The New New York"

B Y 2003, I would find myself moving even deeper into the "other side." That was the year that I found myself within the inner circle of Murder Inc., the hip-hop label best known for spawning superstars like rapper Ja Rule and R&B siren Ashanti. Almost as well known in rap circles as the label's stars is Murder Inc.'s founder, Irv "Gotti" Lorenzo.

Irv Gotti is a colorful character, a charismatic music-biz don who models his persona after gangster movies (Gotti himself conceived and directed the *Goodfellas* homage video for Ashanti's breakthrough hit, "Foolish"). Despite his thugged-out image, Gotti is more than anything a real music man. He started as a D.J. in Queens, gaining local fame as "D.J. Irv"; I'd often see the young Gotti spinning at parks and block parties around the 'hood. He would later become tour D.J. for Jay-Z (who gave Gotti his *mafiosi* nickname) before becoming a powerful record-label executive. The mogul-in-the-making then parlayed his ability to choose the right song in the D.J. booth to becoming a rap producer, making beats for rap stars like DMX. Gotti's "ears" eventually landed him A&R positions first with independent label TVT Records and then Def Jam Records. In 1999, after signing DMX and churning out hits for Jay-Z, Gotti was given backing by Def Jam to start his own subsidiary label, Murder Inc.

If there's a theme to Murder Inc.'s saga, it's that Gotti's relentless about *Godfather*-style family loyalty. If you're an insider within the Murder Inc. camp, you're expected to "ride or die" for the crew; in The Inc., "one for all and all for one" goes for everyone, from the man on top through the artists down to the street teams and interns. It was no surprise to me, then, that Irv Gotti chose his brother Chris for Murder Inc.'s second-in-command lieutenant. And it was Chris who would be my way in to the Murder Inc. world.

When I was first retiring from the NYPD, Chris Gotti approached me about working with him on his personal-security issues. Security was definitely on Murder Inc.'s mind because of the beef between Ja Rule and 50 Cent, which by 2003, was boiling at an all-time high. 50's debut album, *Get Rich Or Die Tryin'*, had just come out, and it was a smash multi-platinum hit. On numerous songs throughout *Get Rich . . .* , 50 brutally taunts Ja Rule as a "wanksta" wannabe. Meanwhile, as 50's star grew, he flaunted their beef in every interview he did, dissing Ja from every concert stage he stood on.

Apparently 50's flagrant taunting got to someone. On January 16, 2003, a shooter went to the offices of 50's management company, Violator, leaving six rounds of retaliatory bullets in his wake. No one was hurt, but the incident left significant property damage—and an omnipresent feeling that no one was safe, anywhere. The beef between Ja and 50 was, and remains, a hip-hop crisis, a hot zone that could go off at any time. Considering the street reputations involved, when that beef comes to its inevitable end, it's going to be a bloody war to the death.

Beef aside, what made things especially tough for Murder Inc. was that success is always the best revenge, and 50 now had it in spades. *Get Rich Or Die Tryin'* would set records by selling 872,000 units alone in the week following its release on February 6, 2003, and would go on to sell over *ten million* copies. Alternatively, while most of Ja Rule's releases have gone at least "platinum," his 2003 album, *Blood In My Eye*—filled with retaliatory rants against 50— couldn't even reach "gold" status (the Record Industry Association of America's classification for albums that ship at least 500,000 copies).

Yes, in 2003, Murder Inc. was a company under the gun—and not just from other rappers. As I would soon learn, the stakes with Murder Inc. were bigger than any mere street shit. With all this turbulence around the company, Chris Gotti wanted someone with him who was reputable, so he reached out to yours truly. After all, who was more reputable than an ex-homicide detective from the NYPD? As for working with a label with such an infamous reputation in the rap game, well, I was nervous—but I wanted to see for myself and experience hip-hop from the *inside*-inside for once. I wanted to see if all my research and intelligence compiled during my NYPD years really added up.

Now Murder Inc. was watching *me*. Chris Gotti and I met up at the BP gas station on Francis Lewis Boulevard and Hollis Avenue one night to talk business. He had heard of me from Kurt, one of Irv Gotti's regular bodyguards. I'd gotten to know Chris a little bit from my rap investigations; he was always a nice guy, and I never had a problem with him.

The co-head of Murder Inc. was no saint, though. Chris had some juvenile assault on his record, and he *did* throw some punches in the incident at the Hit Factory, which left 50 Cent's stabbed by Inc. rapper Black Child (50 would eventually request an order of protection against Murder Inc. due to this assault, although he has repeatedly denied it). But generally Chris kept things far more low-key than his brother and the label's rappers with their thuggish entourages. Chris was still anxious, however. He had good reason to be.

What I liked best about working at Murder Inc. was that it humanized a lot of people whom I'd only known via surveillance in my hip-hop squad days. Inside The Inc. I eventually got upfront and personal with everyone that was around. I don't think everyone trusted me at first, because in this "family" trust was earned. But once I earned that trust, I learned something I couldn't while I was still in the police department: I got to really know the individuals from the Murder Inc. camp, guys I knew about through photograph arrays or from seeing them around inner-city Queens. Working there, I got to know their character, their personalities. One never knows what to think about people, as it's so easy to prejudge from

appearances (or rap sheets). But behind closed doors, I saw a different side of these guys. I saw them play basketball, chase girls,
everything—just living life.

What I learned gave me hope. Some of the crew had had their run-
ins with the law, some were on parole—but I saw how being part of
the Murder Inc. family gave them something that was positive. Most
of these guys, even those with priors, wanted to put the bullshit behind them, clean up their acts, and succeed in the music business.
Often, people like Irv were the only ones that would take them in; he
gave them jobs to keep them off the streets, and they really did want
to stay out of trouble. "A part of the investigation on me is because I
hired so many niggas on parole," Gotti commented in a March 2003
article in the hip-hop magazine *XXL*. "I probably got like 20, 25 niggas that's on parole. I think from a federal standpoint, they may look
at it like, 'This nigga is assembling an army of criminals.' But I'm
not. I'm changing lives." After what I saw, I'd have to agree.

As Chris Gotti's security detail, I stayed primarily in the label's
offices, as Chris traveled infrequently. Chris was always even-
tempered—I never saw him get mad once. He'd work long, hard
hours, after which he liked a little recreation; maybe he'd go to a
club, but more likely he'd just play cards with his boys—sometimes
all night long. This crew stayed up *late*: they'd either be making music until the wee hours at Murder Inc.'s Soho-based studio known as
"The Crackhouse," or maybe Chris's people would just chill out and
watch TV. Ja would came through occasionally, and Irv would come
and go. Irv was always incredibly busy making sure the music got
made and the business was straight. As far as I could tell, Murder
Inc.'s business was legit, and totally professional: Chris paid me in
checks made out to my security company, no problem.

Not everyone was so convinced that Murder Inc.'s business activities were totally on the up-and-up, however—like the F.B.I. While I
was working with Chris Gotti, such rumors began to bubble with increasing velocity. I turned to the law-enforcement grapevine, where
I learned the Feds were about to begin a major investigation into
Murder Inc. I called a friend who told me to be careful and to watch
my back as a federal probe into Murder Inc.'s business practices and

connection to other crimes loomed imminently. I told him that I was working directly with Chris Gotti and if there were any kind of problem, he should contact me immediately. Christ, I didn't want him to think *I* was doing anything illegal.

The Feds began their investigation into Murder Inc. in 2002. The first overt sign of their probe came on January 3, 2003, however, when the agency raided Murder Inc.'s offices in the Def Jam building at Fiftieth Street and Eighth Avenue in midtown Manhattan. In the raid, federal authorities turned the office upside down, snatching up computers, hard drives, documents, and other materials. As well, the Feds found a .25 caliber burner on an employee's desk, which resulted in a gun possession charge for Murder Inc. executive Dexter Ottley.

That gun was the least of the legal headaches for Irv Gotti and Murder Inc., however. In their raid, the Feds were looking for proof that Murder Inc. received drug money and then "laundered" that illegal cash through Murder Inc. accounts to make it "legit" taxable income. The source of this supposed drug money was none other than Kenneth "Supreme" McGriff. The Gottis and Murder Inc. do have ties to McGriff, which they freely admit; Irv Gotti openly claims that he's known McGriff for years. The Gottis became friends with the gangster from hanging around the inner-city Queens 'hood they shared. But that wasn't the full extent of their relationship, which is what drew the Feds' interest in the first place.

After 'Preme was released from a prison bid in the mid-'90s, on the surface it appeared he was on the path to finding a new career outside of drug dealing. In 1997, the veteran felon and ex-con approached Murder Inc. kingpin Gotti about collaborating on a straight-to-DVD movie called *Crime Partners 2000*, based on a Donald Goines novel McGriff had optioned. It was to star Murder Inc.'s flagship star Ja Rule alongside Snoop Dogg and Ice-T; naturally, Murder Inc. would be perfect to handle the movie's soundtrack.

The only thing was, the authorities still had their eye on McGriff: they were convinced that his narcotics operations were up and running—and funding his new "legit" business attempts like *Crime Partners 2000*. To the federal agencies involved, *Crime Partners 2000* was an all-too-apt title: for them, the film was the smoking gun they needed to take down Murder Inc. *and* Supreme. That idea became even more vivid when they discovered McGriff paid Gotti a $500,000 fee for his involvement in the movie, and then Gotti paid McGriff half of his million-dollar "soundtrack fee" right back—a setup that smelled more than anything of money laundering to investigators on the case.

Red flags would repeatedly lead law enforcement to McGriff's connection with Murder Inc. At one point, in July 2001, McGriff was arrested in Harlem for gun possession; the police soon discovered that the weapon in question had originally been lawfully purchased by the Gottis' older brother, Rory Lorenzo. In that last instance, McGriff gave a false name and told NYPD officers that he was an employee of Def Jam; in another brush with the law, a pager on McGriff at the time was found to be registered to Murder Inc.

These leads drew federal authorities to investigate the possibility that McGriff may have been involved in funding the birth of Murder Inc.—just as Los Angeles drug kingpin Michael "Harry O" Harris allegedly backed Death Row Records as Suge Knight's silent partner. In their indictment of Supreme and the Gotti brothers, Federal authorities would charge that McGriff was an employee of Murder Inc.'s—and that the Gottis were conversely partners in Supreme's criminal pursuits.

From my perspective, I guessed rightly that the Feds' focus would add up to nothing—as proved by the Gottis' full acquittal on all charges on December 2, 2005. To my eyes it's pretty clear that Def Jam, not Supreme, devoted the initial millions to start up Murder Inc. If I had conducted the Feds' investigation, I would focus more on areas where the cash aspect can be played with—things like merchandise sales and concert revenues. In my mind, trying to prove that Murder Inc. was funded with drug money was overreaching up there with Bogdanos's "Puffy is the shooter" prosecution in the Club New York case. And with the Gottis' victory, I was ultimately shown to be correct.

For evidence, however, law enforcement would point to clues coming from the very music released by Murder Inc. "Funds unlimited, backed by my 'Preme Team criminal representatives" raps Ja Rule on "Survival of the Illest," suggesting an outside-the-law connection between the label and McGriff. And in liner notes to Ja Rule's 2004 album *R.U.L.E.*, the rapper pays further homage to McGriff: "'Preme, I'm sittin' under the tree and that apple's about to fall in my lap . . . Hold ya head . . . We'll see U soon." Even 50 puts in his own two, er, cents on the situation on a mixtape diatribe against Murder Inc. called "Order of Protection." "You 'Preme's son, nigga," 50 spits, adding "Motherfuckers been getting extorted since day one."

Murder Inc.'s response to the F.B.I. attention was classic hip-hop—that is, outrageous and full of fearless bravado. Most aggressively, Murder Inc. made clear their contempt for the Feds' investigation. While I was working for Murder Inc., the company made a widely publicized music video controversially lampooning the federal probe *as it was still in progress.*

The posse-heavy video was set to "Reign," Ja Rule's Murder Inc. anthem of survival by any means necessary. In the mocking "Reign" clip, conceived and directed by Irv Gotti, the Feds' raid of Murder Inc. gets replicated to a T, with some extra comedy thrown in. In an ingenious bit of stunt casting, Irv hired Patrick Swayze as the bumbling F.B.I. agent in charge of the raid! I was present for the "Reign" video shoot, which took place way out in New Jersey. That night, after the shoot was over, I left the set thinking the Feds weren't going to find this video funny. They didn't.

Around this time, my professional association with Murder Inc. ceased. About three months after I started working there, Chris Gotti became involved in a shooting incident in the courtyard below Def Jam's offices, where he took a bullet in the leg. I was not with Chris at the time of the shooting, alas.

When Chris got shot, all eyes were on Murder Inc. even more. The circumstances surrounding Chris's shooting seemed mysterious: there was talk his wound was self-inflicted. To that end, a friend in the department told me it seemed that most evidence pointed to Chris having shot himself with his own gun because of the gunpowder residue and ballistic burn patterns on the pants he was wearing. I kept what my friend said in the back of my mind; as for Chris, I never asked him about the shooting—I figured it wasn't my business. Of course, the NYPD wanted to know who shot Chris; I can't imagine what they must have thought of me at this time, hanging around all these "rap hoodlums."

About a month and a half after his shooting, Chris began to heal up. At the time, things were changing around Murder Inc.—the feeling of dread was palpable around the office. For one, money was suddenly an issue, as sales were way down, and releases far and few between. One day Chris pulled me into his offices: he told me he no longer required my services. According to him, he now felt safe and couldn't justify the expense. Hearing that, I thanked him and went on my way.

In retrospect, the Feds gave themselves a tall order taking on Murder Inc. With the indictment, it was on the government to prove beyond a reasonable doubt that Irv and Murder Inc. benefited from "ill-gotten gains." But I understood why Irv and Chris might still be worried.

The main thing Murder Inc. had to fear was just who from their camp, and from their enemies, was talking to the Feds. When the government goes so far with an investigation to make an indictment, that means their case is largely based on the testimony of cooperators. Cooperating witnesses are the bedrock of any federal investigation, and the Feds typically won't proceed to an indictment until they feel they have an airtight case. That's how they get their cases to go: they don't want to waste their budget unless they think they have a sure thing. As such, the Feds got to some real insiders with Murder Inc. In August 2003, Jon Ragin, a convicted narcotics dealer, offered a guilty plea in a money-laundering charge connected to *Crime Partners 2000*. Little over a year later, in November 2004, law enforcement arrested Ja Rule manager Ron Robinson (aka "Gutta") and the label's accountant, Cynthia Brent, on charges spanning from money laundering to willful tax evasion. Charges against Robinson were later dropped. Brent pled guilty to a lesser charge of structuring transactions to avoid currency-reporting requirements.

The evidence against The Inc. may not have stopped there. In addition to cooperators, the Feds also have access to phone taps, wires, and methods of surveillance not allowed at the lower levels of law enforcement. They can bring agents in from other agencies and divisions, like the Internal Revenue Service and white-collar crime; it was an IRS agent, in fact, that first made the link in a court of law that Supreme may have been responsible for 50 Cent's 2001 shooting. The Feds' expanding-net approach to gathering witnesses and evidence is exactly what happened to Murder Inc.

Irv and Chris Gotti were arrested on January 19, 2005; agents representing a consortium of four law-enforcement bodies—the Bureau of Alcohol, Tobacco, and Firearms, the Federal Bureau of Investigation, the Internal Revenue Service, and the New York Police Department—indicted the brothers for laundering up to one million dollars in Supreme's drug money. Kenneth "Supreme" McGriff was charged right along with them as their partner-in-crime (although the Gottis made a successful attempt to be tried separately from Supreme when the case goes to trial). With all those agencies involved, it was clear the Feds were going to attempt to try Murder Inc. under RICO laws for criminal conspiracy.

Feds always want to nab the bigger kingpin as the end goal. There's nothing they'd rather do than take down the Enron of the music business; investigating rappers appears to them to be their fastest route to achieving that. And there's political gain to be had in all of this prosecution. Just as Rudy Giuliani gained political capital from his legal takedowns of the Mafia during the '70s and '80s, current New York State Attorney General Eliot Spitzer is hoping to build a career in elected office built on his successful prosecutions of high-profile Wall Street investment banks, mutual funds, and insurance companies for corruption. On July 25, 2005, Spitzer came to a settlement in a payola case against Sony's music companies that most felt was a epic blow to Sony and the entire music industry.

Sony's payola blues are just the beginning, and hip-hop itself could end up a casualty in the Feds' hunt for bigger game in the music industry. The game is on: according to a March 4, 2005, *Newsweek* story by Johnnie L. Roberts, "federal authorities are pressing a wide-ranging investigation into the $1.5-billion hip-hop music industry. . . . According to top industry insiders, federal investigators are digging into a playlist of crimes, ranging from extortion and robbery to the industry's persistent violence and mounting casualties—including the unsolved murders of Tupac Shakur and Notorious B.I.G. Investigators are 'asking about anyone in hip-hop from what I understand,' says a top music lawyer."

As the Feds increase the heat, the public becomes more enthralled in the cat-and-mouse game between rappers and law enforcement. The public knows that whoever wins or loses, it's going to be a fascinating, lurid, gory end, full of guns and "bling" and beautiful women on the arms of charismatic villains. The only thing is, the public has nothing to lose, and rap could lose it all.

It's unclear how all this will ultimately affect Murder Inc. I'm amazed at how those guys handle the stress: since I left Murder Inc.'s employ, I've seen Chris around; he's always friendly and says hello. The last time I saw Chris, in fact, was on the very day he was released on bail from the Feds. It was at a boxing match at New York City's Hammerstein Ballroom, for which my company had been hired to do the event's security. Despite the legal turmoil embroiling him and his brother, Chris was smiling, cool, and collected that night amidst the media circus. He wore a sweatshirt that featured a tough bulldog wearing a menacing spiked collar, and effortlessly worked the room as if everything was business as usual.

Maybe I shouldn't be so surprised: if anybody understands that controversy is just part of doing business in the hip-hop game, it's Irv and Chris Gotti. Controversy makes for big business; nothing sells rap albums better—ask 50 Cent about that. For that reason alone, we may see no end to hip-hop-related crime, with the result that rap will continue to be pilloried as the root of so many of society's problems—crime, community unrest, drugs. From my perspective, though, hip-hop is the symptom, not the cause.

CONCLUSION: CHECK YOURSELF
BEFORE YOU WRECK YOURSELF

I expect that the number of cases like the one the government waged against Murder Inc. will grow. If they couldn't bring down

Murder Inc., they'll find another target. It's a take-no-prisoners, scorched-earth policy—the government is determined to make an example of an organization like Murder Inc., and get them on something big. The Feds' zeal here might have edged into overreach, as is clear to me from their attempts to link a 2004 shooting involving Ja Rule to the case.

On December 27, 2004, an incident ensued as Ja Rule and his entourage were exiting a midtown Manhattan hotspot, Club LQ around 3:45 in the morning. On their way out of the club, Ja and crew encountered two individuals: Troy Moore and William Clark. Clark is better known by his street aliases, "Willie Bang Bang" or "Billy Bang."

After words were exchanged between the two parties, a shootout ensued, injuring Moore and killing Clark. Reportedly Ja had left by the time the gunplay occurred, which was a good thing. According to newspaper reports, a fan had been shot outside a Ja Rule afterparty just a week earlier in Peoria, Illinois, where allegedly a partygoer was shot after hurling a drink in the rapper's face.

Although, according to police, videotapes indicated that Ja's bodyguards fired weapons at Moore and Clark, as of early January 2006 they have not been charged with any crime. However, authorities wanted to know what knowledge the rapper might have about the incident so as to tie it to their then-ongoing Murder Inc. investigation. The Feds were especially curious about the fact that Troy Moore is the brother of Supreme Team associate Tyran "Tah-Tah" Moore, which could have made this incident criminal conspiracy if linked to other aspects of Murder Inc.'s indictment (Tah-Tah refused to participate willingly in the Murder Inc. investigation, and was sentenced to six years and change).

Personally, I think the Feds were overreaching here in their attempt to link the Club LQ shootings to the money-laundering charges—and the reason I know this is actually personal. When this homicide came up, a detective from the Midtown North squad called me about it, theorizing that Ja Rule had something to do with the murder. Hearing his take, it was clear to me NYPD didn't have the right story. I knew they were wrong when I later found out that Billy

Bang went to the club to rob celebrities from a reputable source: his family.

I grew up with Willie Bang Bang, and that intimate connection has led me to information in the case that law enforcement either doesn't have, or doesn't think much of. Either way, I think they're on the wrong track. For one, I knew Billy very well, and he wasn't involved in organized crime. Nope, Billy was a classic stick-up kid, only out for himself.

William "Billy Bang" Clark lived across the street from me in Queens throughout my entire childhood. I never thought Billy would turn out to be such a badass, especially as he came from such a good family. But even back in the day, Billy already had a reputation of robbing and shooting people. In fact, it was a chance run-in with Billy's younger sister Lisa on August 13, 2005, that shed new light on the Club LQ shootings. Lisa was frustrated: she and Billy's mother had been meeting with the police to make sure they had an accurate account of what happened with Billy in the incident. She had become frustrated because the NYPD was only obsessed with linking Billy's homicide to Ja Rule, Murder Inc., and Supreme.

When negotiations dissolved between Billy's family and the police, it was a shame: NYPD could have found out a lot more information about the many crimes Billy certainly was involved in—and likely might've closed a number of unsolved cases. This example shows how the police must do a better job when interviewing witnesses and family members, especially when it involves hip-hop. Instead, Billy Bang's family left with a bad feeling about the police, even after they were initially very willing to cooperate.

Talking to Lisa, I realized that in neglecting to get Billy Bang's real story, law enforcement had passed up a treasure trove of information. For one, Billy loved boasting to his family about his exploits, and they were numerous. Lisa told me that, before the shooting, Billy had recently just come home from jail. Billy told Lisa that he had "angles"—that is, he had plans to rob people, especially celebrities. Even fresh out of prison, Billy was already hot: according to Lisa, Billy had jacked several celebrities—notables like Foxy Brown's brother, Gavin Marchand (who got hit twice by Billy), as well as Red

Café, an up-and-coming Brooklyn rapper, and T. I., a Georgia-based hip-hop star. Billy even had some jewelry that supposedly belonged to Big Noyd of Queens's Mobb Deep family, which Billy bragged about taking in one of his stickups.

As for the Club LQ incident, whatever brought Troy and Billy there, the results proved fatal, when Ja's camp responded with gunfire. But what really drew the cops' attention to the Ja camp was the fact the shooters did not stick around on the scene.

Regardless, the events at Club LQ on December 27, 2004, did not involve the criminal conspiracy charges the government was pursuing at the time against the Gotti, and Murder Inc. I understood why the authorities proved so desperate to link a homicide to the Murder Inc. case: the thinking goes, if they up the ante, maybe they can get someone in the case to "flip." "Flipping" is when the authorities put extreme pressure on a defendant in the hopes that they will make a deal for a lesser sentence which involves giving up even more valuable information.

Ultimately, the Feds aren't that interested in the Gottis on their own. No, they see people like the Gottis and businesses like Murder Inc. as a means to an end—a means to put away an even bigger fish like Supreme or Def Jam or, even better, the music industry itself. The same thing almost happened to Lil' Kim. In 2003, Kim perjured herself in front of a grand jury when she testified about the 2001 Hot 97 shooting. There she claimed she didn't see the shooters Damion "D-Roc" Butler and Suif "Gutta" Jackson at the scene and couldn't point them out in photographs, even though video and photographic surveillance, as well as other eyewitness testimony, indicated the opposite. Her time on the stand was especially damning as the shooters were Kim's intimate associates—D-Roc was her manager at the time and Gutta her bodyguard.

At the conclusion of her perjury trial, the jury determined Kim had lied under oath nearly twenty-nine times; the judge sentenced Kim to a little over a year in prison, along with three years' probation and $50,000 in fines. The thing is, I don't think the Feds wanted to send Kim to jail—I think they wanted her to flip and rat out a bigger prize.

I had many goals when I began this book project. I wanted people to know the truth about the rap music industry. I wanted people to see the mechanisms within the NYPD and how law enforcement deals with hip-hop from the inside. I hoped readers would see why things happen the way they happen and how things should happen, and be able to read between the tabloid headlines. I wanted to clear the air about misconceptions about racial profiling and other things in the hip-hop squad, and maybe inspire both law enforcement and the rap industry to take a good, hard look at themselves before either becomes vulnerable to destruction. Indeed, the music business has opened itself to federal legal exposure in a way from which it may never recover. Then again, what else can you expect, considering their role models?

In the decades I spent working one of the world's most dangerous jobs, I saw society's ugliest face every day, in particular how changes in drugs habits, law enforcement, politics, and the economy affected real people on the margins. I can't deny that it affected me. During my long tenure with the NYPD, I learned more than anything about society's gray areas. I worked under numerous political and law-enforcement administrations, each of which brought its own brand of seismic change to New York's mean streets. But throughout that time, I was always the one actually working those streets, encountering different ethical issues, setbacks, and success stories every day that would constantly challenge and shape my world view.

Through law enforcement's shifting cultures and eras, I saw first-hand the cultural ignorance and racism that can still taint police work today, and how it created the divide that now exists between law enforcement and the hip-hop community. It's a crucial chasm: as so many young African-Americans view rap as their cultural voice, this situation continues to drive a bigger wedge between those wearing badges and the future of black America.

In the process of navigating that chasm on daily basis, I discovered my own personal definition of justice rather than the one dictated to me by police chiefs and politicians. It's this very idea of doing the right thing that drove me to devote myself to solving the senseless killing of Jam Master Jay even after I left the force. To me,

Jam Master Jay's shooting is a classic inside job displaying all the tics of hip-hop crime. Queens authorities, however, continue to insist on treating it as just another conventional homicide.

Indeed, hip-hop ushered in a violent new epoch of revolutionary music, drugs, and crime, but the law-enforcement response wasn't equally as innovative. On the job, I found had to rewrite the rule book to cope with the seemingly insurmountable divide between the NYPD and the hip-hop world—and the self-destructive impulses that pulse through both. In retrospect, my story is that rare kind of stranger-than-fiction tale where organized crime meets big business, where Wall Street, ghetto kids, political candidates, cops, and street hustlers all coexist together.

Despite some high-profile busts, the criminal element within hip-hop is only increasing its activities of late, with law enforcement seemingly continuing grow less equipped to deal with rap even as it becomes obsessed with it. In fact, recent years have been particularly notable in the rise of hip-hop crime, despite supposed efforts to stem it: the phenomenon has evolving into a nationwide epidemic highlighted by a slew of stabbings, killings, shootings, assaults, alleged rape, and other incidents involving rap superstars.

There are so many hip-hop-related crimes, I can't even list all of them in this book. New York–based lyricist Keith Murray got three years in 1999 for his role in a Connecticut barroom assault. New Orleans rapper Mystikal got six years in prison for sexual battery in 2004, while Texas rapper Pimp C of the group UGK got sent to the slammer on an aggravated-assault charge in 2002. DMX was arrested on charges and for impersonating a federal officer after allegedly using a hijacked car to lead police in a reckless chase at New York's John F. Kennedy Airport; he ended up pleading guilty to violating the terms of an earlier conditional release. In Philadelphia, Jay-Z associate Beanie Sigel was recently released from prison after working through a number of shooting, assault, and drug charges, while local rapper Cassidy was arrested and did time for his involvement in a 2005 shooting homicide. On the West Coast, Xzibit—the famous host of *Pimp My Ride*—was slashed in the face by two assailants at a suburban Los Angeles mall in 2004. Snoop Dogg also recently settled a $25 million lawsuit filed by Emmy-winning makeup artist Kylie Bell, who claimed Snoop and crew drugged and raped her during a 2003 appearance on the *Jimmy Kimmel Live* show, a charge that Snoop consistently denied. These are just a few examples, but they're indicative of a larger trend, which knows no boundaries. From the East to the West, from the South to the Midwest, hip-hop crime is happening everywhere.

Celebrity gatherings have become open season for looting in particular. Los Angeles's NBA All-Star Weekend event has become a favorite place to jack b-boy bigshots of their bling: it's rumored that rappers Cam'ron and the Clipse were robbed of some jewelry during the 2004 All-Star festivities. It's hard to know where the hip-hop ends and the crime begins. Rap has indeed become so pervasive that now it's the criminals who are emulating rappers, and not the other way around. In a true life-imitating-art moment, law enforcement in Tulsa, Oklahoma, has been tracking a violent gang called "G-Unit," named in homage to 50 Cent's crew, who may be connected to a number of shootings in the area, including the murder of an innocent sixteen-year-old girl.

As such, the South is particularly under watch as the next major hotbed for hip-hop crime. Ironically, the man who is said to have helped fuel the fire in the '90s East Coast to West Coast rap war, longtime Puff Daddy associate Anthony "Wolf" Jones, was killed in the very same spot that set it off. Wolf ignited East vs. West tensions when he allegedly shot and killed Suge Knight associate Jake Robles outside an Atlanta, Georgia, nightclub in 1995. In November 2003, however, an early-morning shootout outside the Chaos nightclub in Atlanta's Bucktown district left Wolf dead. This time, however, there would be no retaliation, although whispers on the street linked Wolf's murder to the Black Mafia Family, or BMF, a hip-hop entertainment group with ties to gang activity.

I knew that the BMF organization, which has been making moves to become the Southern equivalent of Death Row Records, was being watched: a source of mine who works in Atlanta claimed that federal authorities cut down a number of trees in front of a popular Bucktown nightspot in order to do better surveillance on BMF's activities. He appears to have been telling the truth. On October 28,

2005, allhiphop.com reported that "the Drug Enforcement Administration (DEA) in the United States has arrested 30 members of the self-named Black Mafia Family (BMF) and has seized over $3 million in money, asset, 2½ kilograms of cocaine and weapons. . . . The DEA said prior to today's arrests, they had already arrested 17 members and seized over 632 kilograms of cocaine, $5.3 million in money and $5.7 million in assets." According to the article, the government considered BMF "a large-scale cocaine and money laundering operation operating in Detroit, Michigan; Columbus and Atlanta, Georgia; Los Angeles, California; Miami, Fort Lauderdale, and Orlando, Florida; St. Louis, Missouri; Greenville South Carolina; and Louisville, Kentucky. . . . BMF allegedly distributed thousands of kilos of cocaine and dealt at least 2,500 kilos out of Atlanta, BMF's home base."

Atlanta's hip-hop community is apparently aware of the unwanted federal attention on it, which extends beyond the BMF: "I don't give a fuck about the Feds' investigation on me," Atlanta rapper (and ex-con/drug dealer) T. I. raps on his hit, "You Don't Know Me."

One of BMF's alleged associates, Young Jeezy, is now one of the biggest rappers out today. Signed by Jay-Z to Def Jam, Jeezy's solo album *Let's Get It: Thug Motivation 101* exploded into a national hit in 2005. Earlier in the year, though, Jeezy became involved in a beef with another Georgia-based rapper named Gucci Mane, supposedly over ownership of a song, "Icy," that both appear on. Their beef escalated to the point where Jeezy offered a bounty to whomever could snatch Gucci Mane's chain. Of course, in the 'hood, if you're gonna take a tough guy's chain, you'd better make sure he's dead first. And on May 10, 2005, Gucci Mane was attacked by five men in what appeared to be a setup. Mane then allegedly retaliated, opening fire as he fled the scene. Mane's shots left one man, Henry "Pookie Loc" Clark, dead. That wasn't the end of the story: Clark's rap group, Loccish Lifestyle, was supposedly under contract to Young Jeezy. Jeezy denied all involvement in the incident, which continued to reverberate. On September 20, 2005, a jailed Gucci Mane was assaulted in prison, resulting in numerous injuries; the same day, an Atlanta S.W.A.T. team raided the offices of Mane's label, Big Cat Records, after police received-reports of an armed man on the premises.

The biggest troublemakers of 2005 have to be by far rap superstars 50 Cent and The Game. In mid-2004, 50 Cent heated up his legal situation when he allegedly assaulted a fan after a bottle was thrown onstage during a Springfield, Massachusetts, concert by his G-Unit compadre Lloyd Banks. But 50's all-out attack began in the preparations for the marketing of his 2005 album *The Massacre*. 50 sparked beef by leaking the dis track "Piggy Bank," which called out 50's hard-core-rap peers Fat Joe and Jadakiss for appearing on a song with 50's nemesis Ja Rule; 50 also had some choice words in the song for his fellow Queens rapper Nas. Most shocking was 50's eyebrow-raising beef with his own G-Unit protégé, The Game.

The Game was discovered by Dr. Dre, who saw in the young rapper a chance to revive the West Coast's rap fortunes. The good doctor's instincts were right—Game's album *The Documentary* went straight to number one in early 2005, selling over one million units in just three weeks; one of the biggest rap releases of the year, it's now achieved multi-platinum status. Still, Game, an acknowledged member of a Compton, California, charter of the Bloods gang, attracted trouble like a true gangsta.

Like 50, Game heavily publicized the fact that he survived a drug-related gang shooting before he found rap fame. Similar troubles continue to follow him: shots have been reported fired at Game's vehicles and Compton compound, and the rapper and his manager Jimmy "Henchmen" Rosemond were accused of delivering a beatdown to a Washington, D.C.–area radio jock. (Charges against Game were later dropped.) Game advertises his capacity for deadly violence openly, down to the tattoo of a teardrop that marks his face— it's all part of his thoroughly marketed myth. "They say when you've got a teardrop you've either murdered someone or done a long stretch in jail," The Game told *The New York Times*. "Let's just say I've never been to jail."

Game himself followed 50's "beef marketing" lead by dissing rappers like Memphis Bleek, Yukmouth, Joe Budden, and even

Jay-Z in his raps and interviews. But it was Game's shocking red-meat feud with mentor 50 that raised the most eyebrows. Sensing like minds, Dr. Dre entrusted Game to 50 Cent for a little artist development; 50 subsequently served as an executive producer on Game's hit album *The Documentary* from late 2004. Not only did 50 provide the hooks for many of the album's hits, he embraced Game as a member of his tight G-Unit clique. When Game balked at standing with 50 Cent on his beefs with Fat Joe, Nas, and Jadakiss, however, 50 publicly kicked Game out of G-Unit in a live radio interview on Hot 97 on February 28, 2005.

This ouster caused immediate repercussions. Game's crew quickly mobilized outside Hot 97; in the ensuing altercation a member of Game's entourage, Kevin Reed, was shot in the leg. Later, shots were fired at the offices of Violator, the management company that handles 50 as a client. There was speculation that it might have been retaliation. Despite a heavily hyped peace treaty, animosity between 50 and The Game continues: Game relentlessly trashes G-Unit from stages and mixtapes, and has even started selling T-shirts stating "G-U*not.*"

Whether on purpose or not, beef works too well as marketing for many of today's highest-profile rap releases. In the wake of mega-hyped beef, 50 Cent's *Massacre* album set records by selling well over a million copies in its first week alone, and The Game's *Documentary* is on course to sell four million copies. Now every rapper makes their supposed criminal activities part of their media strategy, boasting about how many times they've been shot, and how many other people they've shot. In the same way, sparking a beef or two with a prominent rapper is now de rigueur for fomenting tabloid headlines and Web site chatter.

Beef has become an industry in itself, as the hundreds of thousands in sales of the *Beef* DVD documentary series makes clear. There are now even successful rap-oriented magazines like *F.E.D.S.* and *Don Diva* devoted to hip-hop's criminal associations. It's not just about who's on the cover, either—even those on the masthead can cause legal headaches: two executives from *The Source* magazine, for example, were arrested and charged with attempted murder in a July 2005 shooting incident outside a New York bar after a dispute allegedly over the bar's choice of music.

Yes, it's gotten to the point where bragging about surviving shootings and threatening beef has become an utter-hip-hop cliché. These beefs can become a public hazard, as they often play out in public arenas like music-industry awards shows. In November 2004, Dr. Dre was assaulted by an audience member while picking up a lifetime-achievement award at the Second Annual Vibe Music Awards. In the ensuing fracas, Dre's assailant was stabbed in retaliation. G-Unit member Young Buck was arrested as the stabbing's prime suspect. Months later, he pled no contest to a lesser charge and was sentenced to perform community service.

Reports floated that Suge Knight, who was present at the Vibe Awards' televised taping, was responsible for commissioning Dre's slugging, though he denied any involvement. But whenever Suge attends an awards show, something always seems to go down. At events surrounding the July 2005 Black Entertainment Television awards show, meanwhile, Suge Knight and The Game reportedly scuffled, and rumors abounded that a Suge associate may have snatched Game's chain.

Suge's awards-show carnage continued with 2005's edition of the MTV Video Music Awards, which were held in Miami. At an awards show pre-party for Kanye West at Miami Beach's glitziest hotel/nightspot the Shore Club, Suge Knight was shot in the leg either by an unknown assailant or, as some police reports indicated, by himself by accident. Thankfully Knight was the only person hurt in the incident; some six hundred people were attending the party, and if there had been additional confrontation or panic, who knows how many would be injured or dead?

Even if Suge's latest brush with violence doesn't involve any rap beef (initial rumors speculated that it was payback from Game for the B.E.T. scrap, but Game vigorously denied any involvement), investigations into the incident still suffer from the traditional problems that come with solving rap-related crime. Miami Beach P.D. spokesperson Bobby Hernandez told *The Miami Herald* that the department's investigations into the matter were being held back by—*surprise, surprise!*—a lack of cooperative eyewitnesses. "We don't have any physical description. We don't know how many subjects were involved, which is mind boggling, with all those people around," Hernandez claimed.

Those within the hip-hop community, meanwhile, were outraged at the "same ol', same ol'" behavior exhibited in the incident by both law enforcement and those representing the rap game. "It's disturbing that someone can let off six shots in a packed club and can escape without being arrested," noted Elliott Wilson, editor-in-chief of leading rap magazine *XXL*, in an Associated Press report. "The hip-hop community doesn't trust the police to confide info to them, and in turn the police have done little to make us feel like they give a damn about our safety. It's a vicious cycle."

That cycle continued to spin at the VMA show's taping, where the sad lessons of hip-hop crime fell on deaf ears, even after a stirring symphonic tribute to Notorious B.I.G. led by Sean "Diddy" Combs himself. From the awards-show stage, Fat Joe taunted nemesis 50 Cent, noting, "I feel safe with all the police protection—courtesy of G-Unit." 50 Cent immediately attempted to storm the stage, but was halted by security. Later, during 50 Cent's own performance, the G-Unit leader chanted, "Fat Joe's a pussy! Fuck Joe—fuck Terror Squad!"—all bleeped out, however, on the international telecast.

After so many problems, rappers soon may no longer be welcome at awards shows—no matter how many records they sell. Then again, what are the awards shows thinking when they bring together Fat Joe, 50 Cent, The Game, Suge Knight, and other beefing rappers and crews together? With combinations like that together in one room, are you going to tell me sparks *aren't* gonna fly, even with cameras rolling The VMA's incidents were, in fact, bigger than *just* hip-hop—after all, Suge got shot around an event of international significance. These developments suggest how the hip-hop crime phenomenon is not just spreading—instead, it's *transforming* a new era where the criminal element has entrenched itself into legitimate business.

In particular, corporations are getting in bed with known criminals and convicted felons more and more, preferring to look the other way due to the profits involved. Some of hip-hop's greatest impresarios and moguls lived a life of crime before entering the music industry—and it might've been the best business education they could've gotten. In fact, just as rappers are now expected to come fully formed with a criminal background in narcotics and death, now it's not unusual for executives behind the scenes to have a serious rep on the streets, too. Jimmy "Henchmen" Rosemond is one of hip-hop's biggest manager moguls. In addition to The Game, he manages the careers of rappers like Big Gipp, Guerilla Black, and Sheek Louch under his Czar Entertainment banner. Throughout his career, Henchmen has been involved in the careers of everyone from Salt-N-Pepa to Biggie and the Fugees; all in all, Henchmen's had a hand in (at his estimate) twenty million records being sold.

As well, Henchmen's done real time behind bars, and is known on the streets as a real tough O.G. Henchmen's not afraid to get into beefs himself, either. 50 Cent is no fan of his, and neither was Tupac, as a line from the late rapper's song "Against All Odds" makes clear: "Promised a payback, Jimmy Henchmen." Recently, the NYPD's investigation into Tupac's 1994 shooting has been reopened to further explore Henchmen's possible involvement, which Henchmen denies. Even notorious Brooklyn drug dealer and Jay-Z role model Calvin "Klein" Bacote, fresh from a prison bid, is starting his own hip-hop record label, according to a report on mtvnews.com. And why not? If the public wants hip-hop that represents the streets, these are the kind of guys that know them.

For legitimate businesses like major record companies, however, doing business with known felons represents a real risk—not just from what the felon might do, but from the legal exposure such associations engender. The end result of such practices is a pressure-cooker situation that could take down some of the biggest corporate entities in America and the world, as well as the most important African-American art form since jazz.

Organized crime has always been in the music industry. Today, however, the lines are becoming even more blurred. Even after the recent spate of violence and the Murder Inc. investigation, major companies like Reebok continue to partner with former drug dealers like 50 Cent and Jay-Z on endorsement deals; Def Jam recently hired Jay-Z for a senior management position as well. As hip-hop grows in magnitude as a cultural force, such partnerships increasingly represent a new business model—and a potentially profitable playground for a more advanced style of corporate thuggery. And when such partnerships implode on themselves, as in the Murder Inc. situation, the result is a lethal cocktail of race, drugs, politics, prejudice, fame, and greed.

Most conglomerates look the other way, though, due to the potential multimillion dollar profits involved; today, a record full of priors won't keep anyone out of a record-company boardroom if what they've got is hot. For example, Def Jam, a subsidiary of major international conglomerate Universal, has made a vice president out of Jay-Z, an admitted former drug dealer who pleaded guilty to stabbing someone in public. Even after his appointment, Jay-Z continues to be involved in high-profile cases: in November 2004, R. Kelly sued the rapper and label executive for $75 million after a Jay-Z associate allegedly assaulted Kelly with pepper spray at the Madison Square Garden stop on the performers' joint tour in progress.

Chances are, most Fortune 500 companies on Wall Street wouldn't hire someone with such a background. However, hip-hop remains a new, uncharted frontier in the Wild West of the music biz—and beyond. Major industries like sports, fashion, movies, and telecommunications are opening their doors to those whose criminal pasts might've never got them past the receptionist in different times. In 2004, Sean "P. Diddy" Combs was named top menswear designer of the year by the Council of Fashion Designers of America for his hugely successful Sean John clothing line; chances are that previous winners like Ralph Lauren and Michael Kors didn't have Puffy's history of arrests. As well, Snoop Dogg currently stars in ads for T-Mobile and Chrysler amidst numerous major motion-picture deals, all while catching cases and boasting about his affiliation with the infamous Crips gang on his recent number-one smash, "Drop It Like It's Hot." Even the rappers themselves are surprised at what they're getting away with. "[I] can't believe Reebok did a deal with a psycho," 50 Cent raps about his shoe-endorsement deal with the sneaker giant on G-Unit's anthemic hit "Stunt 101."

This is not to put down rappers, especially the likes of 50 Cent or Jay-Z. It's clear from their successes that these men are not only major artistic talents but genius business strategists as well. Their acumen is to be envied: both 50 Cent and Jay-Z run hugely successful empires that go far beyond releasing their own albums as performers. Both rappers own clothing companies, hit-generating record labels, and in the case of Jay-Z, sports teams (Jay-Z owns a minority stake in the New Jersey Nets).

For anyone to have achieved as much as Jay-Z and 50 Cent have in business is commendable. As for their criminal tendencies, to my mind, they are more than anything products of their environments. If you live by the 'hood, you die by the 'hood, no matter how rich you might be. But sometimes I wonder if they'd been given more privilege, if they'd been born anywhere *but* the ghetto, could a Jay-Z or a 50 Cent take their natural intelligence and drive and become president of the United States—or at least a Colin Powell? I think so.

In truth, hip-hop has always proven to be a litmus test, a mirror for society's ills. On that level, I see the combination of lawless and legit that performer-businessmen like Jay-Z and 50 flaunt as simply reflecting what's going on in the world at large. As businessmen, are they any more corrupt or unlawful then the once-dignified suits that drove companies like Arthur Andersen and Enron into the ground—or are they less so? And how does the color of their skin affect how their behavior is judged?

The thing is, we live in a gangsta society, where gangsta values are rewarded, from politics to business on down. "Don't get caught," rather than "do the right thing," is the new corporate paradigm. And if that's how the big boys play, isn't it hypocritical to expect rappers to do something different? If the rules of the street work for top-tier executives, why punish a Jay-Z for bringing them into the boardroom, too? Don't think ambitious, business-minded leaders of the rap game don't notice and absorb the methods of those holding absolute power—they're too smart *not* to notice the parallels. Indeed, it's not for nothing that The Game calls his company the "Black Wall Street": he's not content to stay in the ghetto—he wants to be with the Robb Report power brokers, the real barbarians at the gates. As such, rappers are the new wealth, the new money set, the new "society": when Lil' Kim was sentenced to jail for perjury, for example, she was rightly compared to none other than Martha Stewart. The truth is, hip-hop crime is a top-down problem throughout our culture: both society and hip-hop have some cleaning up to do before the causes of rap-related crime will ever be substantially addressed. The fact that the NYPD and the hip-hop community both in their own way have allowed Jam Master Jay's killers to run free is proof of that.

In hindsight, I couldn't believe that the man I suspected to be Jay's murderer had brazenly walked the pews and paid respects at his funeral: on top of everything else, such a gesture of cold-blooded disrespect directed at one of rap's most cherished idols made me consider losing hope. If hip-hop doesn't love it own icons enough to give up their killers, then I'm sure that law enforcement will never successfully prosecute a high-profile hip-hop crime case.

At the same time, if authorities don't do everything they can to address hip-hop crime, then these problems will multiply exponentially. As such, hip-hop crime isn't just just a black thing anymore, but now crossing color and class lines. Chinese-American rapper Jin was the intended target in a 2003 Asian gang-related shooting incident in New York's Chinatown, for example. Latinos, the largest- growing minority in the United States, have seen their share of rap-related legal controversy: in 2002, Houston, Texas, rapper South Park Mexican was sentenced to forty-five years in prison after being convicted of sexual assault involving a nine-year-old child. Eminem, the world's most famous Caucasian rapper, had to serve out probation for his share of weapon and assault charges.

Every passing day suggests that hip-hop crime is rapidly becoming a *global* problem as well. Today, rap is the universal sound of struggle—all over the world, those on the margins identify with hip-hop's rebellious rise and make it their own. But like a computer virus, wherever rap goes, it seems to bring its violent legacy with it.

Africa has seen its share of hip-hop-related violence. Nigerian rapper Eedris Abdulkareem got into a physical dispute with 50 Cent's entourage on a plane during 50's appearances at Nigerian music festivals. Meanwhile, Ja Rule provoked a confrontation with a South African D.J. in front of tens of thousands of people when the spinner played 50 Cent's "21 Questions" immediately following Rule's performance. In England, meanwhile, East London rapper Dizzee Rascal survived a stabbing, which added to his legend à la 50 Cent's shooting; a murder charge against another chart-topping U.K. hip-hopper, Megaman of the So Solid Crew, recently ended in a mistrial. In a November 4, 2005, allhiphop.com article headlined, "London Mayor Blames Rap Artists for Surge of Crime In England," London mayor Ken Livingstone takes it there. "Gun crime, knife crime—they are the only crime categories that continue to rise," Livingstone is quoted as saying. "With role models like rap groups there is almost an inevitability about that and people in the public eye should consider the role models they set."

Europe is especially feeling its own homegrown hip-hop crime. In France, Arab and African immigrant youth have seized upon rap music as the soundtrack to their marginalization in Parisian ghettos, adopting the provocative dress and confrontational manner of their hip-hop heroes. As well, rappers are being perceived of as threats to the political powers that be in their own countries. According to a August 9, 2005, *New York Times* article by Andreas Tzortzis, a German gangsta rapper named Bushido was recently placed on a watch list created by Germany's Federal Department for Media Harmful to Young Persons. This list was originally set up twenty-some years ago to monitor the propaganda activities of neo-Nazi activists. Being on it is one step away from being banned entirely: music on the list is illegal for sale to minors, and advertising it is *verboten*. In Asia, Korean rapper Tiger JK has been imprisoned and forbidden from performing by the South Korean government due to his involvement in violent incidents. It's more likely the threatening power of his lyrics, however, that got Tiger JK thrown in jail.

Before we go any further, I want to correct a common misconception: in no way am I implying that all rappers are criminals. Artists like Missy Elliott, the Neptunes, Lil Jon, Mos Def, Talib Kweli, Kanye West, Outkast, and Ludacris have all managed to attain hip-hop stardom without flaunting a reputation as a hard street criminal. These artists are about the music first and foremost, though they don't hold the same kind of street respect as, say, 50 Cent or Mobb Deep do. For some hip-hop insiders, the absence of a criminal background is considered unusual and suspect. "We all grew up street guys who had to do whatever we had to do to get by," Jay-Z said in an interview for a 2005 *Time* magazine cover featuring Kanye West. "Then there's Kanye, who to my knowledge has never hustled a day in his life. I didn't see how it could work."

For some, though, drugs and violence will always appear to be the only way out of the struggle that has plagued black communities since slavery; for others it is hip-hop's only acceptable subject matter. In videos, Young Jeezy constantly shows off his diamond-encrusted platinum pendant in the shape of his trademark "snowman" logo, and his line of "snowman"-adorned clothing has proven controversial. Considering the Georgia heat of his Atlanta hometown, it's not hard to deduce what the "snow" refers to.

Gimmicks like Jeezy's "snowman" make for brilliant marketing. There's no denying the cinematic, taboo power of gangsta rap—it sells for a reason: hard-core MCs have replaced traditional mobsters as the villains we love to hate. Just as gangster flicks like *Scarface* endure like they were released yesterday, there's a subversive thrill in listening to the supposedly authentic details of a drug dealer's violent existence. I'm susceptible to it, too.

This isn't just about lyrics, though, but actions. In the end, if rap truly wants to be free of law-enforcement interference, it needs to clean up its own game as the stakes grow higher and the business becomes more legit. This idea wasn't lost on even a figure like the Notorious B.I.G. "I often say to myself, watch what you're doing, Big, 'cause you're not on Fulton Street anymore," the iconic rapper is quoted as saying in Cheo Coker's *Unbelievable: The Life, Death, and Afterlife of the Notorious B.I.G.* "If a nigga say, 'Fuck you,' you can't shoot at him. You just can't do it. . . ."

At the same time, the streets remain many rappers' Achilles' heel, as one high-level music-industry executive I've worked with complained to me once. "It doesn't matter if they have all the wealth in the world, because they never let go of the street," he told me, throwing up his hands in frustration. "Even if it's in their best interests, they just can't leave the ghetto bullshit alone." It was this Achilles' heel that got Lil' Kim sent to the slammer for perjury. Lil' Kim wasn't being prosecuted herself for a crime, but she was asked to testify in trials relating to the 2001 Hot 97 shooting. Even when it was clear that the Feds had the goods, Kim still had to live by the code of the streets: she just didn't want to be known as a snitch, even if that meant jail time. Kim's example demonstrates the streets' powerful influence—even Jam Master Jay couldn't shake this Achilles' heel.

The thing is, when rappers play themselves like Lil' Kim did, they're just opening themselves up to even more pressure to snitch and cut a deal. Feds look to arrest rappers so they'll flip and turn state's witness on even bigger probe targets. The government figures that, even if rappers aren't such big criminals themselves, they're the connective tissue to the bigger fish—and they have more to lose. Putting rappers in jail isn't the Feds' main goal: they're just stepping stones to prosecute large companies on crimes like payola and mail fraud. To government law-enforcement agencies, rappers are just the crack dealers on the corner, while the entertainment conglomerates are the kingpin suppliers in Bolivia.

Ultimately, my work investigating hip-hop crime over the years was never to bring down rap; that was the opposite of what I was trying to do. On some level, I was working to save hip-hop—that was the whole idea. The thing is, my time in law enforcement represented a new-jack era, but the new jacks were operating carelessly in legitimate business with numerous safeguards and regulations. Too many in hip-hop want to bypass these regulations altogether, but you can't succeed doing that: at some point, such activity will catch up to you. The Feds have all the time in the world: they're just watching you, fattening up their dossiers until they have enough to strike. And when it comes to major crimes, they can strike at any time. Future gangstas of America need to remember that the statute of limitations never expires on homicides.

The situation with hip-hop crime is as dire as ever, and remember, I've seen it all. When I retired in 2002 as the New York Police Department's foremost detective specializing in hip-hop-associated crime, I left a void; these days, it seems that everyone thinks they are experts. By now, I've seen inside hip-hop from *both* sides. I had dinner once with the Brooklyn O.G. known as Supreme Magneto—it was like the scene in *Heat* where Robert De Niro the criminal and Al Pacino the seasoned cop finally meet and compare notes from different sides of the fence. Magneto was surprised at how much I knew.

Law enforcement today doesn't know that much, I'm sure. Most hip-hop crime's will never be solved because it's too easy for the police to blame the messenger in most cases. It's not just rap that's on trial in these overpublicized court cases, but society, too. Hip-hop is just another victim of an all-too-deadly combination of money, oppression, racism, the allure of power, and the pressures of fame. Law enforcement has to bring itself to truly comprehend the roots of the rage that drives hip-hop; otherwise, the hip-hop crime epidemic will never become less of a threat to the public, and even to hip-hop itself. If there is any lesson to be learned from the deaths of Biggie, Tupac, and Jam Master Jay, that's it. It's more likely, though, that this vicious cycle will just continue grinding away toward oblivion.

In the end, hip-hop is always about the struggle. The struggle continues, but remember, somebody's always going to be watching. Don't be surprised if that somebody is me—in fact, you should hope it's me and not the Feds. You might see me on the corner, just watching, observing. Maybe I'll see you at the club, or at the concert. Maybe I'll see you on the block. Yeah, I'm still watching. Yeah, I'm still there, with my eyes open and my ear to the street. That's right—I'm still here. And if the truth hurts, I'll keep on bringing the pain.

How ya like me now?

BIBLIOGRAPHY

The following books, films, publications and Web sites were highly inspirational and useful in the creation of *Notorious C.O.P.*

BOOKS

Coker, Cheo Hodari. *Unbelievable: The Life, Death, and Afterlife of the Notorious B.I.G.* New York: Three Rivers Press, 2003.

Light, Alan, ed. *The VIBE History of Hip-Hop.* New York: Three Rivers Press, 1999.

Ro, Ronin. *Have Gun Will Travel: The Spectacular Rise and Violent Fall of Death Row Records.* New York: Broadway Books, 1998.

Sullivan, Randall. *LAbyrinth.* New York: Atlantic Monthly Press, 2002.

FILMS

Broomfield, Nick. *Biggie & Tupac: The Story Behind the Murder of Rap's Biggest Superstars.* London: FilmFour/Lafayette Films, 2002.

PUBLICATIONS

Rolling Stone

SPIN

The Source

VIBE

XXL

ARTICLES

Bruck, Connie. "The Takedown of Tupac." *The New Yorker* (July 7, 1997).

Sullivan, Randall. "The Unsolved Mystery of the Notorious B.I.G." *Rolling Stone* (December 5, 2005).

WEB SITES

www.allhiphop.com

www.mtv.com

www.ohhla.com

www.sohh.com